MOTHER IS COMING

Other FoxTrot Books by Bill Amend

FoxTrot
Pass the Loot
Black Bart Says Draw
Eight Yards, Down and Out
Bury My Heart at Fun-Fun Mountain
Say Hello to Cactus Flats
May the Force Be with Us, Please
Take Us to Your Mall
The Return of the Lone Iguana
At Least This Place Sells T-shirts
Come Closer, Roger, There's a Mosquito on Your Nose
Welcome to Jasorassic Park
I'm Flying, Jack . . . I Mean, Roger
Think iFruity
Death by Field Trip
Encyclopedias Brown and White
His Code Name Was The Fox
Your Momma Thinks Square Roots Are Vegetables
Who's Up for Some Bonding?
Am I a Mutant or What!
Orlando Bloom Has Ruined Everything
My Hot Dog Went Out, Can I Have Another?
How Come I'm Always Luigi?
Houston, You Have a Problem
And When She Opened the Closet, All the Clothes Were Polyester
Math, Science, and Unix Underpants
FoxTrot Sundaes
Jasotron: 2012
AAAA! A FoxTrot Kids Collection
Some Clever Title

Anthologies

FoxTrot: The Works
FoxTrot en masse
Enormously FoxTrot
Wildly FoxTrot
FoxTrot Beyond a Doubt
Camp FoxTrot
Assorted FoxTrot
FoxTrot: Assembled with Care
FoxTrotius Maximus
Jam-Packed FoxTrot
Wrapped-Up FoxTrot
The Best of FoxTrot

MOTHER IS COMING

A FoxTrot Collection

by Bill Amend

Andrews McMeel
PUBLISHING®

Introduction

On April 10, 1988, at the age of 25, I officially became a professional cartoonist. I had previously drawn cartoons for my college paper, but those were editorial cartoons, and I was largely just doing them to amuse my friends and as an excuse to put off studying. This was to be a whole different ball game. My little bitty, until-then-unpublished comic strip *FoxTrot* had been signed by the same syndicate that represented such giants as *Doonesbury*, *The Far Side*, and *Calvin and Hobbes*, and on that Sunday, they launched it into about 70 newspapers around the country. And over the next few weeks, as the giddy excitement of seeing my work in print started to give way to the reality of my new occupation, something occurred to me: I had no idea what I was doing.

Fortunately, I was a quick learner, and I rapidly absorbed important syndicated cartoonist lessons such as the importance of golf jokes, how the word "hell" can get you canceled, and which FedEx stations stayed open the latest. However, when it came to a lot of things, I was basically making it up as I went, and crossing my fingers that my hunches and guesses would steer me right more often than wrong and that I'd still have a job in a year.

One such hunch was my suspicion that if I enjoyed a topic or subject, there was a decent chance that at least some other people did as well and that I should include it in my strip. This probably seems like a pretty safe, no-brainer sort of thing, but you have to keep in mind that I was a rather nerdy young man, and a lot of my interests weren't exactly normal fodder for newspaper comics, particularly back in those days: things like math and science and coding and gaming. Writing jokes about Ohm's law in a family strip wasn't the sort of thing a person who "knew what they were doing" would probably do. But I was young and crazy and followed my hunch (cautiously at first—I was young and crazy, but not completely stupid), and as I reflect back now 30-plus years later, I think it was one of the best creative decisions I've made. Newspaper comics, when successful, can last a looooong time. If I weren't writing about things I cared about, I don't know how I'd do it.

FoxTrot isn't everyone's cup of tea—of that I am well aware. But for those of you who've supported my strip in books and papers and online, I guess it's close enough, and for that I am profoundly grateful. Not only for the many years that I've been able to make a living at this but also for the opportunity to write comics about things I enjoy and to share them with others who enjoy those things, too. I hope you enjoy this latest collection.

Bill Amend
May 2018

Dum da Dum Dummm

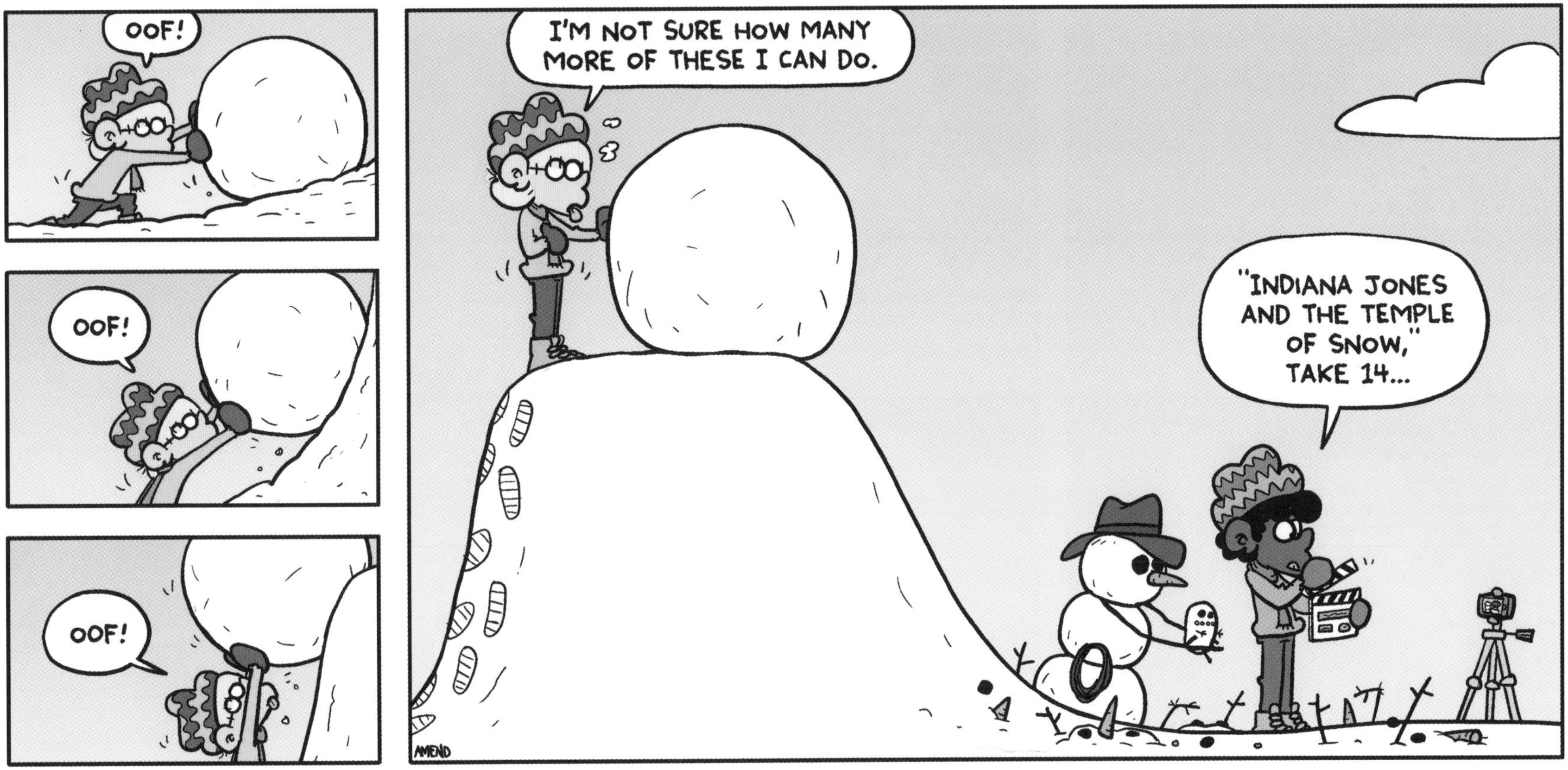
OOF!
OOF!
OOF!
I'M NOT SURE HOW MANY MORE OF THESE I CAN DO.
"INDIANA JONES AND THE TEMPLE OF SNOW," TAKE 14...
AMEND

Kazap!

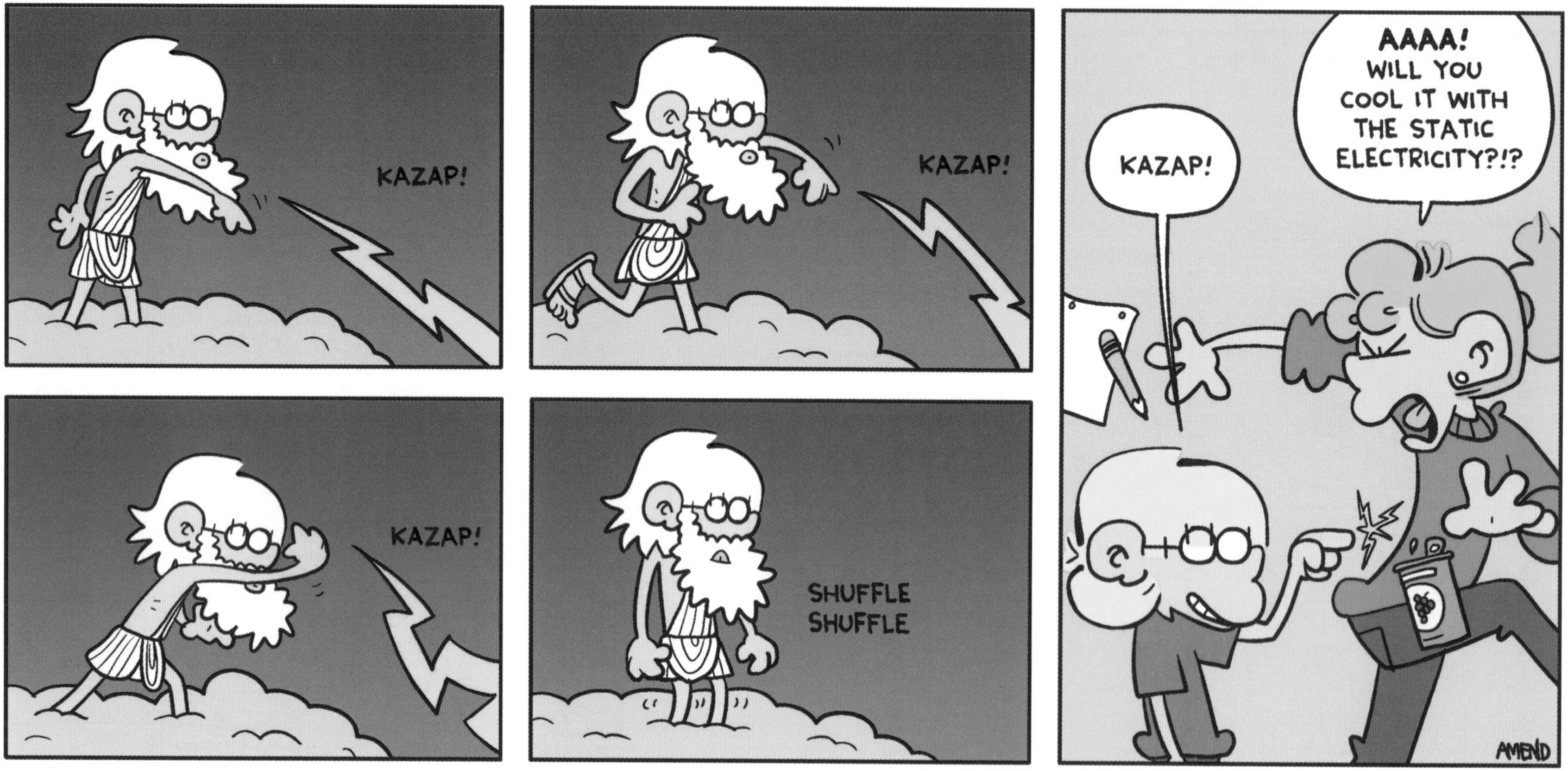
KAZAP!
KAZAP!
KAZAP!
SHUFFLE
SHUFFLE
KAZAP!
AAAA! WILL YOU COOL IT WITH THE STATIC ELECTRICITY?!?
AMEND

Dig Dugged

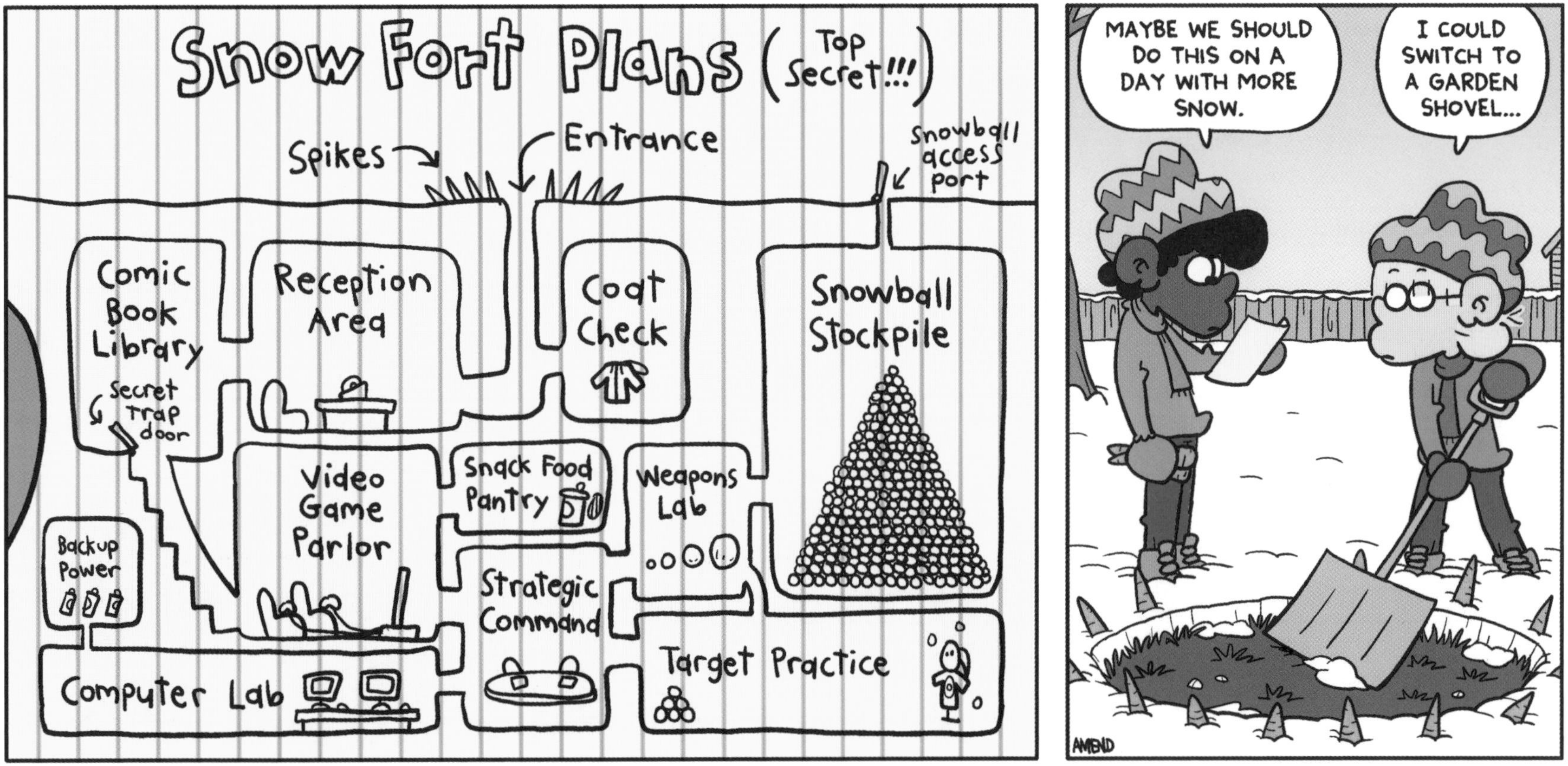
Snow Fort Plans (Top Secret!!!)
Spikes
Entrance
Snowball access port
Comic Book Library
Secret trap door
Reception Area
Coat Check
Snowball Stockpile
Video Game Parlor
Snack Food Pantry
Weapons Lab
Backup Power
Strategic Command
Target Practice
Computer Lab
MAYBE WE SHOULD DO THIS ON A DAY WITH MORE SNOW.
I COULD SWITCH TO A GARDEN SHOVEL...
AMEND

Petey the Procrastinator

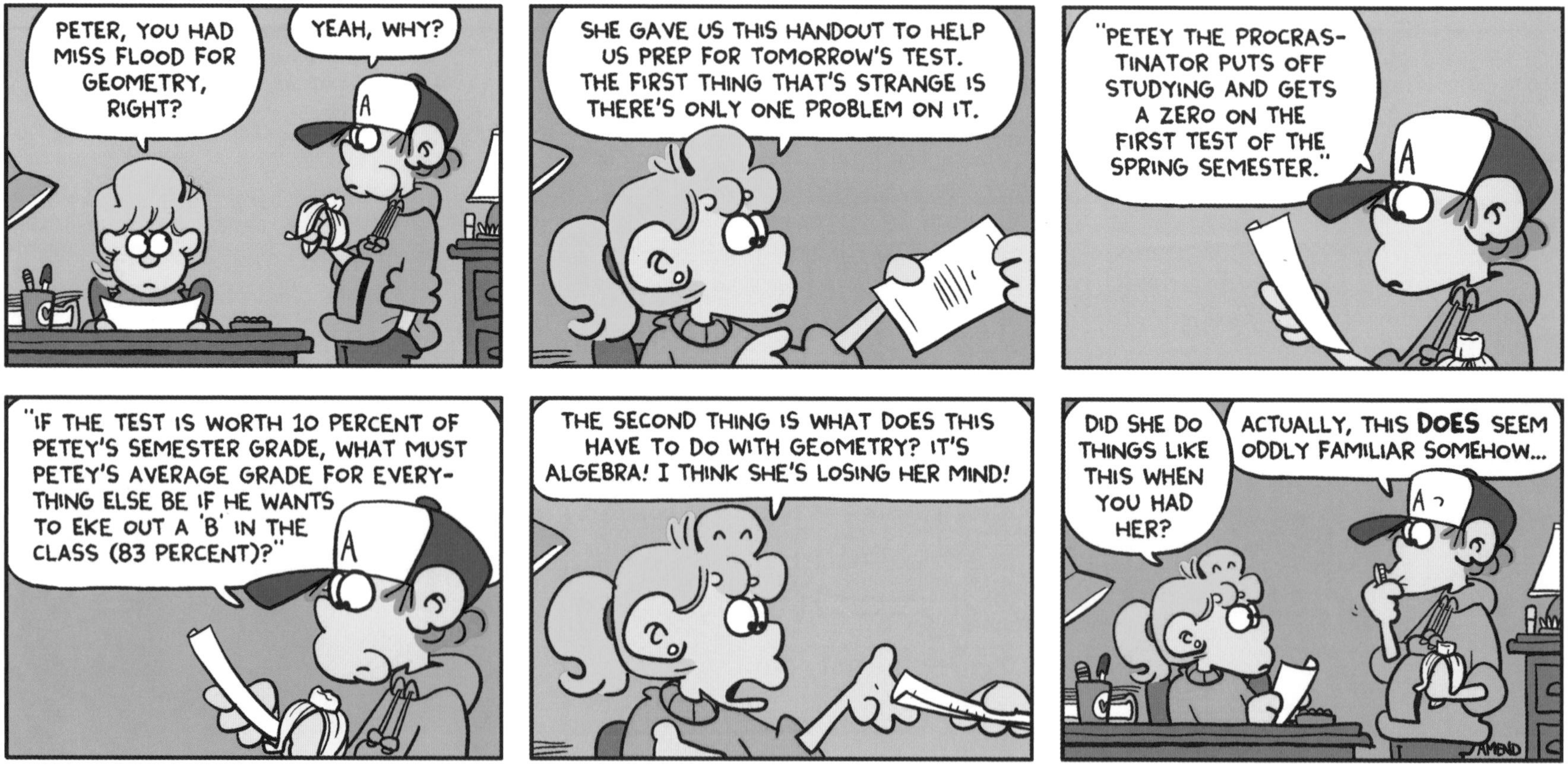
PETER, YOU HAD MISS FLOOD FOR GEOMETRY, RIGHT?
YEAH, WHY?
SHE GAVE US THIS HANDOUT TO HELP US PREP FOR TOMORROW'S TEST. THE FIRST THING THAT'S STRANGE IS THERE'S ONLY ONE PROBLEM ON IT.
"PETEY THE PROCRAS-TINATOR PUTS OFF STUDYING AND GETS A ZERO ON THE FIRST TEST OF THE SPRING SEMESTER."
"IF THE TEST IS WORTH 10 PERCENT OF PETEY'S SEMESTER GRADE, WHAT MUST PETEY'S AVERAGE GRADE FOR EVERY-THING ELSE BE IF HE WANTS TO EKE OUT A 'B' IN THE CLASS (83 PERCENT)?"
THE SECOND THING IS WHAT DOES THIS HAVE TO DO WITH GEOMETRY? IT'S ALGEBRA! I THINK SHE'S LOSING HER MIND!
DID SHE DO THINGS LIKE THIS WHEN YOU HAD HER?
ACTUALLY, THIS **DOES** SEEM ODDLY FAMILIAR SOMEHOW...
AMEND

Super Ready

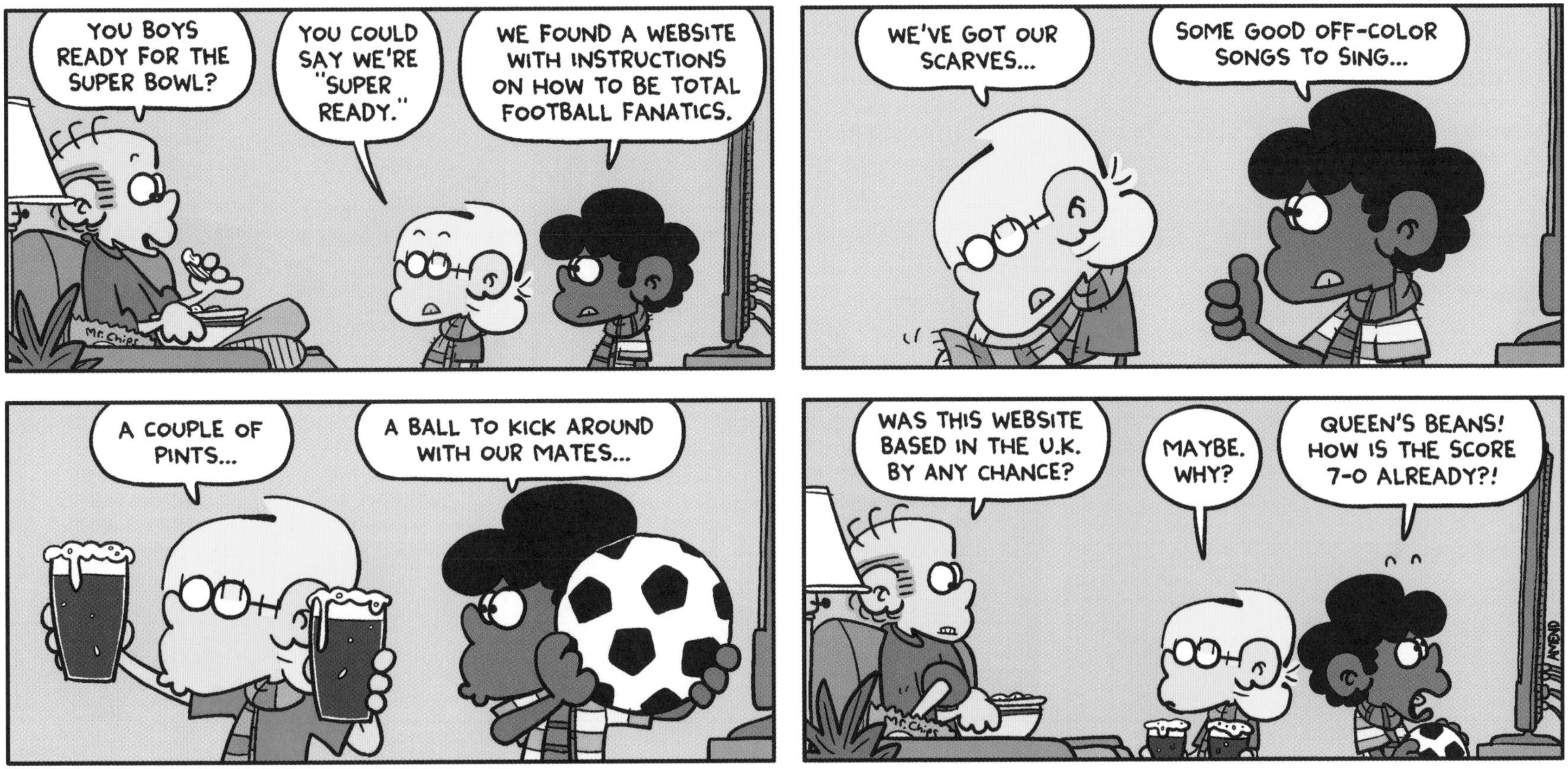

YOU BOYS READY FOR THE SUPER BOWL?
YOU COULD SAY WE'RE "SUPER READY."
WE FOUND A WEBSITE WITH INSTRUCTIONS ON HOW TO BE TOTAL FOOTBALL FANATICS.
Mr. Chips
WE'VE GOT OUR SCARVES...
SOME GOOD OFF-COLOR SONGS TO SING...
A COUPLE OF PINTS...
A BALL TO KICK AROUND WITH OUR MATES...
WAS THIS WEBSITE BASED IN THE U.K. BY ANY CHANCE?
MAYBE. WHY?
QUEEN'S BEANS! HOW IS THE SCORE 7-0 ALREADY?!

Calling All Florists

HI, I WAS INTERESTED IN ORDERING A VALENTINE'S BOUQUET FOR MY SISTER.

HOW EXPENSIVE WOULD AN ARRANGEMENT FEATURING AN AMORPHOPHALLUS TITANUM BE?

YOU DON'T? ARE YOU SURE? IT MIGHT BE LABELED "TITAN ARUM" OR EVEN JUST "CORPSE FLOWER."

NO? COULD YOU AT LEAST CHECK IN THE BACK? IT'D SMELL LIKE ROTTING FLESH. YES, FLESH.

PHOOEY. OK, FINE, WHAT ABOUT SYMPLOCARPUS FOETIDUS? IT'D HAVE MORE OF A SKUNK ODOR.

THAT'S THE THIRD FLORIST THAT'S CALLED ME A WEIRDO AND HUNG UP.

DUDE, BUYING VALENTINE'S FLOWERS FOR YOUR SISTER IS PRETTY WEIRD.

Pop(sicle) Art

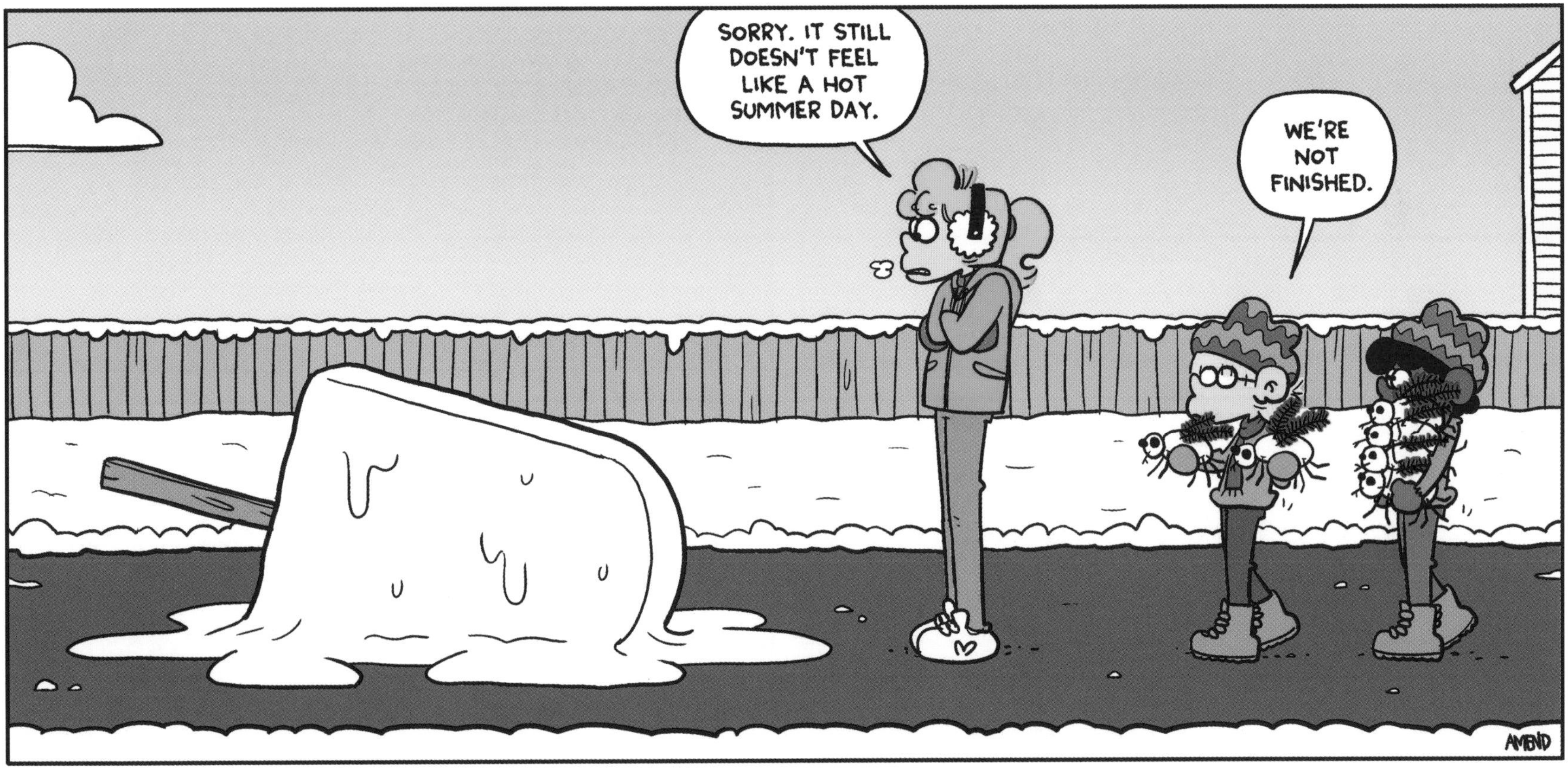
SORRY. IT STILL DOESN'T FEEL LIKE A HOT SUMMER DAY.
WE'RE NOT FINISHED.
AMEND

Lengthy Discussion

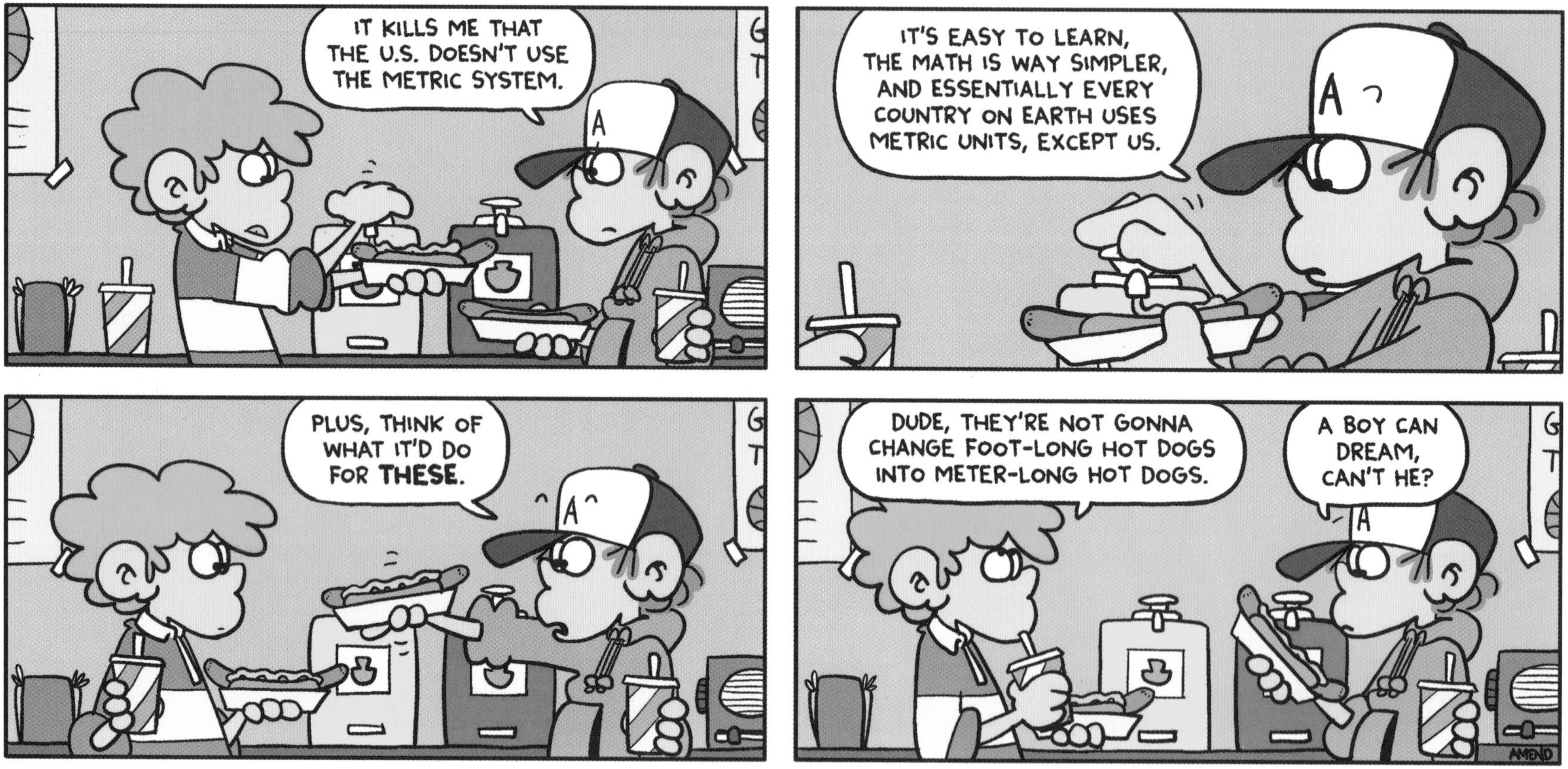
IT KILLS ME THAT THE U.S. DOESN'T USE THE METRIC SYSTEM.
IT'S EASY TO LEARN, THE MATH IS WAY SIMPLER, AND ESSENTIALLY EVERY COUNTRY ON EARTH USES METRIC UNITS, EXCEPT US.
PLUS, THINK OF WHAT IT'D DO FOR **THESE**.
DUDE, THEY'RE NOT GONNA CHANGE FOOT-LONG HOT DOGS INTO METER-LONG HOT DOGS.
A BOY CAN DREAM, CAN'T HE?
AMEND

Fashion Fruit

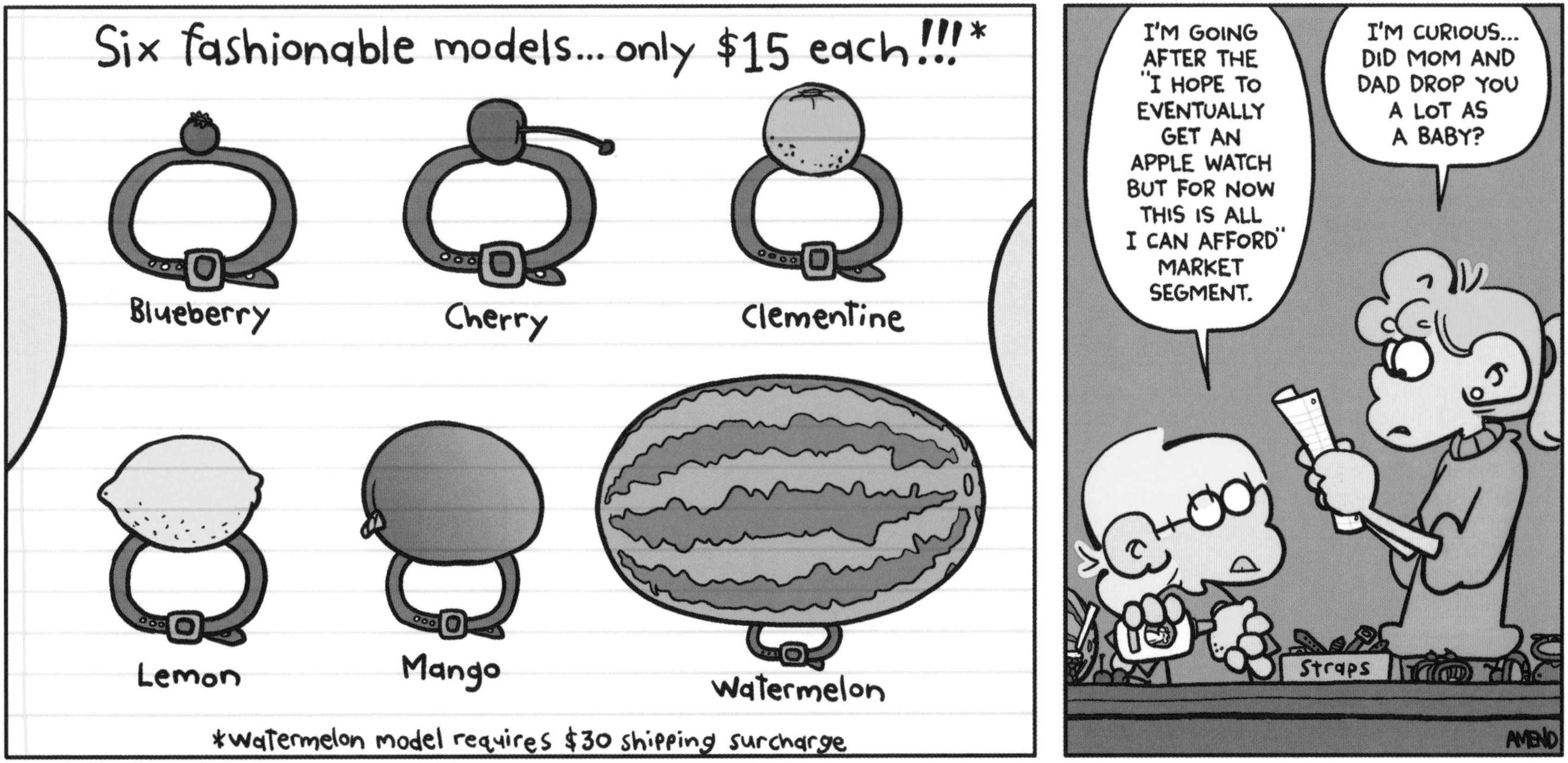
Six fashionable models... only $15 each!!!*
Blueberry
Cherry
Clementine
Lemon
Mango
Watermelon
*watermelon model requires $30 shipping surcharge
I'M GOING AFTER THE "I HOPE TO EVENTUALLY GET AN APPLE WATCH BUT FOR NOW THIS IS ALL I CAN AFFORD" MARKET SEGMENT.
I'M CURIOUS... DID MOM AND DAD DROP YOU A LOT AS A BABY?
Straps
AMEND

Peteritis

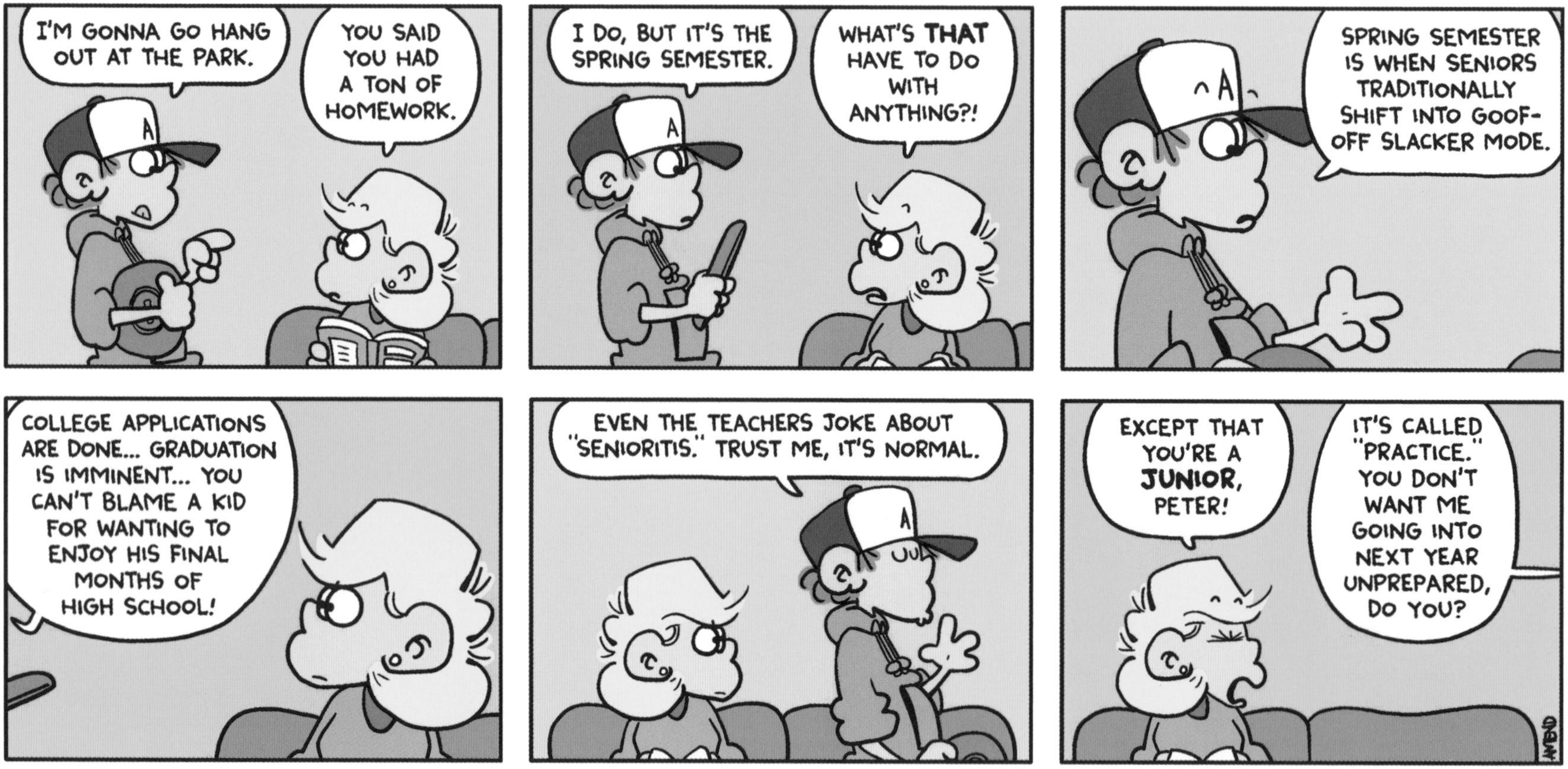

I'M GONNA GO HANG OUT AT THE PARK.
YOU SAID YOU HAD A TON OF HOMEWORK.
I DO, BUT IT'S THE SPRING SEMESTER.
WHAT'S **THAT** HAVE TO DO WITH ANYTHING?!
SPRING SEMESTER IS WHEN SENIORS TRADITIONALLY SHIFT INTO GOOF-OFF SLACKER MODE.
COLLEGE APPLICATIONS ARE DONE... GRADUATION IS IMMINENT... YOU CAN'T BLAME A KID FOR WANTING TO ENJOY HIS FINAL MONTHS OF HIGH SCHOOL!
EVEN THE TEACHERS JOKE ABOUT "SENIORITIS." TRUST ME, IT'S NORMAL.
EXCEPT THAT YOU'RE A **JUNIOR**, PETER!
IT'S CALLED "PRACTICE." YOU DON'T WANT ME GOING INTO NEXT YEAR UNPREPARED, DO YOU?

All Decks on Hand

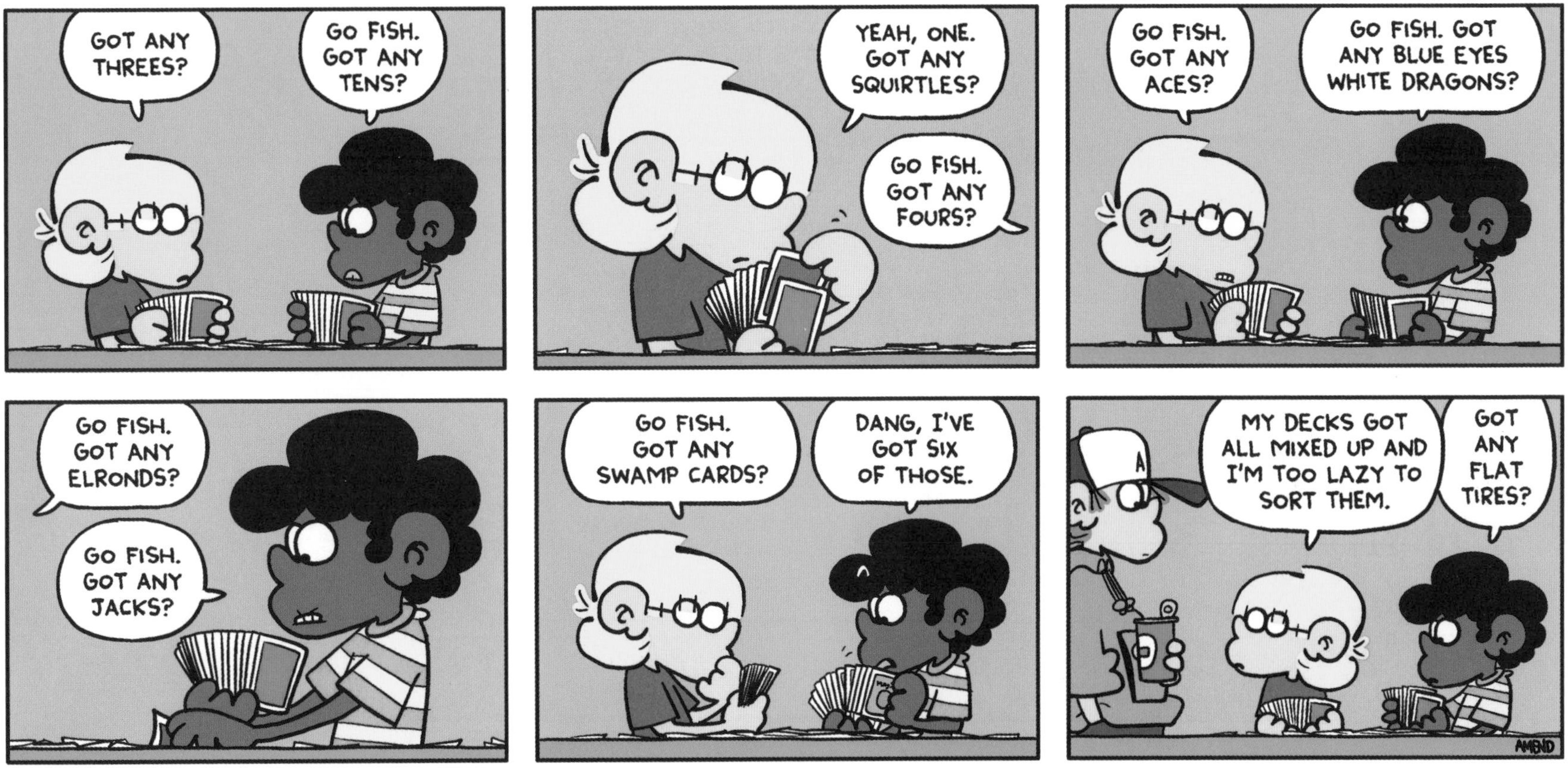
GOT ANY THREES?
GO FISH. GOT ANY TENS?
YEAH, ONE. GOT ANY SQUIRTLES?
GO FISH. GOT ANY FOURS?
GO FISH. GOT ANY ACES?
GO FISH. GOT ANY BLUE EYES WHITE DRAGONS?
GO FISH. GOT ANY ELRONDS?
GO FISH. GOT ANY JACKS?
GO FISH. GOT ANY SWAMP CARDS?
DANG, I'VE GOT SIX OF THOSE.
MY DECKS GOT ALL MIXED UP AND I'M TOO LAZY TO SORT THEM.
GOT ANY FLAT TIRES?
AMEND

Dice Lessoning

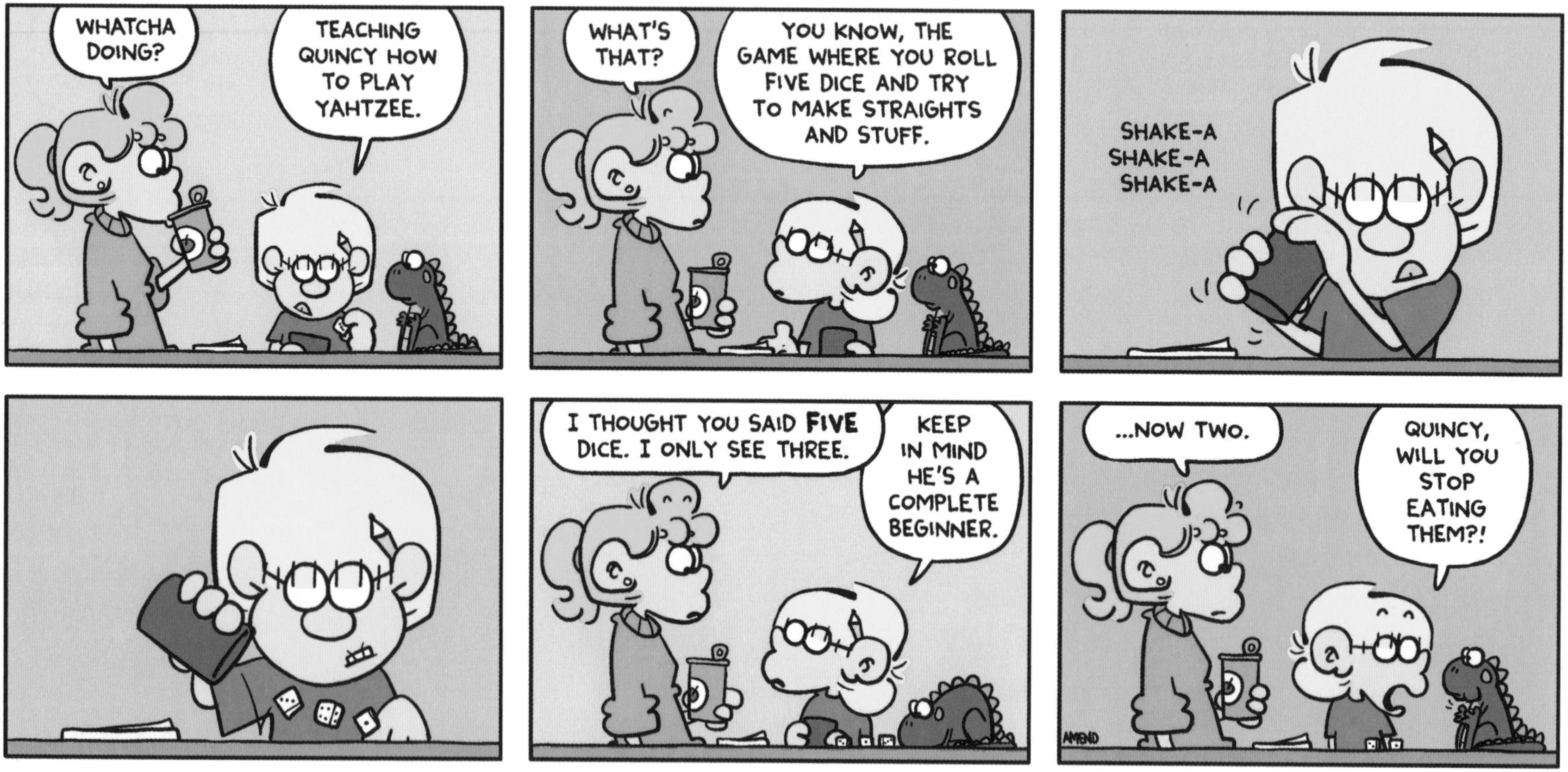
WHATCHA DOING?
TEACHING QUINCY HOW TO PLAY YAHTZEE.
WHAT'S THAT?
YOU KNOW, THE GAME WHERE YOU ROLL FIVE DICE AND TRY TO MAKE STRAIGHTS AND STUFF.
SHAKE-A SHAKE-A SHAKE-A
I THOUGHT YOU SAID **FIVE** DICE. I ONLY SEE THREE.
KEEP IN MIND HE'S A COMPLETE BEGINNER.
...NOW TWO.
QUINCY, WILL YOU STOP EATING THEM?!
AMEND

Minor Assistance

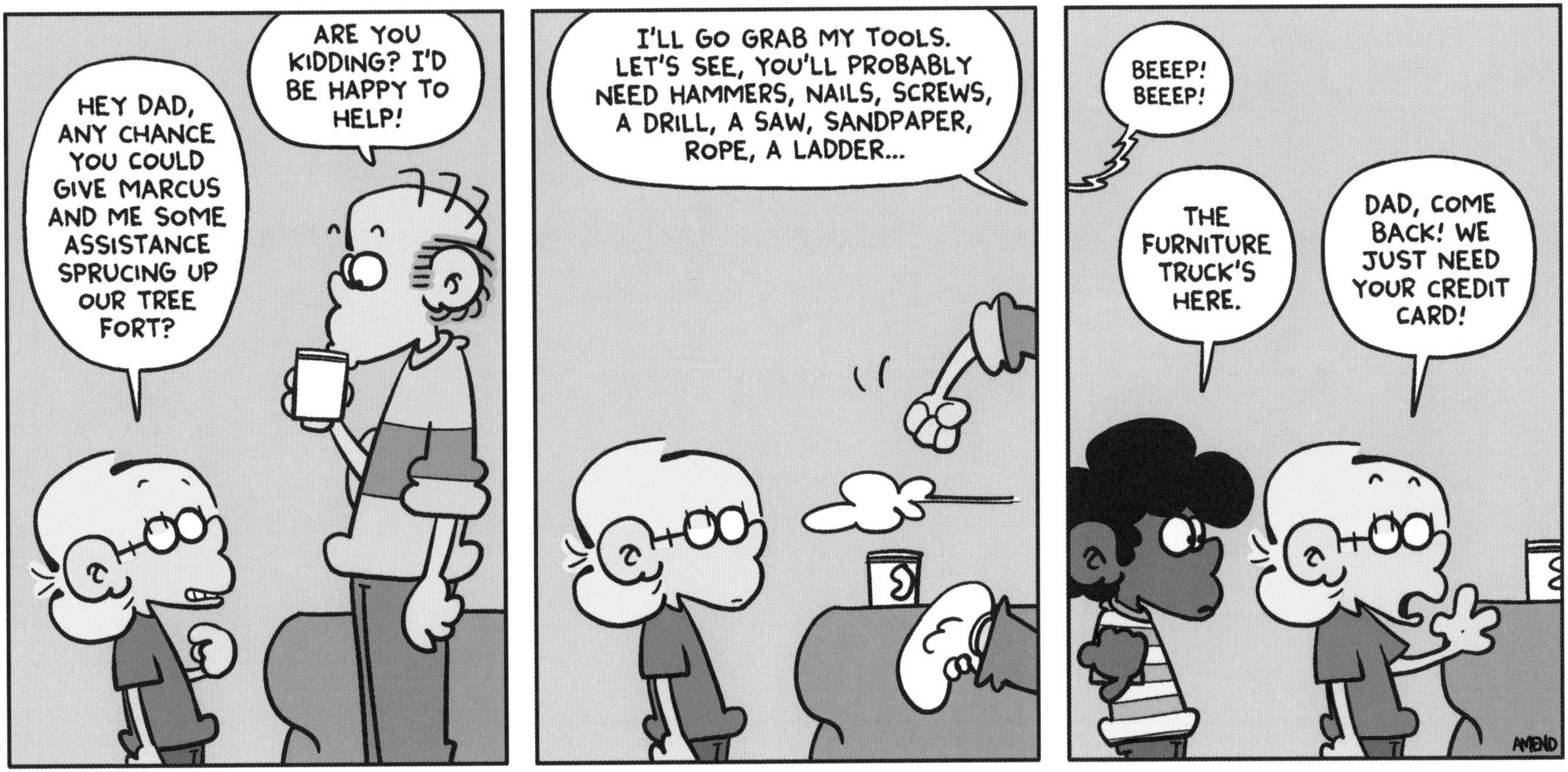
HEY DAD, ANY CHANCE YOU COULD GIVE MARCUS AND ME SOME ASSISTANCE SPRUCING UP OUR TREE FORT?
ARE YOU KIDDING? I'D BE HAPPY TO HELP!
I'LL GO GRAB MY TOOLS. LET'S SEE, YOU'LL PROBABLY NEED HAMMERS, NAILS, SCREWS, A DRILL, A SAW, SANDPAPER, ROPE, A LADDER...
BEEEP! BEEEP!
THE FURNITURE TRUCK'S HERE.
DAD, COME BACK! WE JUST NEED YOUR CREDIT CARD!
AMEND

Jelly Jarred

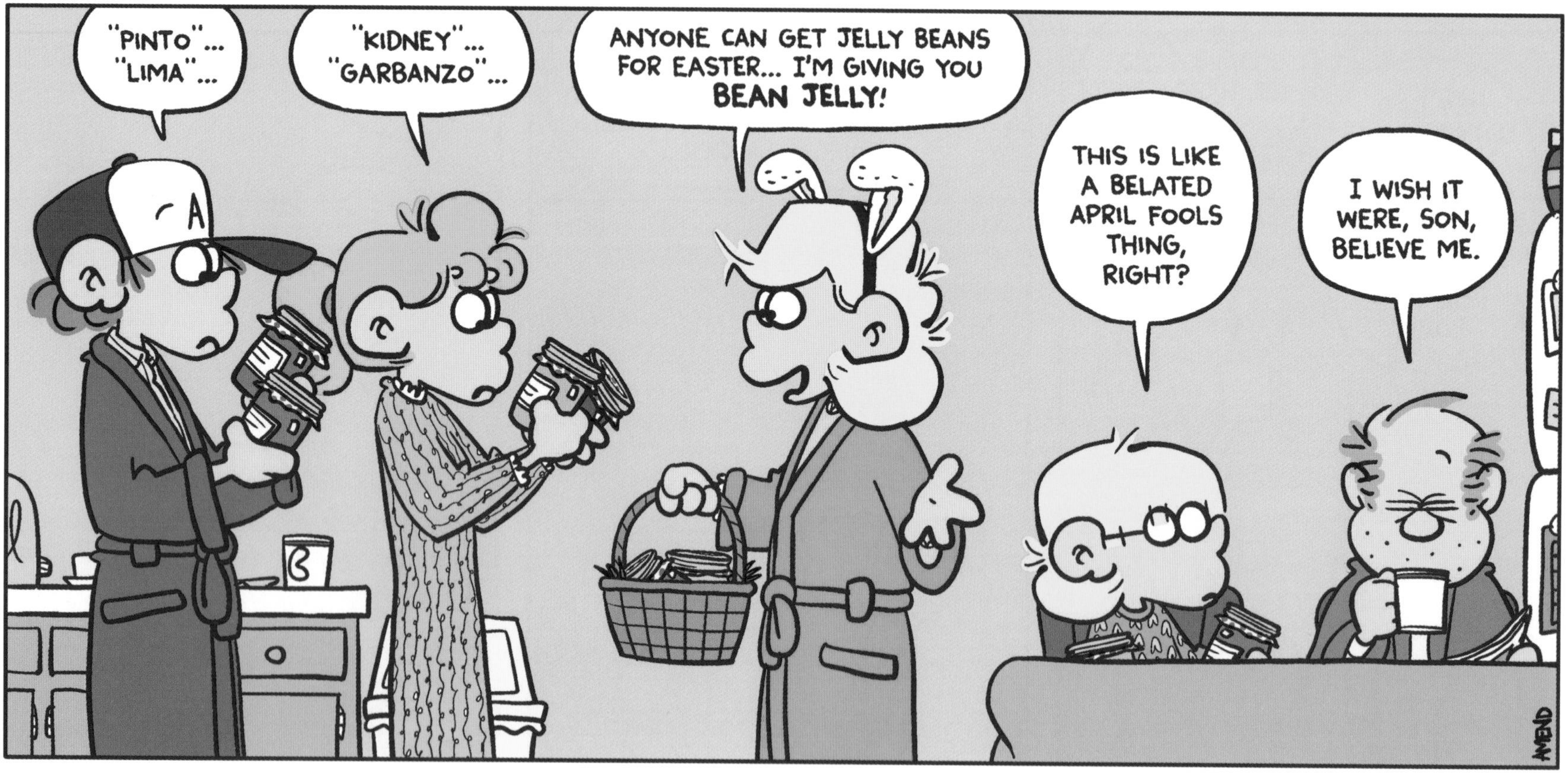
"PINTO"... "LIMA"...
"KIDNEY"... "GARBANZO"...
ANYONE CAN GET JELLY BEANS FOR EASTER... I'M GIVING YOU BEAN JELLY!
THIS IS LIKE A BELATED APRIL FOOLS THING, RIGHT?
I WISH IT WERE, SON, BELIEVE ME.
AMEND

Speedball

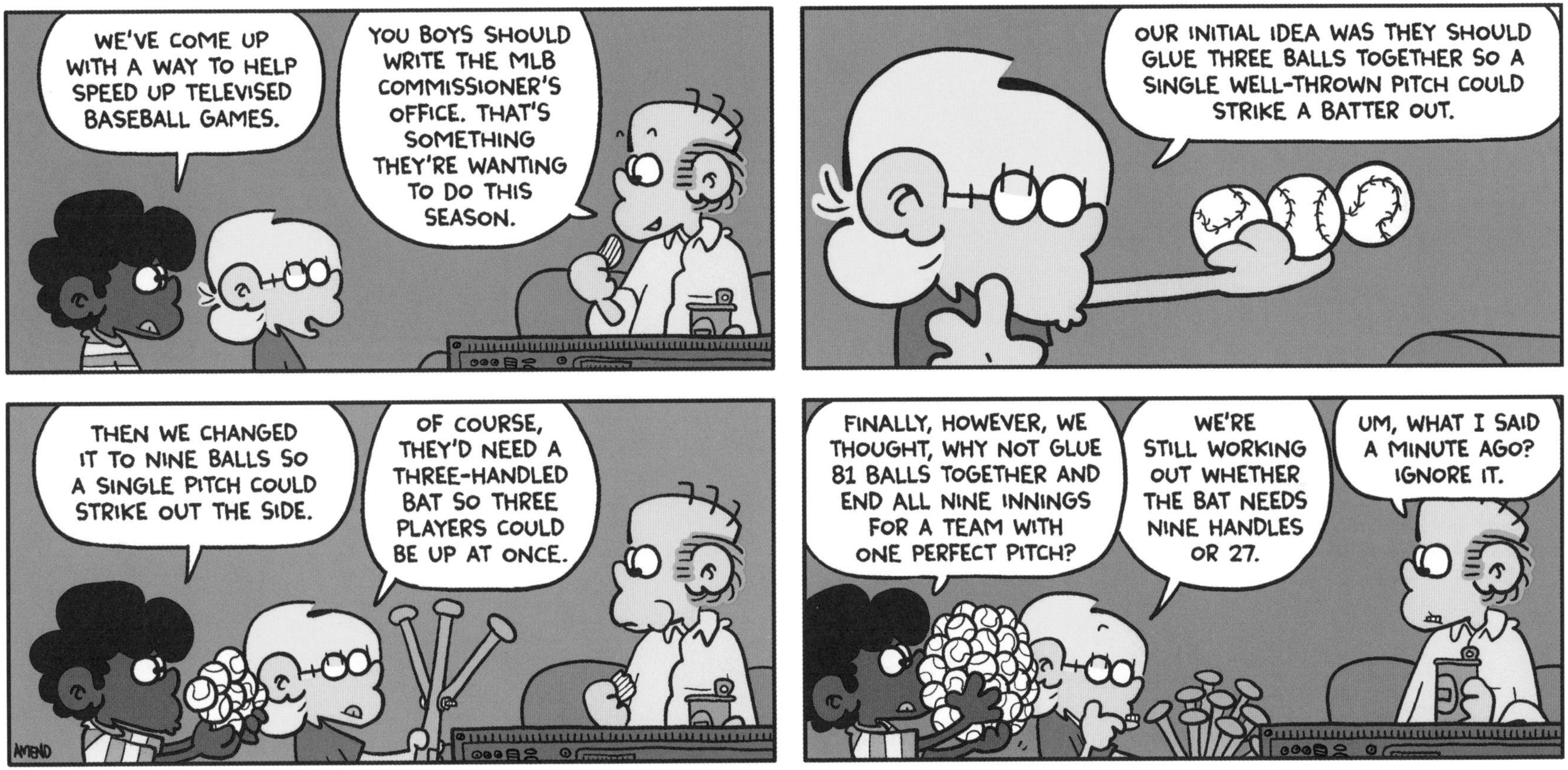
WE'VE COME UP WITH A WAY TO HELP SPEED UP TELEVISED BASEBALL GAMES.
YOU BOYS SHOULD WRITE THE MLB COMMISSIONER'S OFFICE. THAT'S SOMETHING THEY'RE WANTING TO DO THIS SEASON.
OUR INITIAL IDEA WAS THEY SHOULD GLUE THREE BALLS TOGETHER SO A SINGLE WELL-THROWN PITCH COULD STRIKE A BATTER OUT.
THEN WE CHANGED IT TO NINE BALLS SO A SINGLE PITCH COULD STRIKE OUT THE SIDE.
OF COURSE, THEY'D NEED A THREE-HANDLED BAT SO THREE PLAYERS COULD BE UP AT ONCE.
AMEND
FINALLY, HOWEVER, WE THOUGHT, WHY NOT GLUE 81 BALLS TOGETHER AND END ALL NINE INNINGS FOR A TEAM WITH ONE PERFECT PITCH?
WE'RE STILL WORKING OUT WHETHER THE BAT NEEDS NINE HANDLES OR 27.
UM, WHAT I SAID A MINUTE AGO? IGNORE IT.

Squeezy Peezy

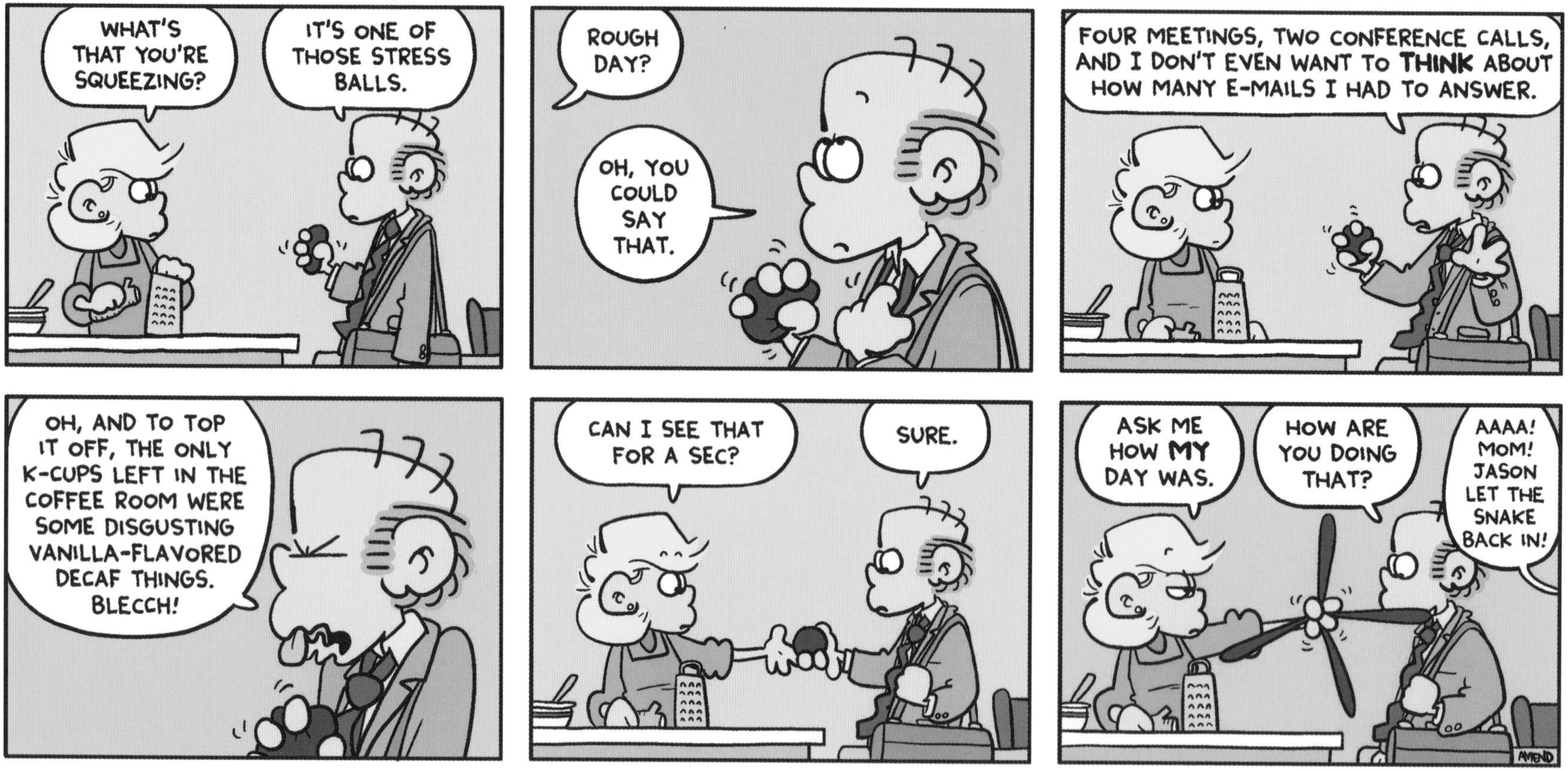
WHAT'S THAT YOU'RE SQUEEZING?
IT'S ONE OF THOSE STRESS BALLS.
ROUGH DAY?
OH, YOU COULD SAY THAT.
FOUR MEETINGS, TWO CONFERENCE CALLS, AND I DON'T EVEN WANT TO THINK ABOUT HOW MANY E-MAILS I HAD TO ANSWER.
OH, AND TO TOP IT OFF, THE ONLY K-CUPS LEFT IN THE COFFEE ROOM WERE SOME DISGUSTING VANILLA-FLAVORED DECAF THINGS. BLECCH!
CAN I SEE THAT FOR A SEC?
SURE.
ASK ME HOW MY DAY WAS.
HOW ARE YOU DOING THAT?
AAAA! MOM! JASON LET THE SNAKE BACK IN!
AMEND

Shields Up

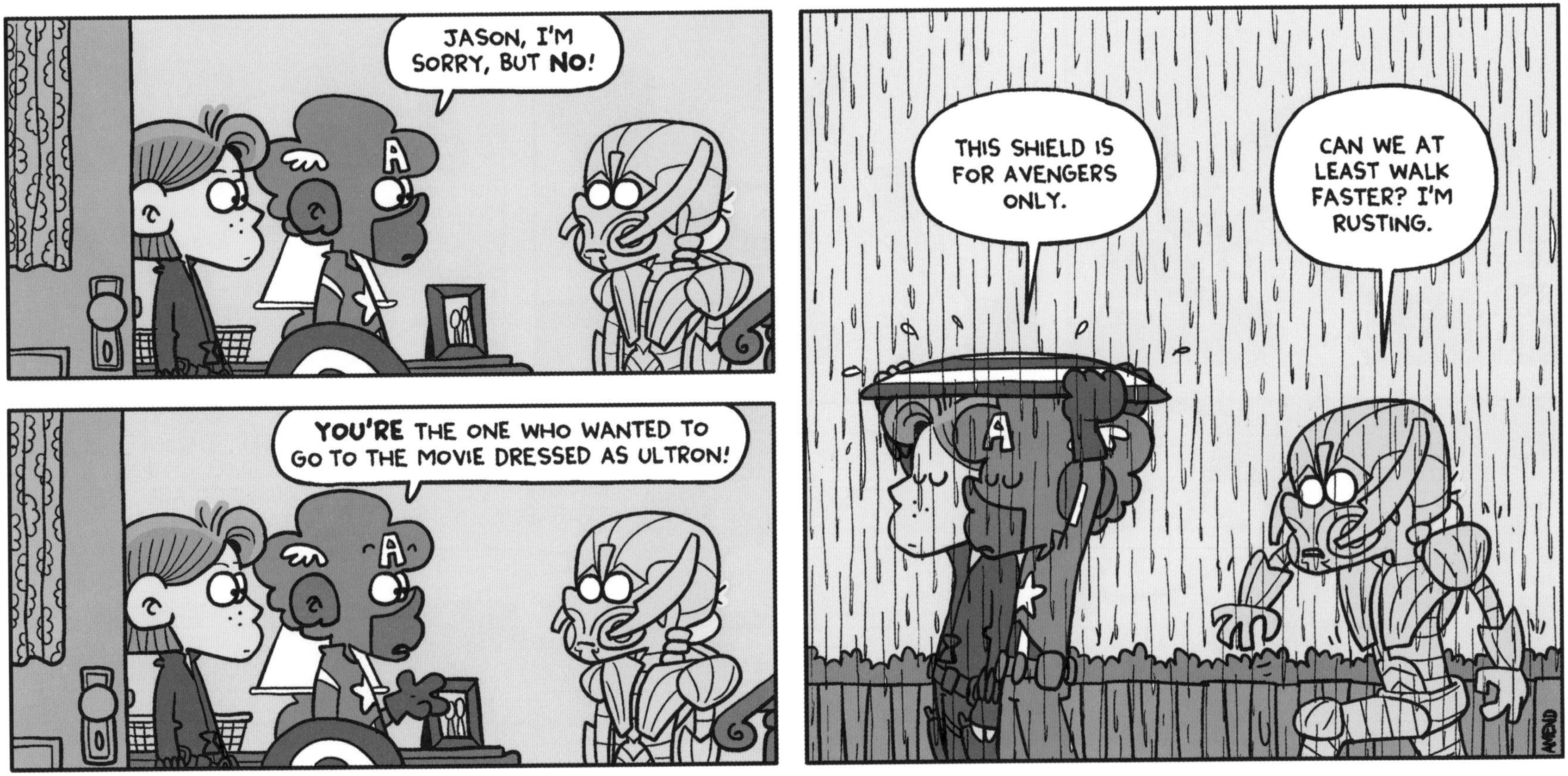

JASON, I'M SORRY, BUT **NO**!
YOU'RE THE ONE WHO WANTED TO GO TO THE MOVIE DRESSED AS ULTRON!
THIS SHIELD IS FOR AVENGERS ONLY.
CAN WE AT LEAST WALK FASTER? I'M RUSTING.

#holycow

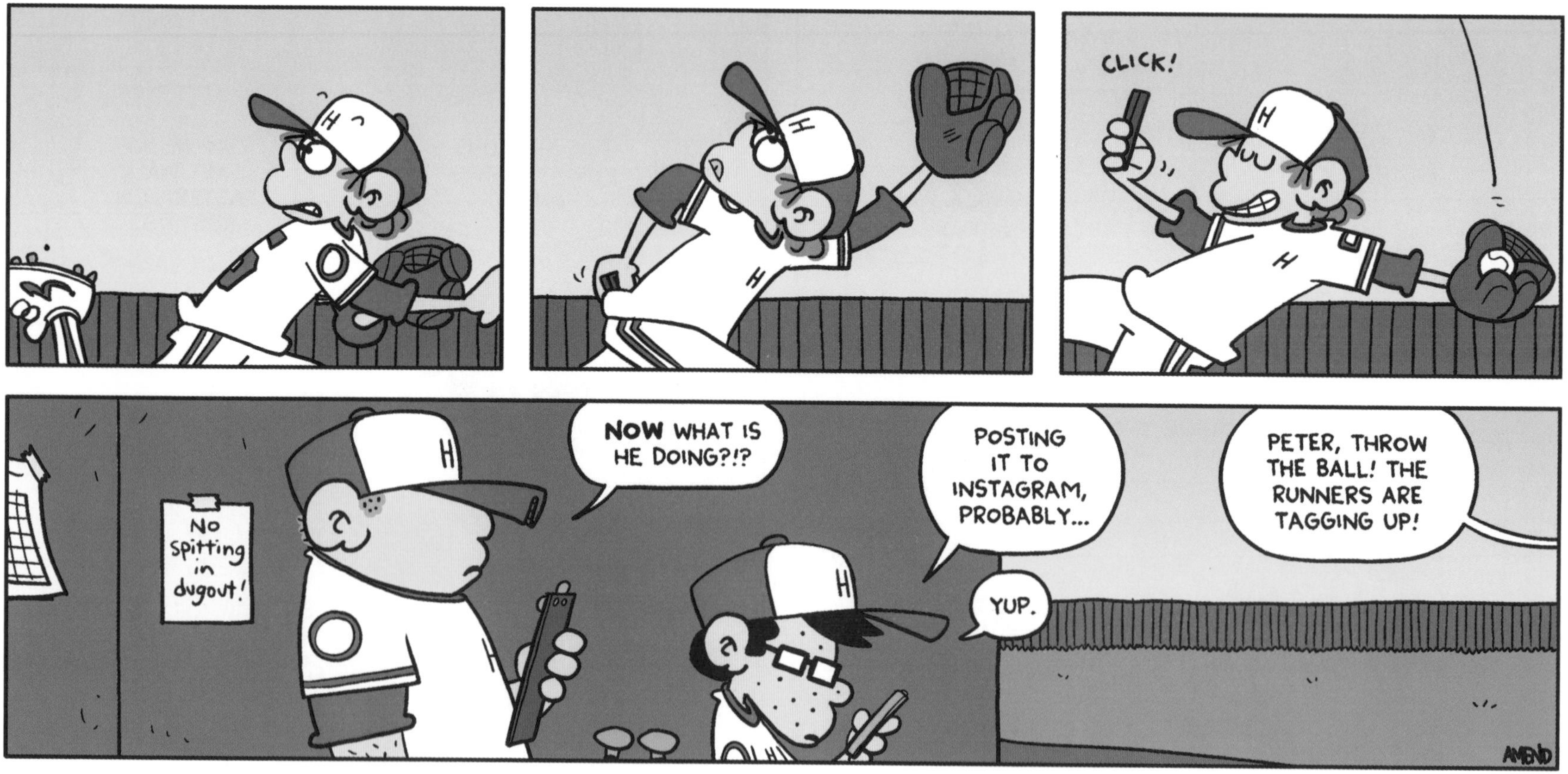
CLICK!
No spitting in dugout!
NOW WHAT IS HE DOING?!?
POSTING IT TO INSTAGRAM, PROBABLY...
YUP.
PETER, THROW THE BALL! THE RUNNERS ARE TAGGING UP!
AMEND

Out of Season

SON, REMEMBER LAST HALLOWEEN WHEN I SAID, "BE SURE TO BRING IN ALL YOUR YARD DECORATIONS"?

KINDA. WHY?

Pointless

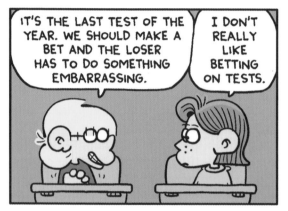

IT'S THE LAST TEST OF THE YEAR. WE SHOULD MAKE A BET AND THE LOSER HAS TO DO SOMETHING EMBARRASSING.

I DON'T REALLY LIKE BETTING ON TESTS.

C'MON, I'LL EVEN SPOT YOU TWO POINTS!

NOT MY THING. SORRY.

OK, FIVE POINTS!

TEN POINTS!

FIFTEEN POINTS!

NOPE.

NOPE.

NOPE.

ALL RIGHT, ALL RIGHT, I'LL SPOT YOU **25** POINTS!

25? OK, FINE.

NOW WE JUST NEED SOMETHING SUPER EMBARRASSING FOR THE LOSER TO DO.

YOU ALREADY DID IT.

A REMINDER, CLASS, THIS TEST WILL BE WORTH 20 POINTS.

Hurl Locker

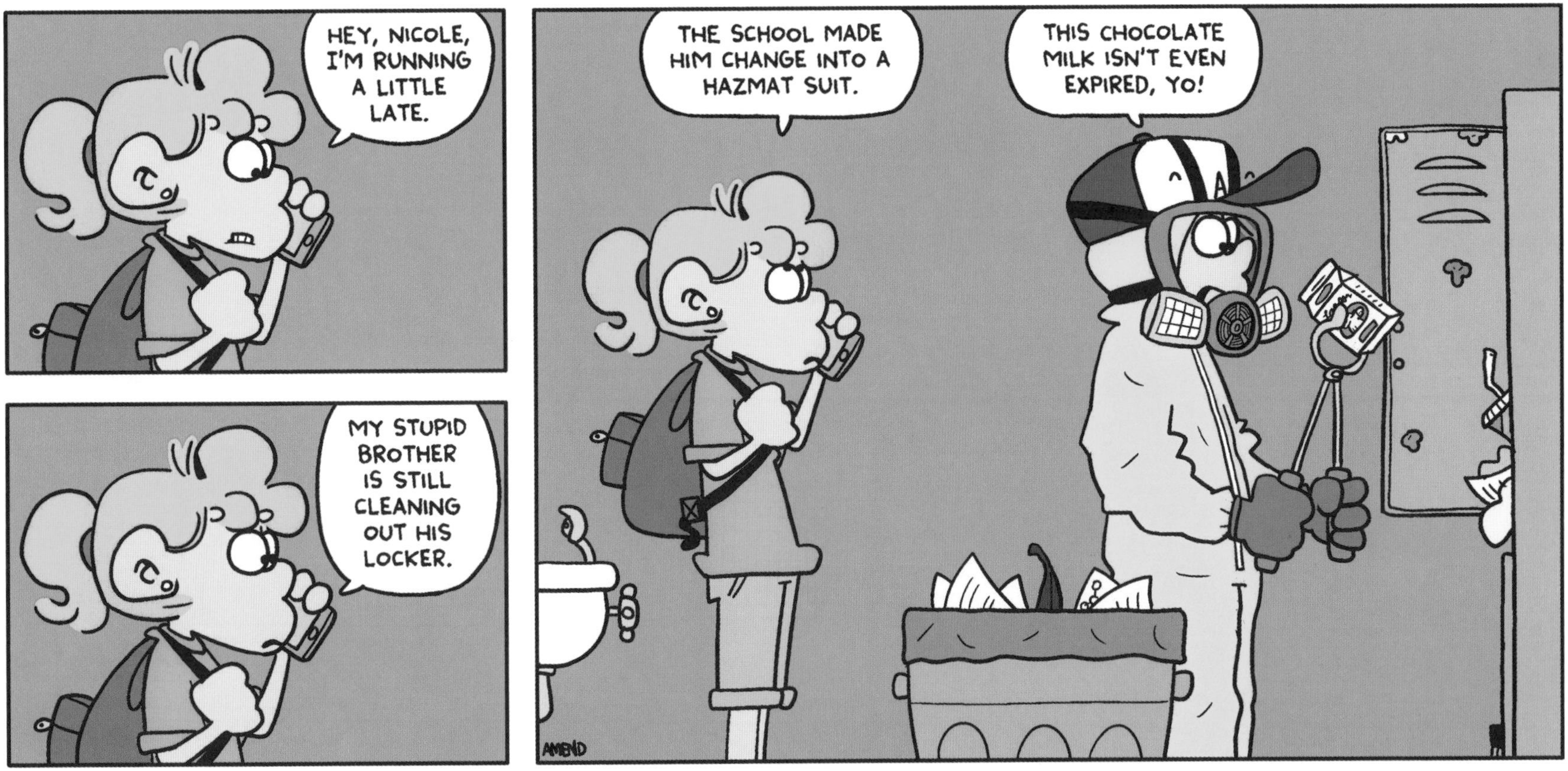
HEY, NICOLE, I'M RUNNING A LITTLE LATE.
MY STUPID BROTHER IS STILL CLEANING OUT HIS LOCKER.
THE SCHOOL MADE HIM CHANGE INTO A HAZMAT SUIT.
THIS CHOCOLATE MILK ISN'T EVEN EXPIRED, YO!
AMEND

Bad Minton

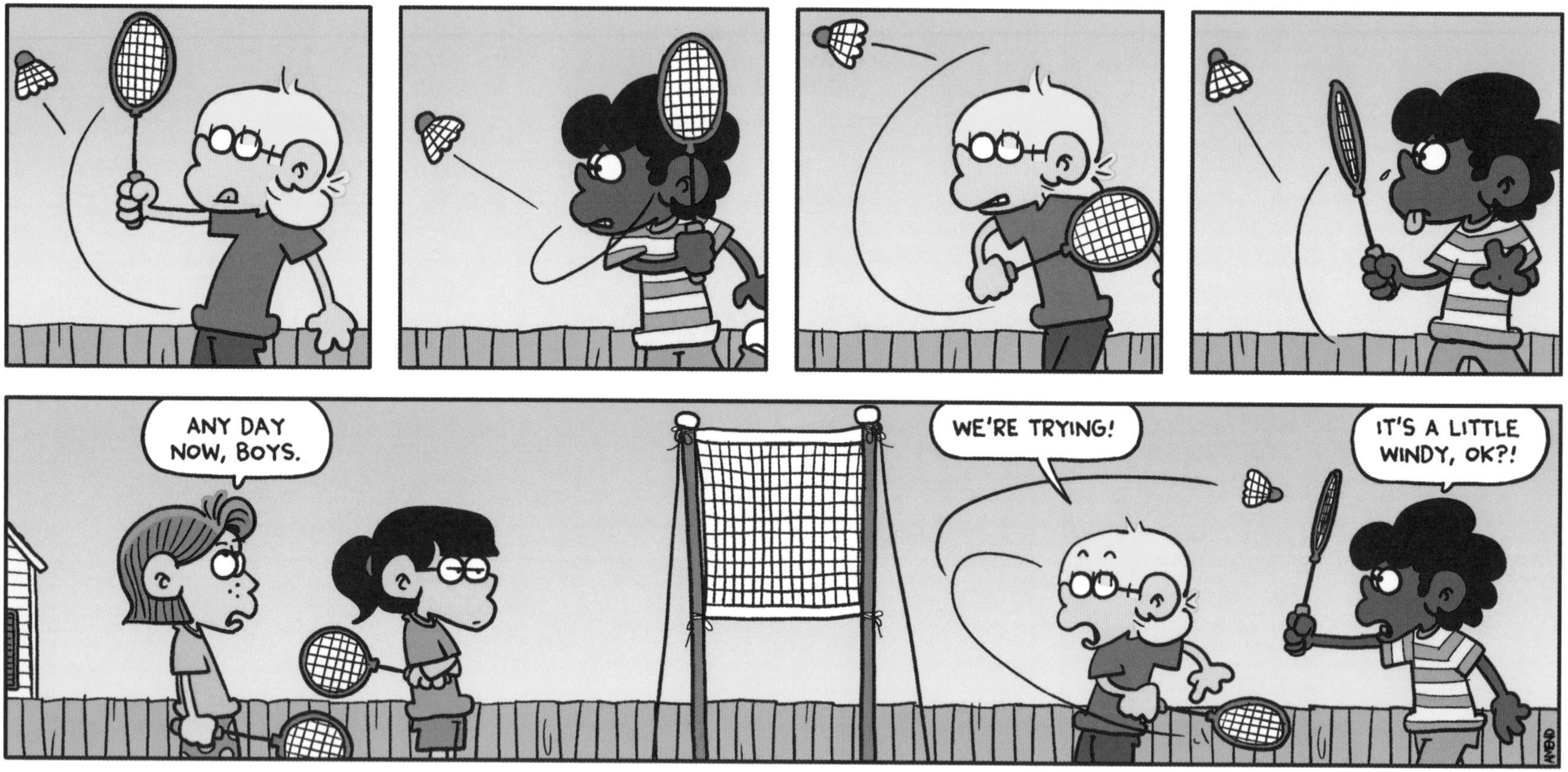
ANY DAY NOW, BOYS.
WE'RE TRYING!
IT'S A LITTLE WINDY, OK?!

Gettin' Triggy Wit It

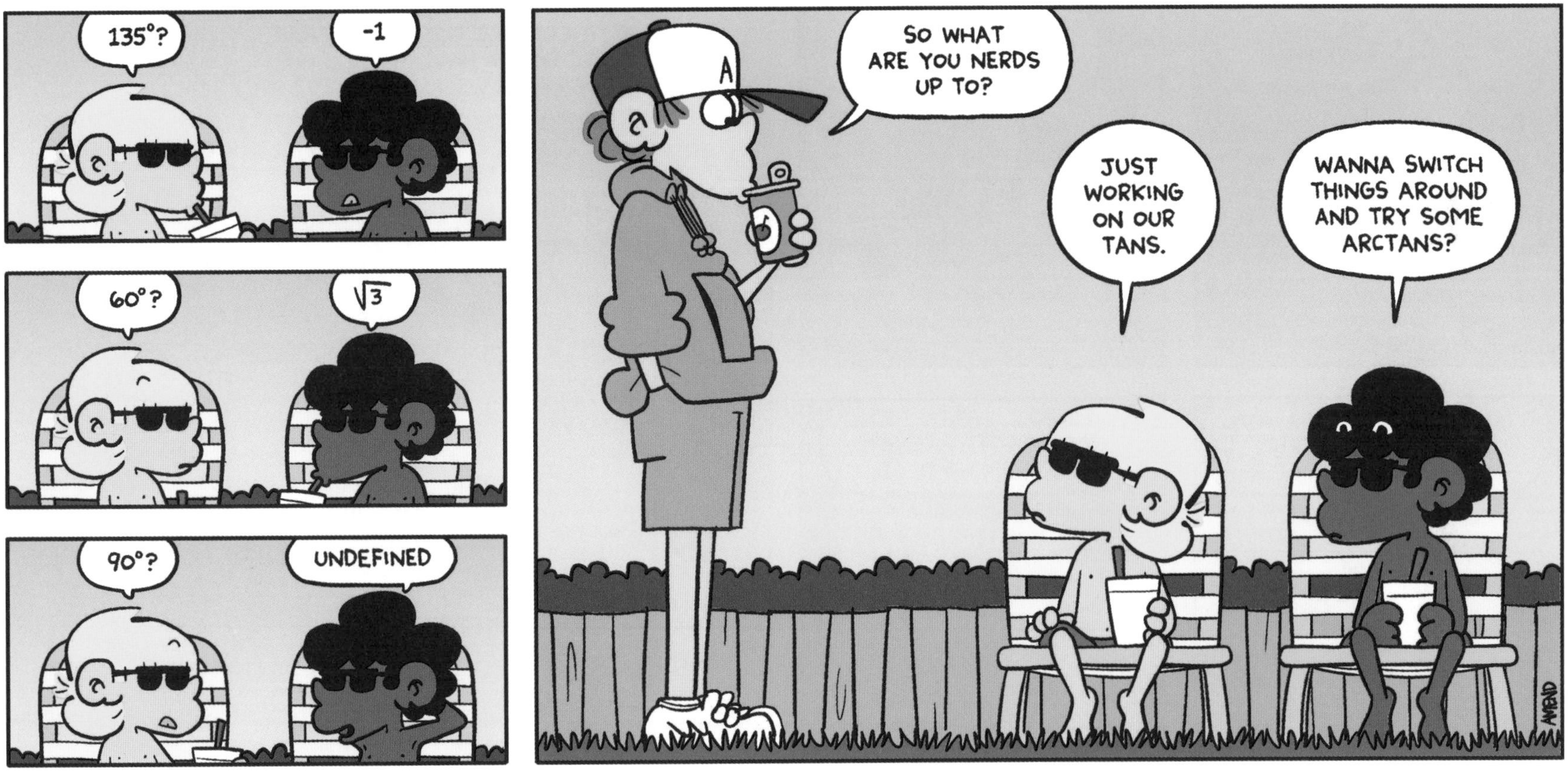

135°?
-1
60°?
√3
90°?
UNDEFINED
SO WHAT ARE YOU NERDS UP TO?
JUST WORKING ON OUR TANS.
WANNA SWITCH THINGS AROUND AND TRY SOME ARCTANS?

Graphic Novice

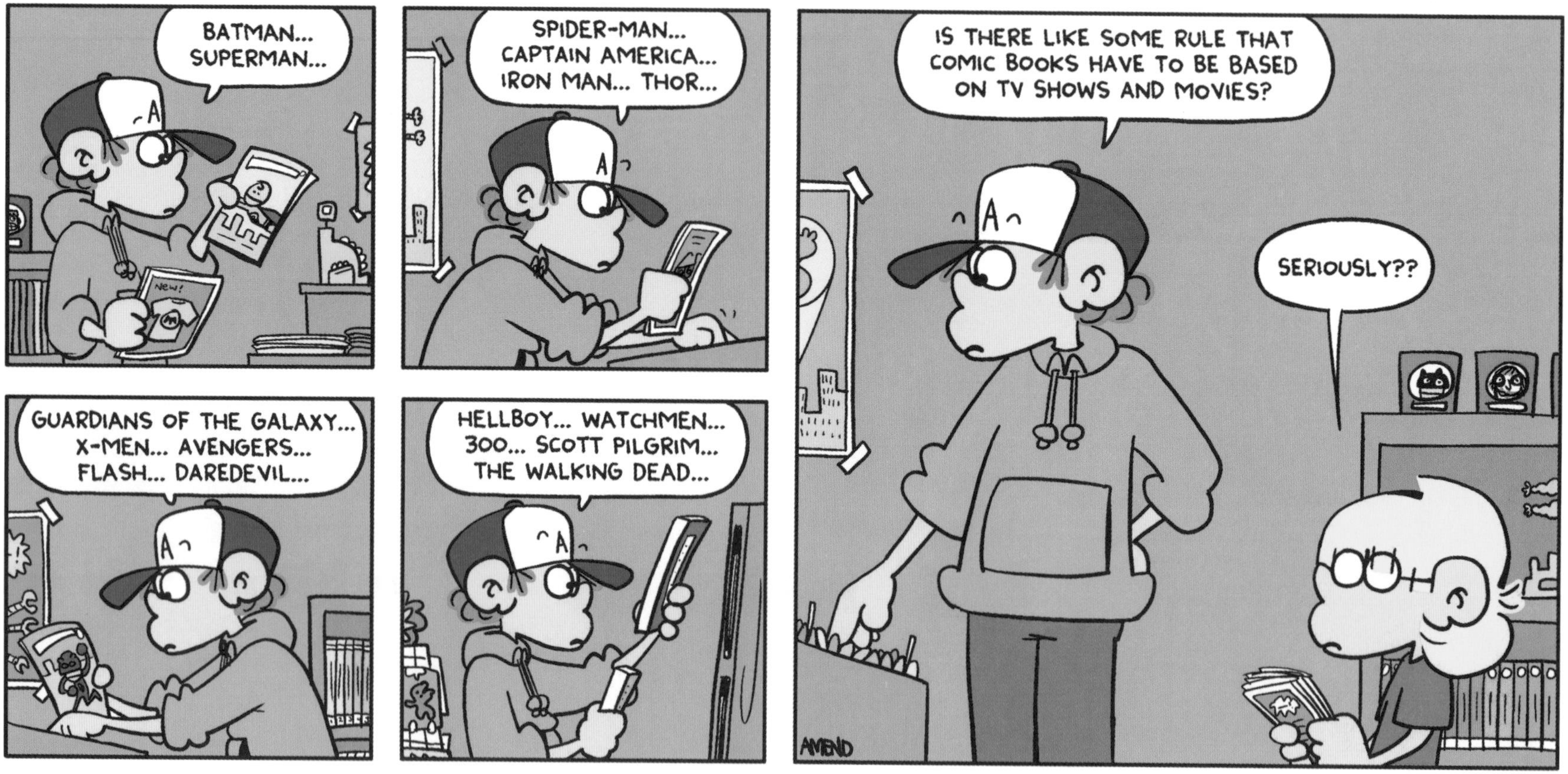
BATMAN... SUPERMAN...
NEW!
SPIDER-MAN... CAPTAIN AMERICA... IRON MAN... THOR...
GUARDIANS OF THE GALAXY... X-MEN... AVENGERS... FLASH... DAREDEVIL...
HELLBOY... WATCHMEN... 300... SCOTT PILGRIM... THE WALKING DEAD...
IS THERE LIKE SOME RULE THAT COMIC BOOKS HAVE TO BE BASED ON TV SHOWS AND MOVIES?
SERIOUSLY??
AMEND

Hole Everything

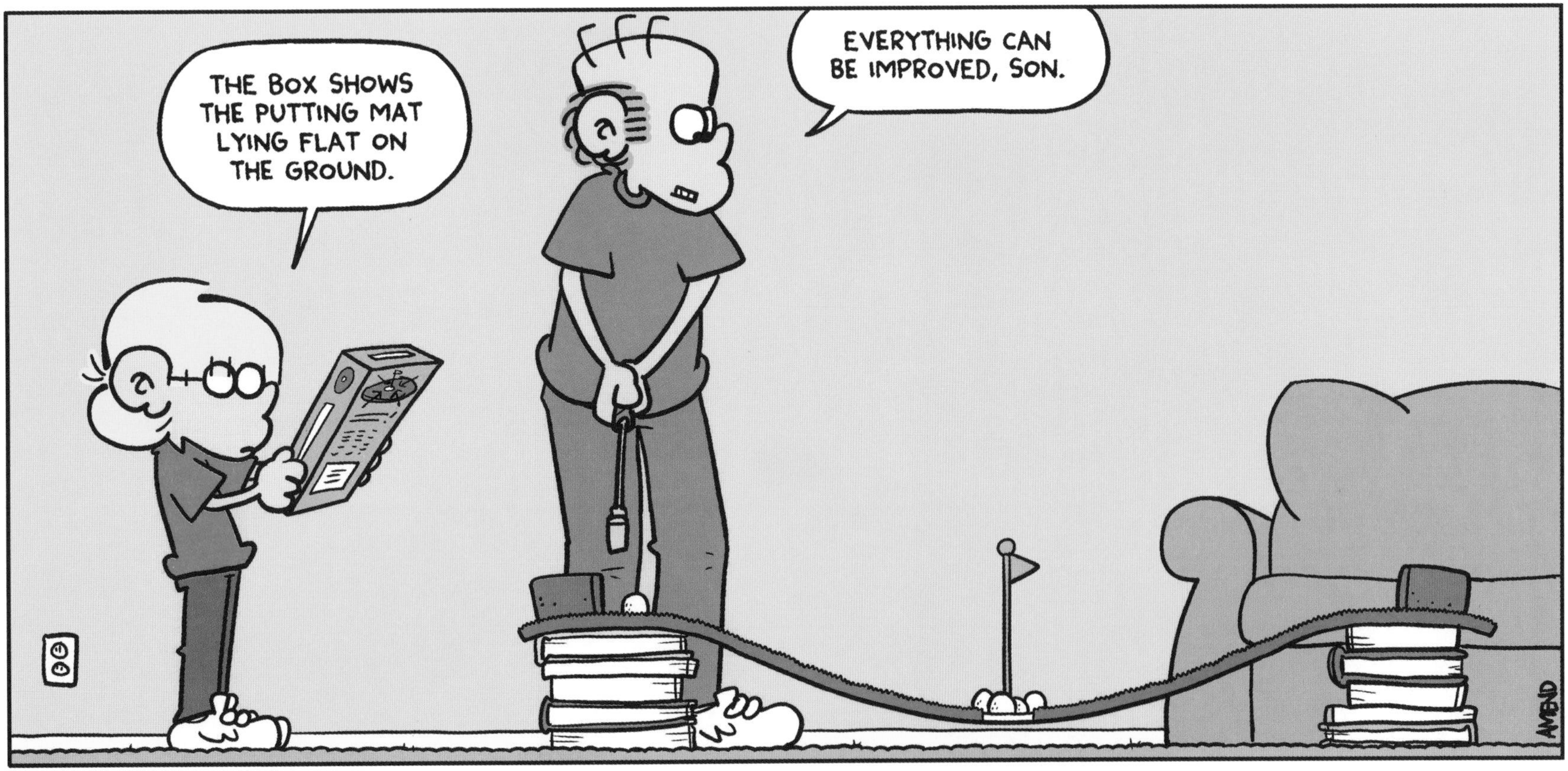
THE BOX SHOWS THE PUTTING MAT LYING FLAT ON THE GROUND.
EVERYTHING CAN BE IMPROVED, SON.
AMEND

Gotta Be a Catch

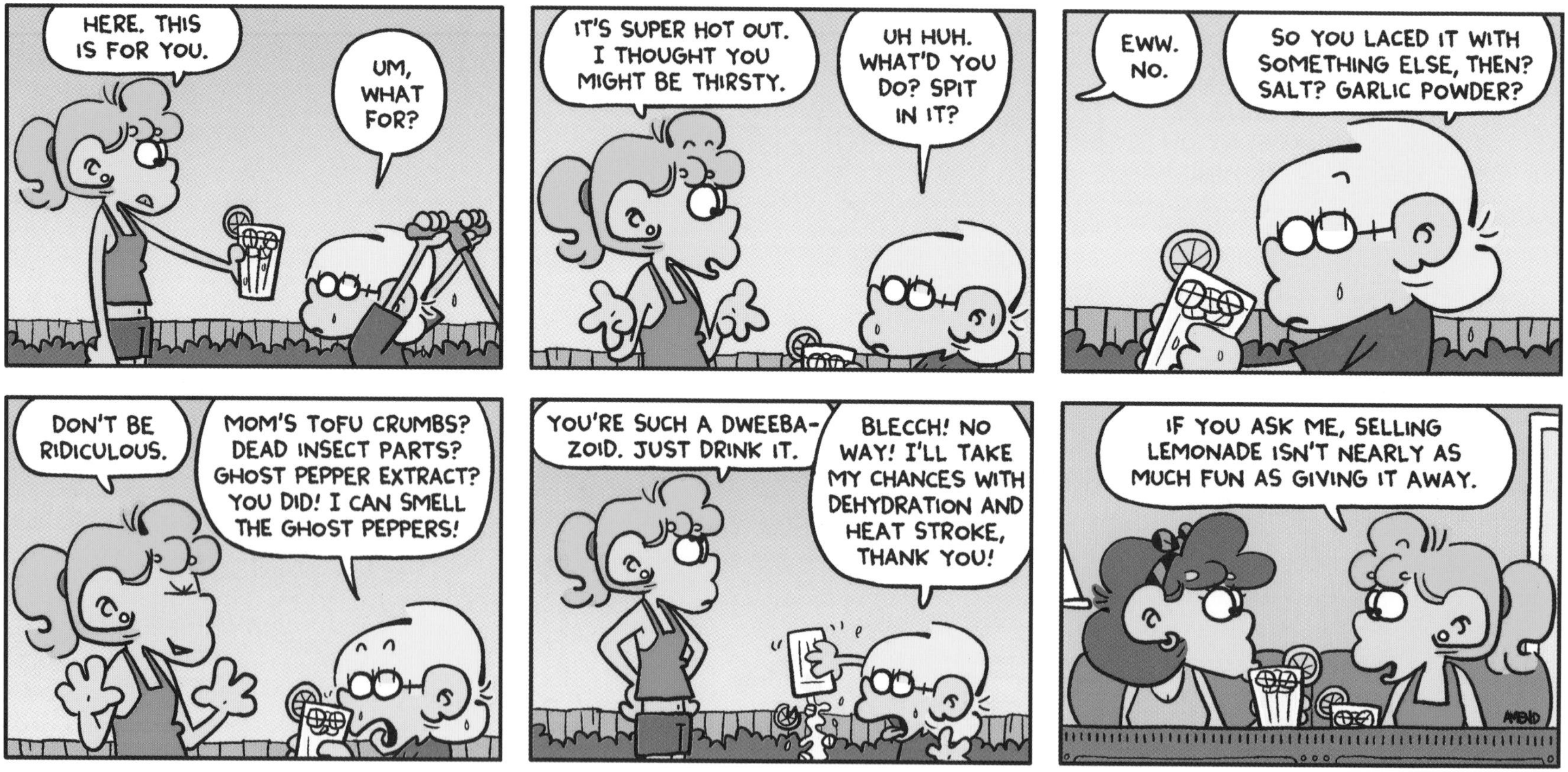
HERE. THIS IS FOR YOU.
UM, WHAT FOR?
IT'S SUPER HOT OUT. I THOUGHT YOU MIGHT BE THIRSTY.
UH HUH. WHAT'D YOU DO? SPIT IN IT?
EWW. NO.
SO YOU LACED IT WITH SOMETHING ELSE, THEN? SALT? GARLIC POWDER?
DON'T BE RIDICULOUS.
MOM'S TOFU CRUMBS? DEAD INSECT PARTS? GHOST PEPPER EXTRACT? YOU DID! I CAN SMELL THE GHOST PEPPERS!
YOU'RE SUCH A DWEEBA-ZOID. JUST DRINK IT.
BLECCH! NO WAY! I'LL TAKE MY CHANCES WITH DEHYDRATION AND HEAT STROKE, THANK YOU!
IF YOU ASK ME, SELLING LEMONADE ISN'T NEARLY AS MUCH FUN AS GIVING IT AWAY.
AMEND

Anticip . . .

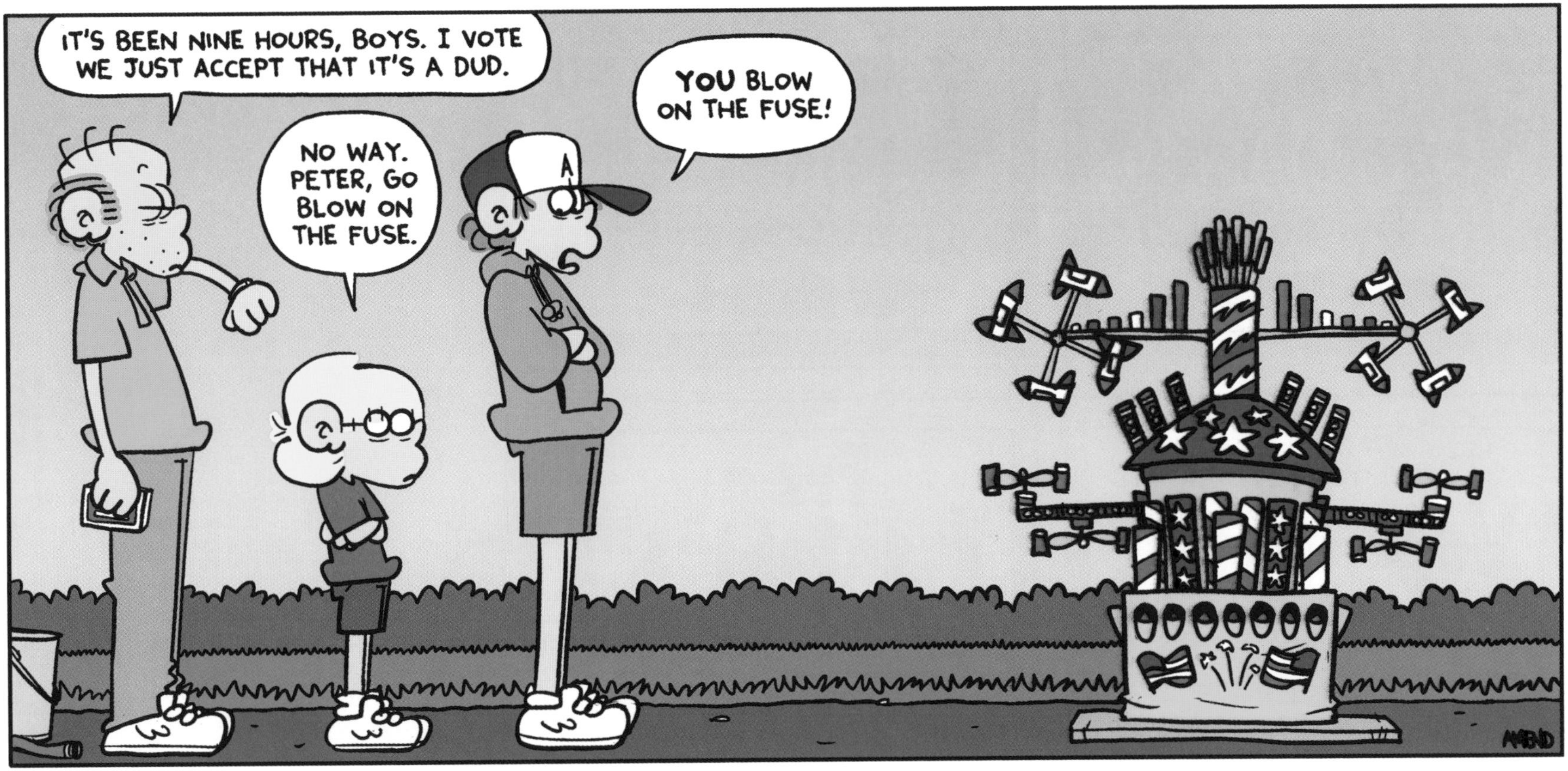
IT'S BEEN NINE HOURS, BOYS. I VOTE WE JUST ACCEPT THAT IT'S A DUD.
NO WAY. PETER, GO BLOW ON THE FUSE.
YOU BLOW ON THE FUSE!

Come On in, Guys!

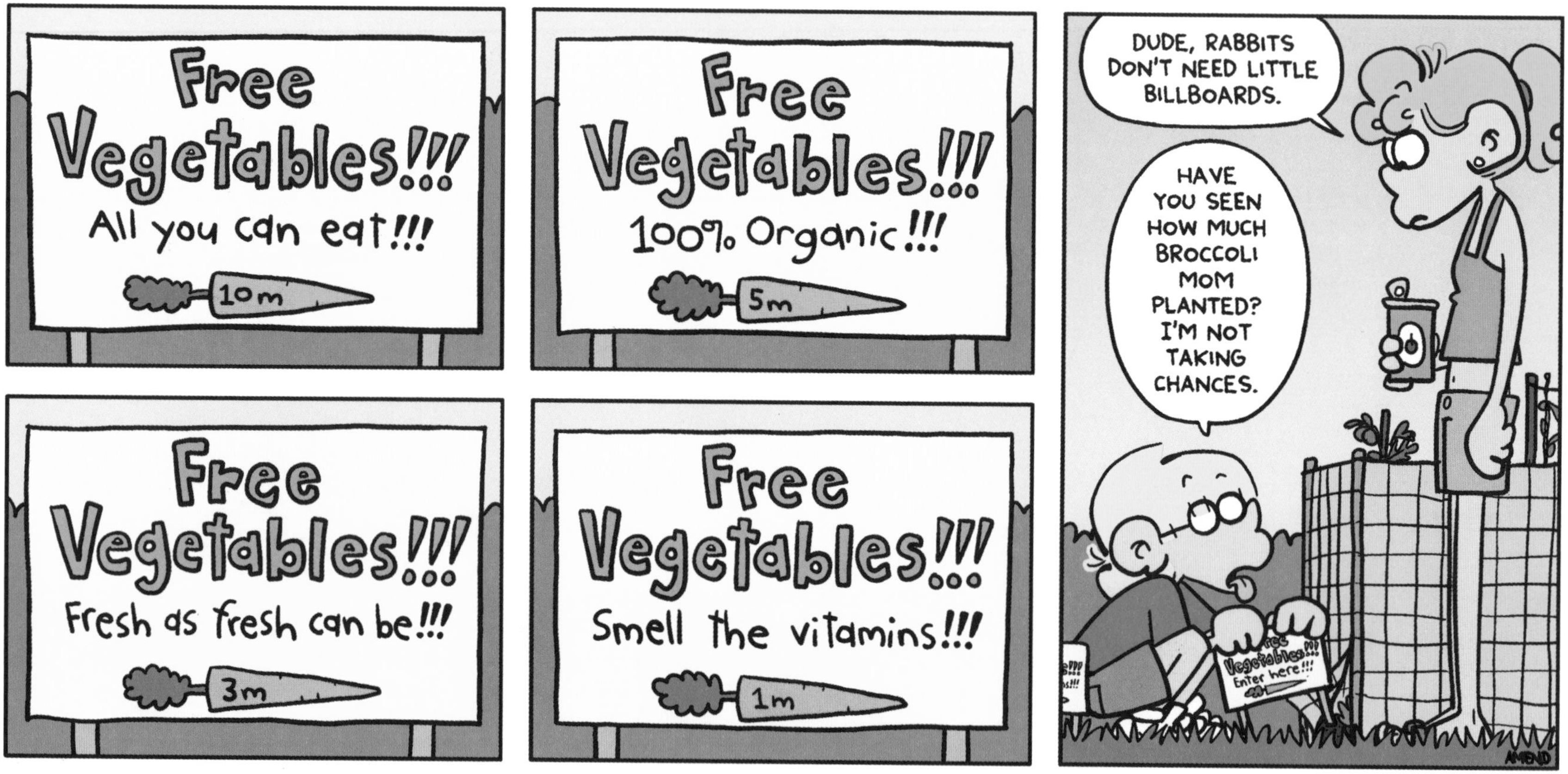

Free Vegetables!!!
All you can eat!!!
10m
Free Vegetables!!!
100% Organic!!!
5m
Free Vegetables!!!
Fresh as fresh can be!!!
3m
Free Vegetables!!!
Smell the vitamins!!!
1m
DUDE, RABBITS DON'T NEED LITTLE BILLBOARDS.
HAVE YOU SEEN HOW MUCH BROCCOLI MOM PLANTED? I'M NOT TAKING CHANCES.
Vegetables!!!
Enter here!!!

Too Cool

WHY ARE YOU WALKING AROUND WITH A DRONE FLYING SIX INCHES ABOVE YOUR HEAD?

BECAUSE I'M SUPER COOL.

YOU. "SUPER COOL."

YES. NOT ONLY AM I THE OWNER OF THE COOLEST RC TOY KNOWN TO MAN...

BUT I AM ALSO USING ITS QUAD ROTORS TO BLOW AIR ONTO MY HEAD, THUS COOLING MYSELF OFF.

AT FIRST I THOUGHT THAT MADE ME DOUBLY COOL, BUT NOW I'M THINKING IT'S MORE LIKE COOL TO THE COOLTH POWER. I SHOULD CHANGE MY NAME TO COOLIO McCOOLESTER OR SOMETHING.

IS THAT THE BATTERY LIGHT THAT'S FLASHING?

UM...

COOL HAIRCUT.

SHUT UP.

Say "AAAAA"

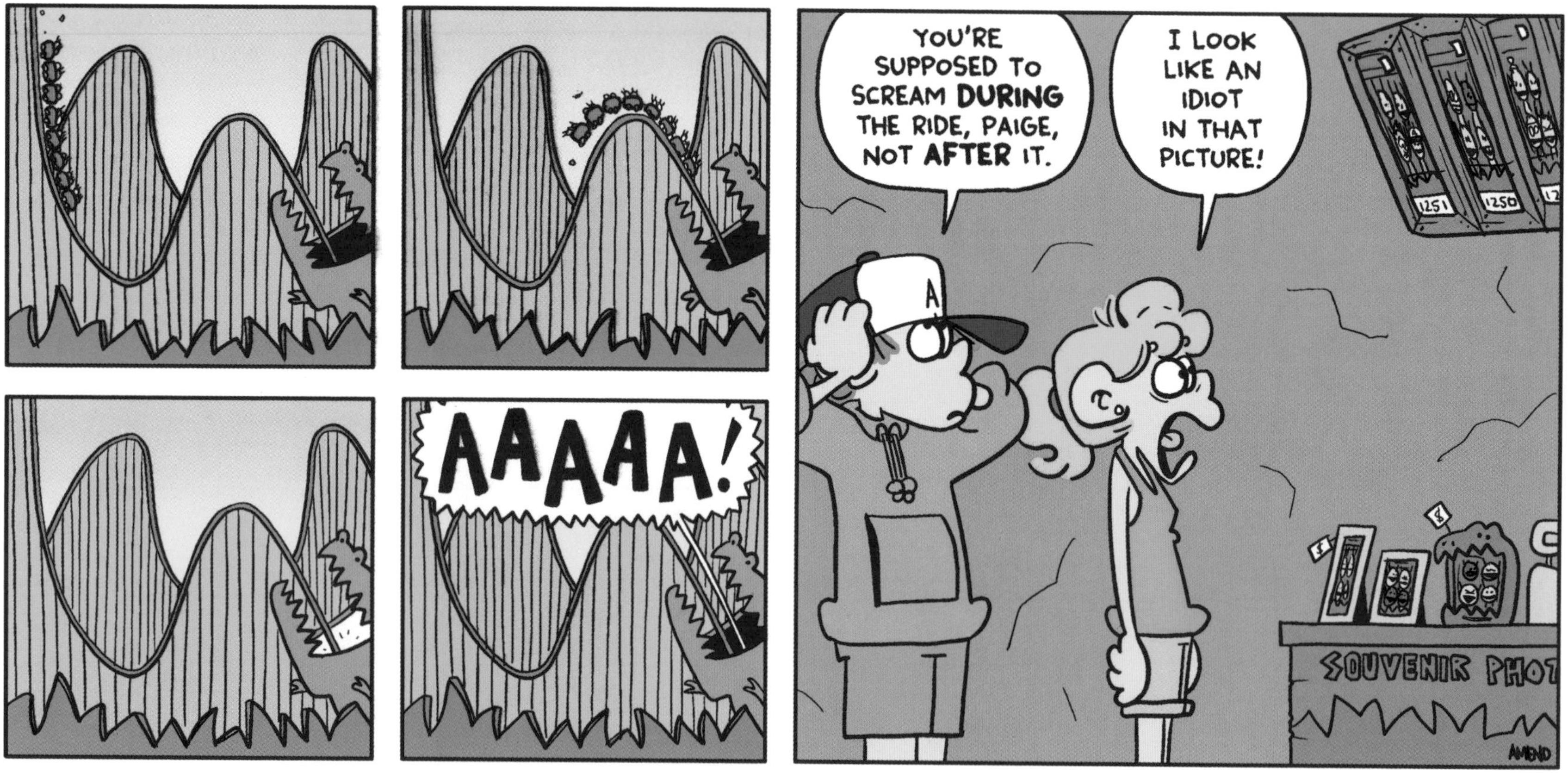

AAAAA!
YOU'RE SUPPOSED TO SCREAM DURING THE RIDE, PAIGE, NOT AFTER IT.
I LOOK LIKE AN IDIOT IN THAT PICTURE!
SOUVENIR PHOT
AMEND

Iguaminus Rex

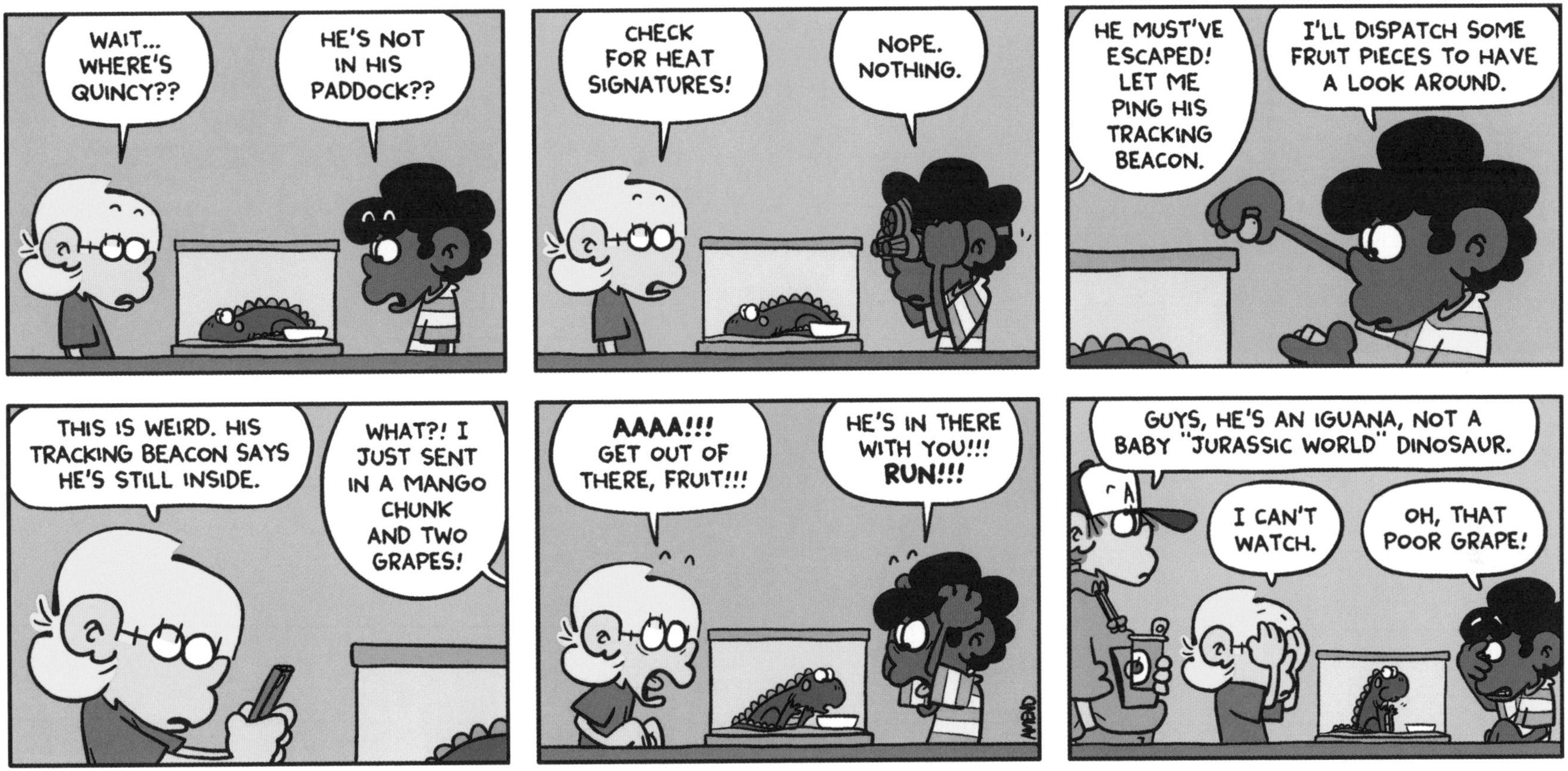
WAIT... WHERE'S QUINCY??
HE'S NOT IN HIS PADDOCK??
CHECK FOR HEAT SIGNATURES!
NOPE. NOTHING.
HE MUST'VE ESCAPED! LET ME PING HIS TRACKING BEACON.
I'LL DISPATCH SOME FRUIT PIECES TO HAVE A LOOK AROUND.
THIS IS WEIRD. HIS TRACKING BEACON SAYS HE'S STILL INSIDE.
WHAT?! I JUST SENT IN A MANGO CHUNK AND TWO GRAPES!
AAAA!!! GET OUT OF THERE, FRUIT!!!
HE'S IN THERE WITH YOU!!! RUN!!!
GUYS, HE'S AN IGUANA, NOT A BABY "JURASSIC WORLD" DINOSAUR.
I CAN'T WATCH.
OH, THAT POOR GRAPE!

Tastyshapes

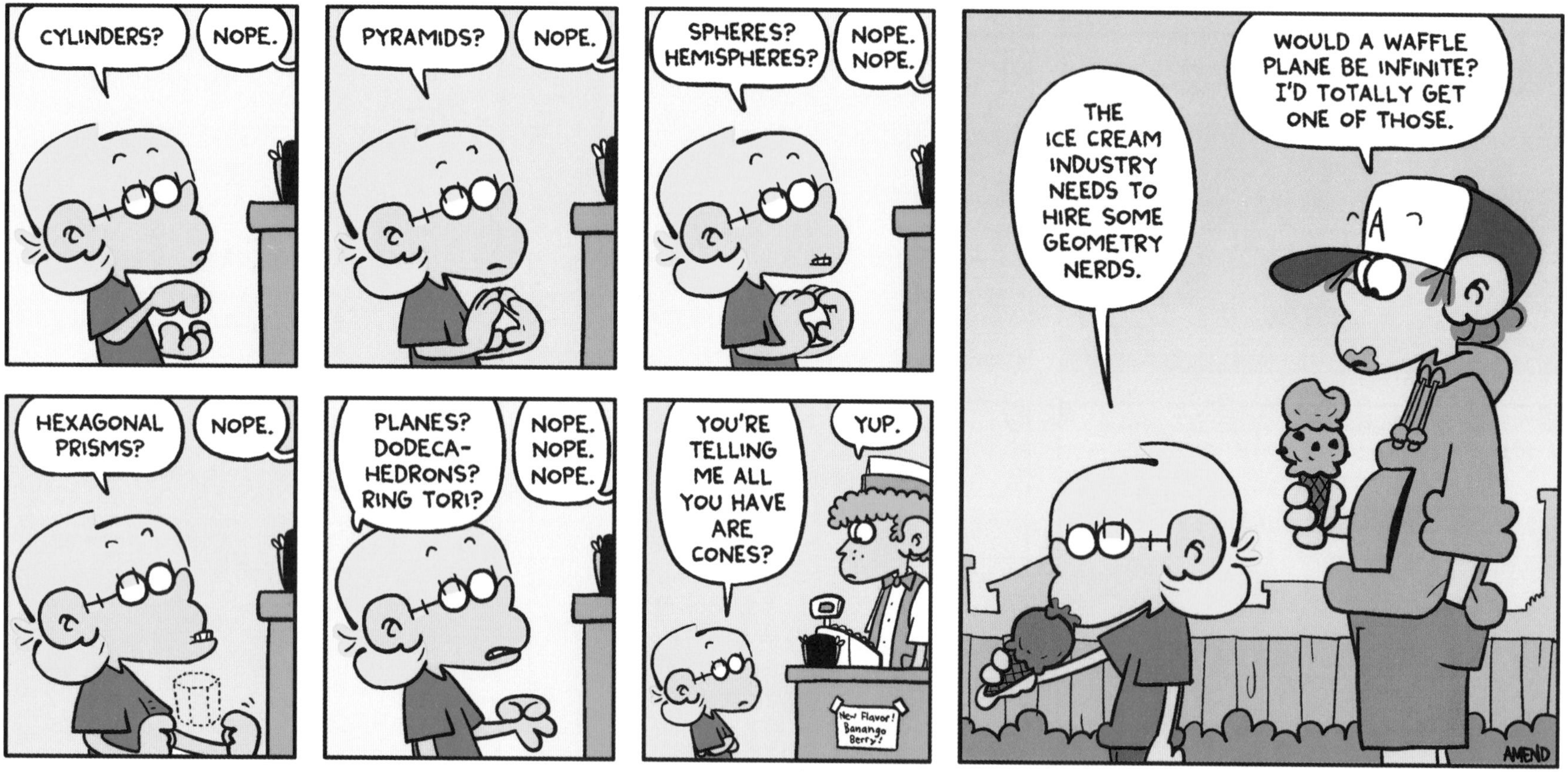

CYLINDERS?
NOPE.
PYRAMIDS?
NOPE.
SPHERES? HEMISPHERES?
NOPE. NOPE.
HEXAGONAL PRISMS?
NOPE.
PLANES? DODECA-HEDRONS? RING TORI?
NOPE. NOPE. NOPE.
YOU'RE TELLING ME ALL YOU HAVE ARE CONES?
YUP.
New Flavor! Banango Berry!
THE ICE CREAM INDUSTRY NEEDS TO HIRE SOME GEOMETRY NERDS.
WOULD A WAFFLE PLANE BE INFINITE? I'D TOTALLY GET ONE OF THOSE.
AMEND

No Worries

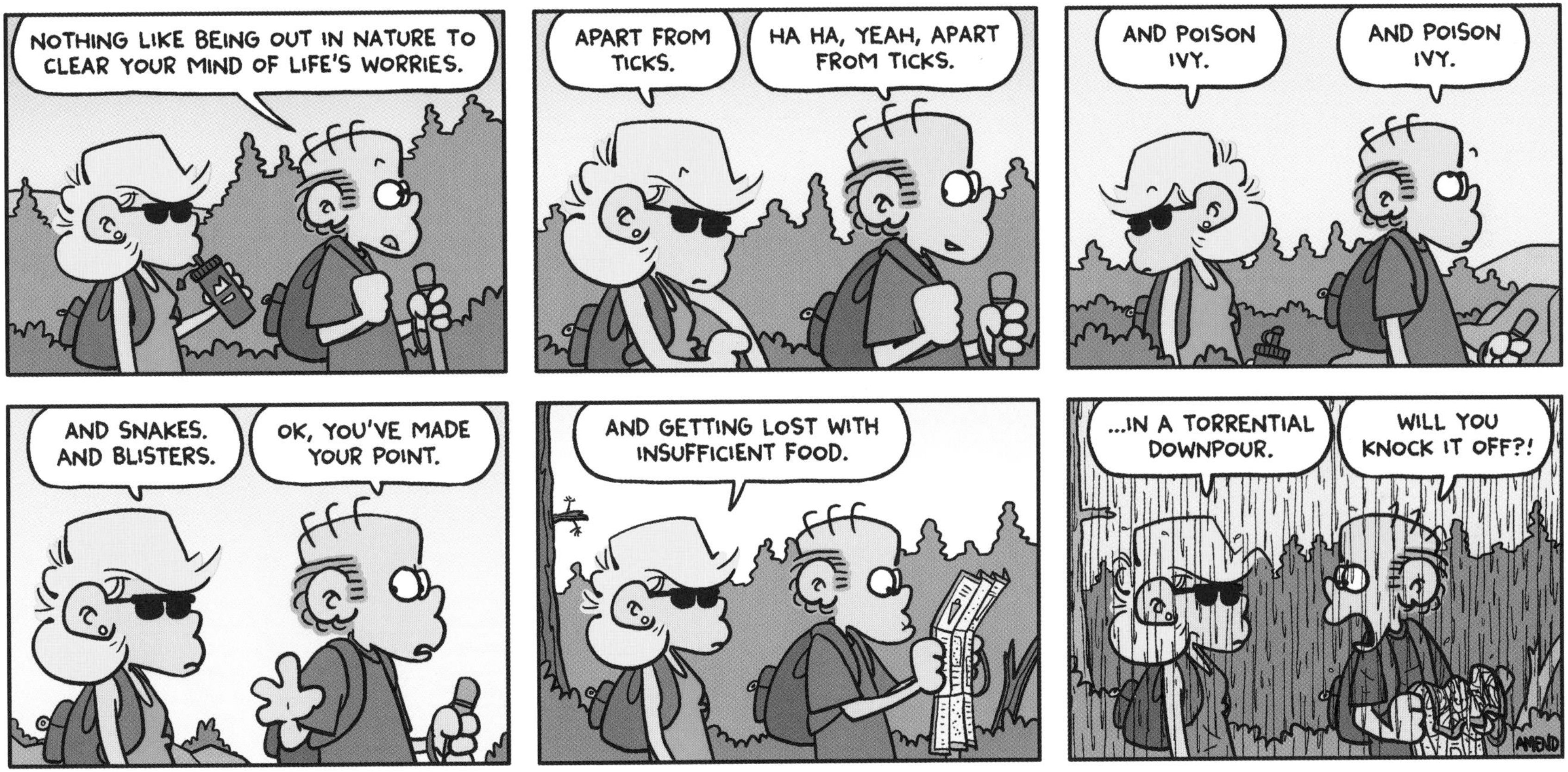
NOTHING LIKE BEING OUT IN NATURE TO CLEAR YOUR MIND OF LIFE'S WORRIES.
APART FROM TICKS.
HA HA, YEAH, APART FROM TICKS.
AND POISON IVY.
AND POISON IVY.
AND SNAKES. AND BLISTERS.
OK, YOU'VE MADE YOUR POINT.
AND GETTING LOST WITH INSUFFICIENT FOOD.
...IN A TORRENTIAL DOWNPOUR.
WILL YOU KNOCK IT OFF?!
AMEND

Watch Out for Sandworms

Shakin' It Way Off

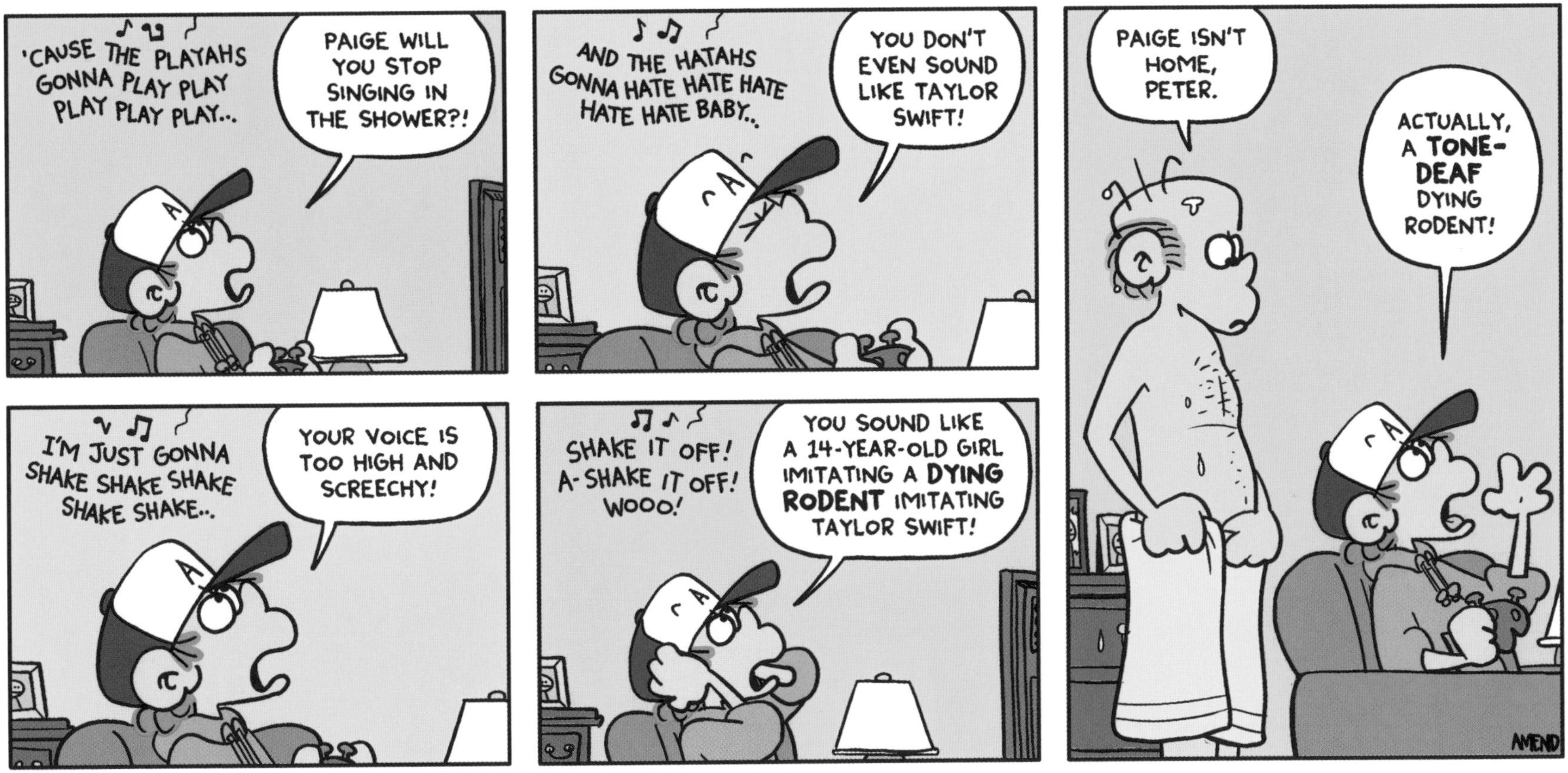
'CAUSE THE PLAYAHS GONNA PLAY PLAY PLAY PLAY PLAY...
PAIGE WILL YOU STOP SINGING IN THE SHOWER?!
AND THE HATAHS GONNA HATE HATE HATE HATE HATE BABY...
YOU DON'T EVEN SOUND LIKE TAYLOR SWIFT!
I'M JUST GONNA SHAKE SHAKE SHAKE SHAKE SHAKE...
YOUR VOICE IS TOO HIGH AND SCREECHY!
SHAKE IT OFF! A-SHAKE IT OFF! WOOO!
YOU SOUND LIKE A 14-YEAR-OLD GIRL IMITATING A DYING RODENT IMITATING TAYLOR SWIFT!
PAIGE ISN'T HOME, PETER.
ACTUALLY, A TONE-DEAF DYING RODENT!
AMEND

Paper Cut

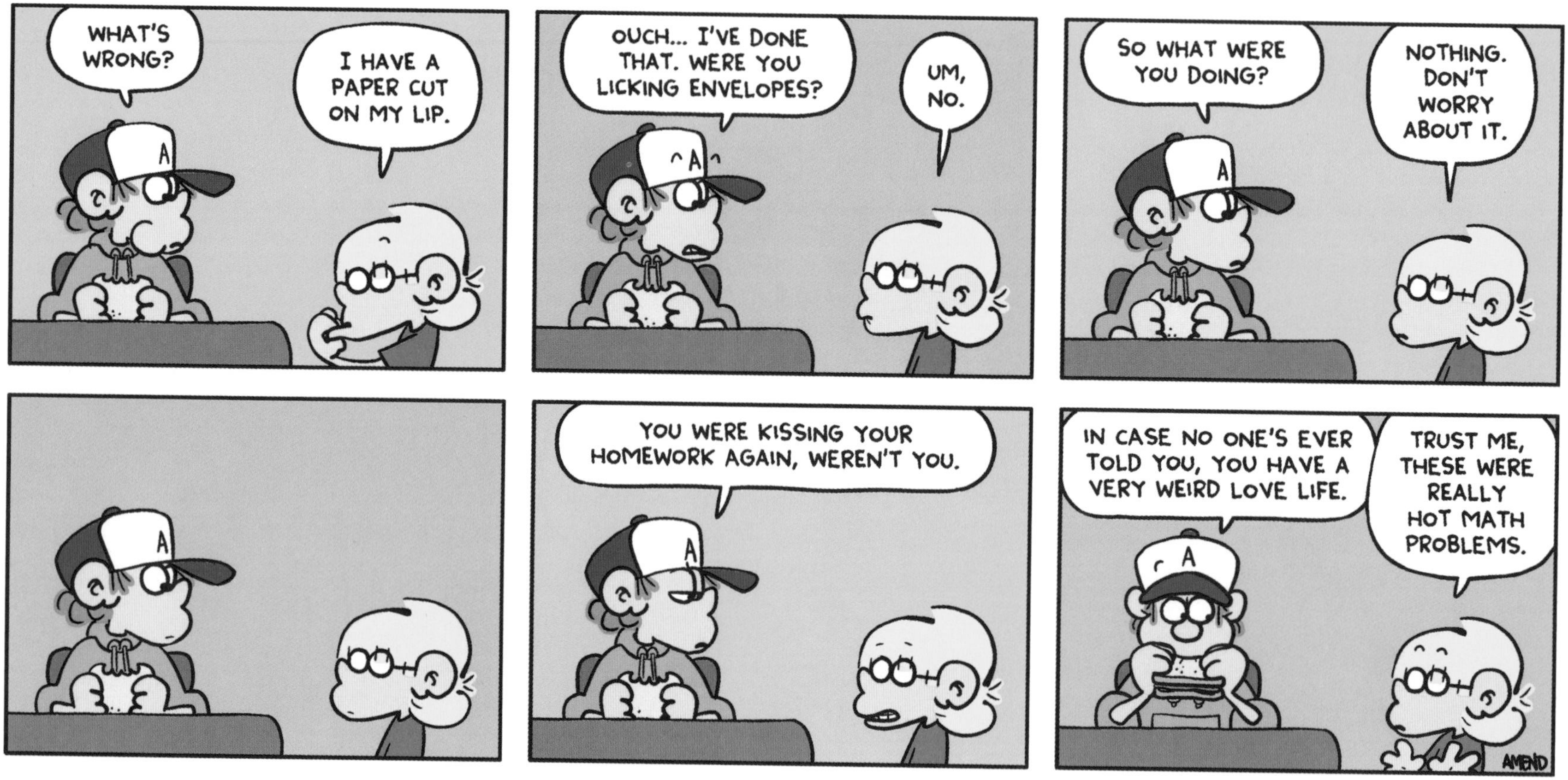
WHAT'S WRONG?
I HAVE A PAPER CUT ON MY LIP.
OUCH... I'VE DONE THAT. WERE YOU LICKING ENVELOPES?
UM, NO.
SO WHAT WERE YOU DOING?
NOTHING. DON'T WORRY ABOUT IT.
YOU WERE KISSING YOUR HOMEWORK AGAIN, WEREN'T YOU.
IN CASE NO ONE'S EVER TOLD YOU, YOU HAVE A VERY WEIRD LOVE LIFE.
TRUST ME, THESE WERE REALLY HOT MATH PROBLEMS.
AMEND

Font Club

WANT TO SIGN UP FOR CHEERLEADING?
MAYBE. I'LL THINK ABOUT IT.
WANT TO SIGN UP FOR DEBATE?
MAYBE. I'LL THINK ABOUT IT.
WANT TO SIGN UP FOR FONT CLUB?
WHAT'S FONT CLUB?
IT'S A LITTLE HARD TO EXPLAIN, SINCE THE FIRST RULE OF FONT CLUB IS NO TALKING ABOUT FONT CLUB.
WANT TO TRY GUESSING OUR SECOND RULE?
NO TALKING ABOUT FONT CLUB?
WRONG. THE SECOND RULE OF FONT CLUB IS NO USING COMIC SANS.
SWEET FLYER, BY THE WAY.
AMEND

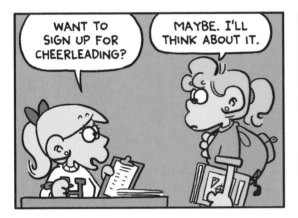

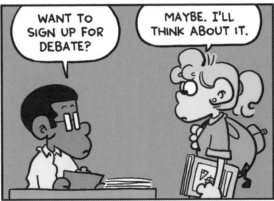

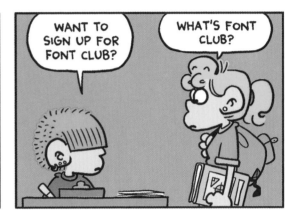

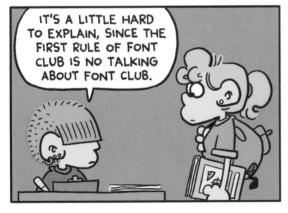

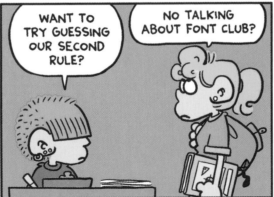

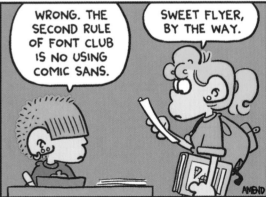

Do Not Breathe In

CLASS, THIS EXPERIMENT HAS THE POTENTIAL TO BE SOMEWHAT DANGEROUS, SO I WANT TO STRESS THE IMPORTANCE OF USING THE FUME HOOD FOR STEPS 4, 7 AND 16.

AND IF AT ANY TIME YOU SHOULD DETECT THE SMELL OF AMMONIA, ROTTEN EGGS OR SEWAGE, PLEASE STEP AWAY FROM THE CHEMICALS AND LET ME KNOW ASAP.

(SNIFF SNIFF) WHAT ABOUT A FOUL BODY-ODOR-LIKE SMELL?

THAT YOU'D HAVE TO DISCUSS WITH YOUR LAB PARTNER.

I FORGOT TO PUT ON DEODORANT TODAY! I'M SORRY!

UGGH! DUDE! LOWER YOUR ARMS!

Darwin Award Incoming

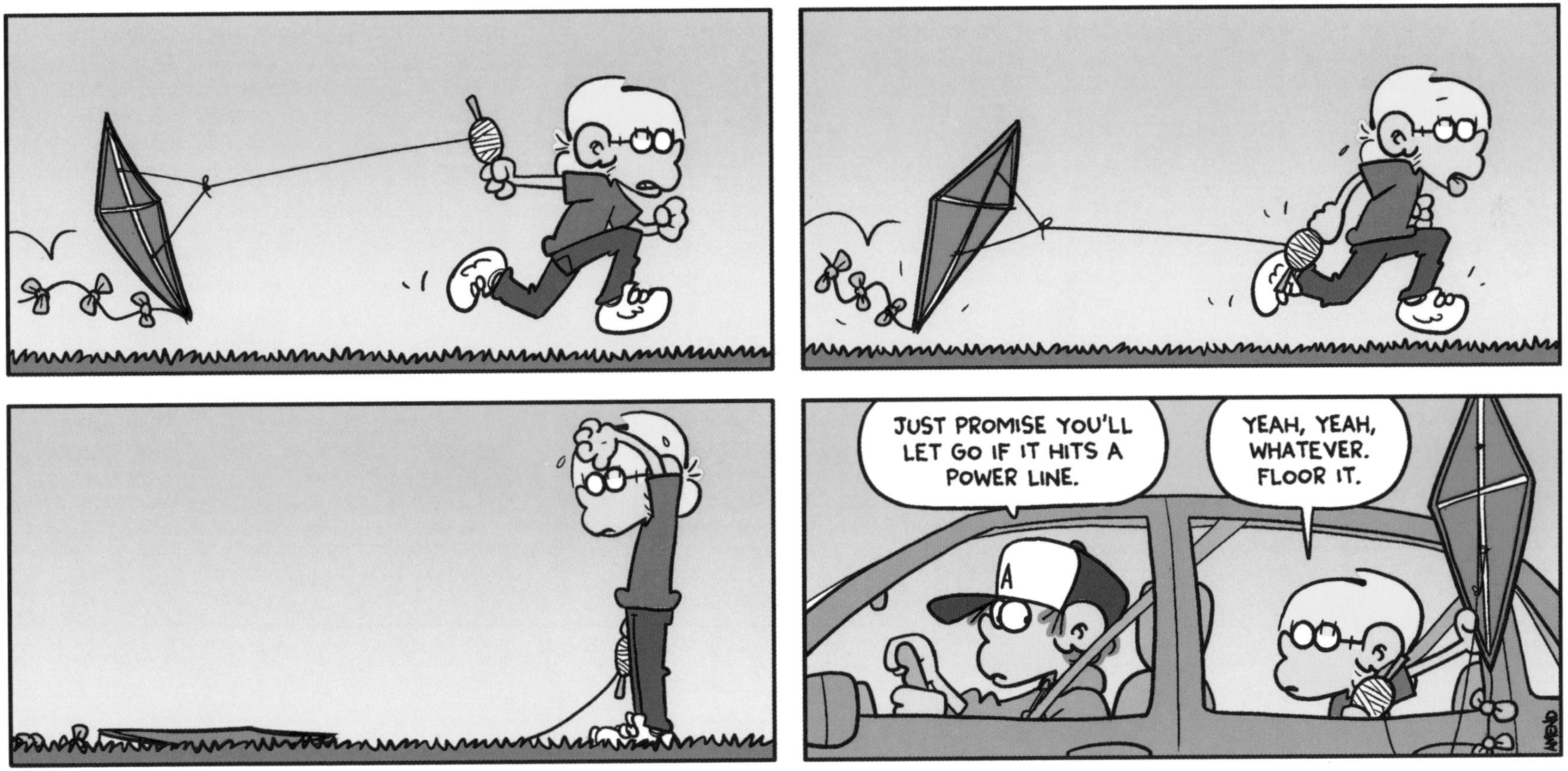
JUST PROMISE YOU'LL LET GO IF IT HITS A POWER LINE.
YEAH, YEAH, WHATEVER. FLOOR IT.

TV Correspondence

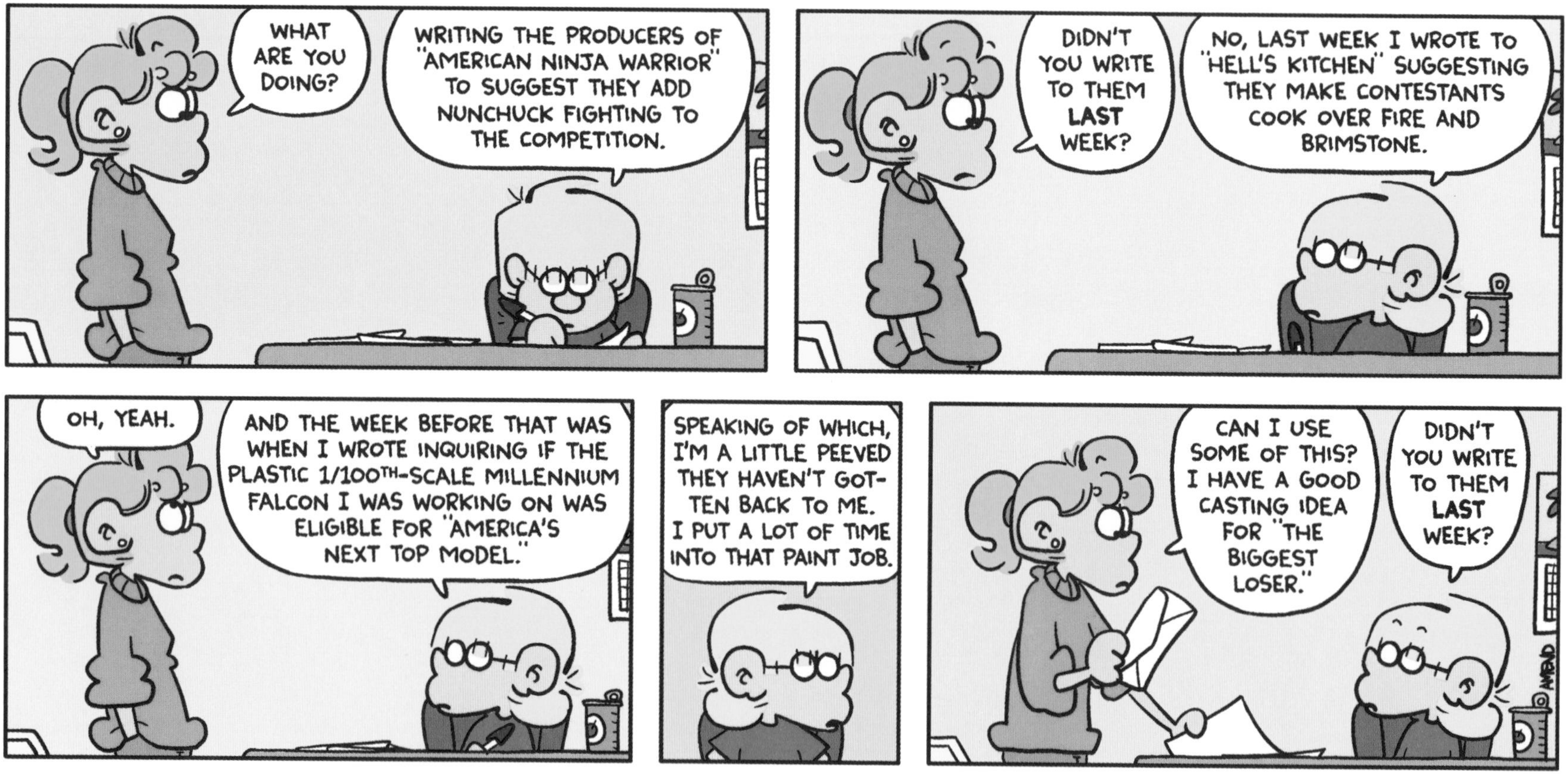
WHAT ARE YOU DOING?
WRITING THE PRODUCERS OF "AMERICAN NINJA WARRIOR" TO SUGGEST THEY ADD NUNCHUCK FIGHTING TO THE COMPETITION.
DIDN'T YOU WRITE TO THEM LAST WEEK?
NO, LAST WEEK I WROTE TO "HELL'S KITCHEN" SUGGESTING THEY MAKE CONTESTANTS COOK OVER FIRE AND BRIMSTONE.
OH, YEAH.
AND THE WEEK BEFORE THAT WAS WHEN I WROTE INQUIRING IF THE PLASTIC 1/100TH-SCALE MILLENNIUM FALCON I WAS WORKING ON WAS ELIGIBLE FOR "AMERICA'S NEXT TOP MODEL."
SPEAKING OF WHICH, I'M A LITTLE PEEVED THEY HAVEN'T GOTTEN BACK TO ME. I PUT A LOT OF TIME INTO THAT PAINT JOB.
CAN I USE SOME OF THIS? I HAVE A GOOD CASTING IDEA FOR "THE BIGGEST LOSER."
DIDN'T YOU WRITE TO THEM LAST WEEK?

Combo Moves

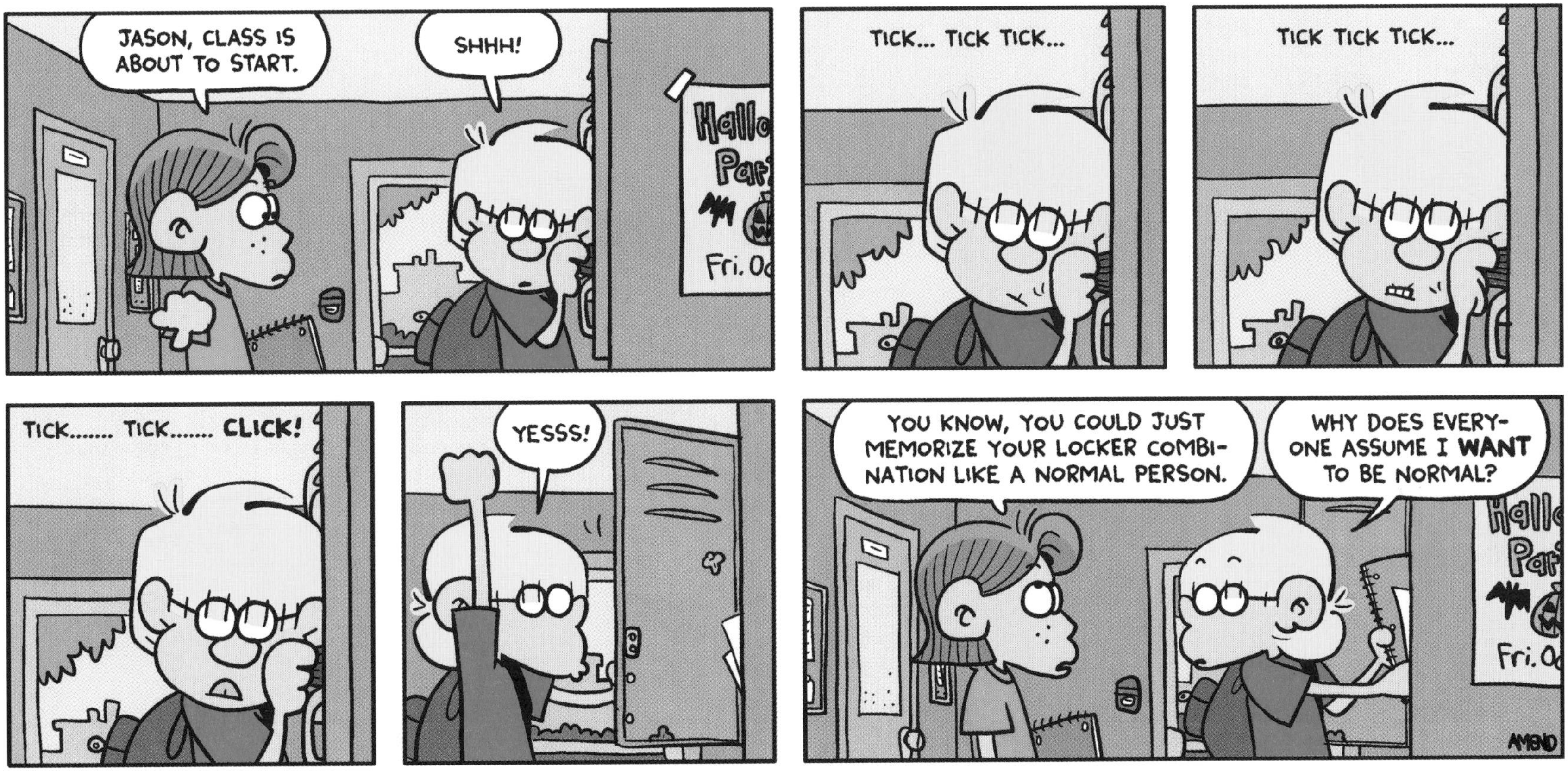
JASON, CLASS IS ABOUT TO START.
SHHH!
TICK... TICK TICK...
TICK TICK TICK...
TICK....... TICK....... CLICK!
YESSS!
YOU KNOW, YOU COULD JUST MEMORIZE YOUR LOCKER COMBI-NATION LIKE A NORMAL PERSON.
WHY DOES EVERY-ONE ASSUME I WANT TO BE NORMAL?
AMEND

Compromising Situation

Uncandy X-Men

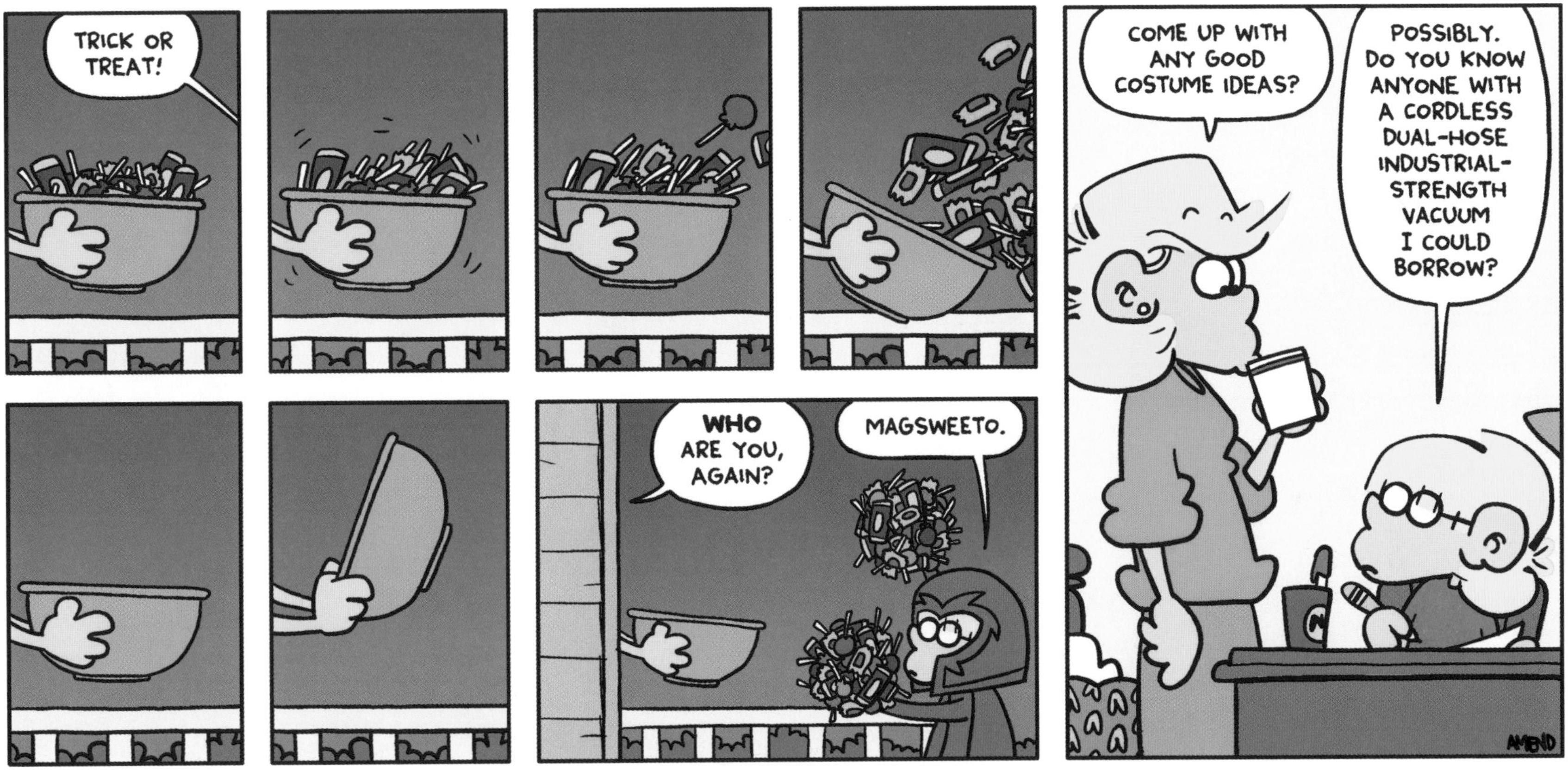

TRICK OR TREAT!
WHO ARE YOU, AGAIN?
MAGSWEETO.
COME UP WITH ANY GOOD COSTUME IDEAS?
POSSIBLY. DO YOU KNOW ANYONE WITH A CORDLESS DUAL-HOSE INDUSTRIAL-STRENGTH VACUUM I COULD BORROW?
AMEND

Fall Classic

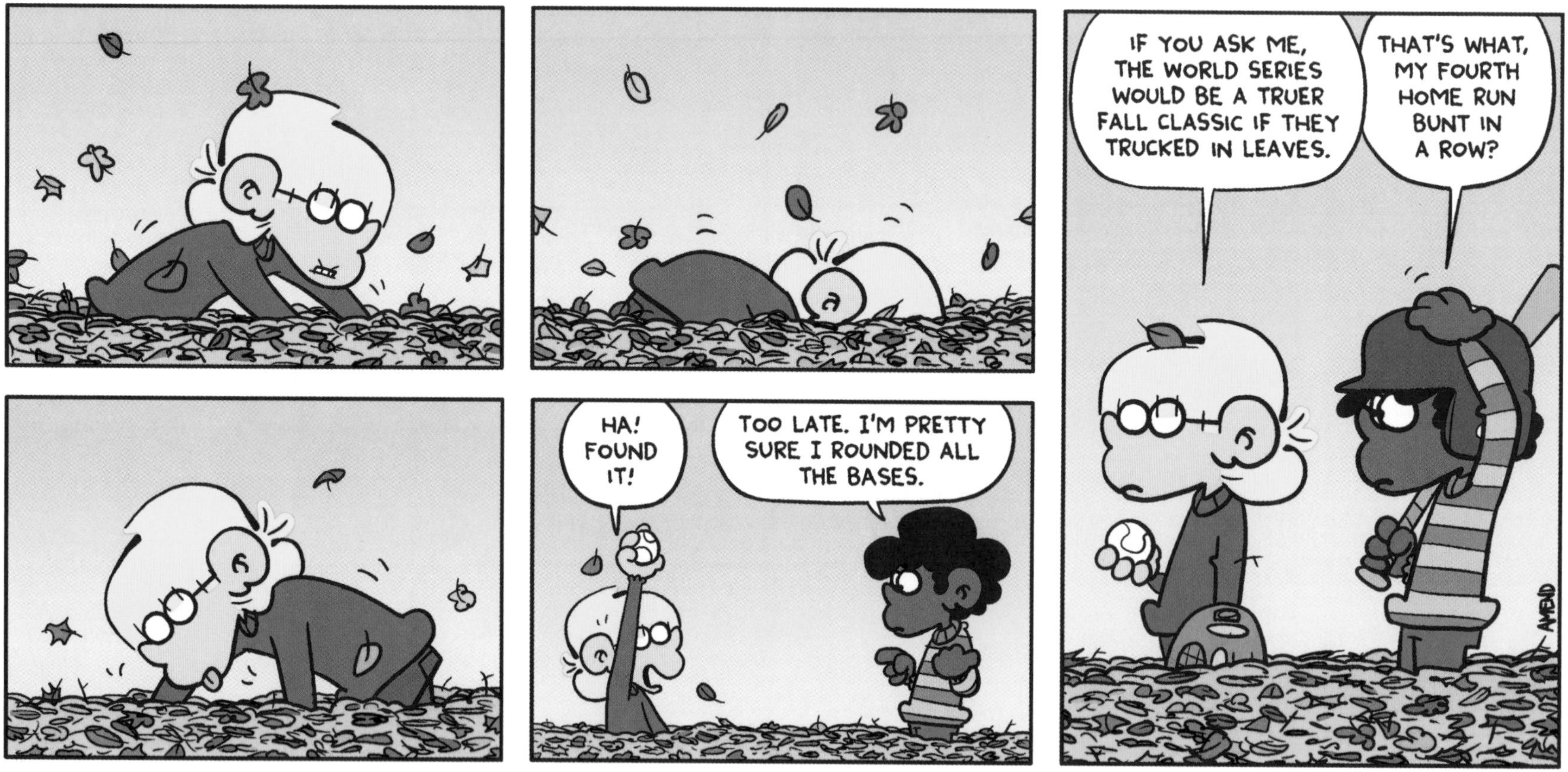
HA! FOUND IT!
TOO LATE. I'M PRETTY SURE I ROUNDED ALL THE BASES.
IF YOU ASK ME, THE WORLD SERIES WOULD BE A TRUER FALL CLASSIC IF THEY TRUCKED IN LEAVES.
THAT'S WHAT, MY FOURTH HOME RUN BUNT IN A ROW?
AMEND

Pain in the Math

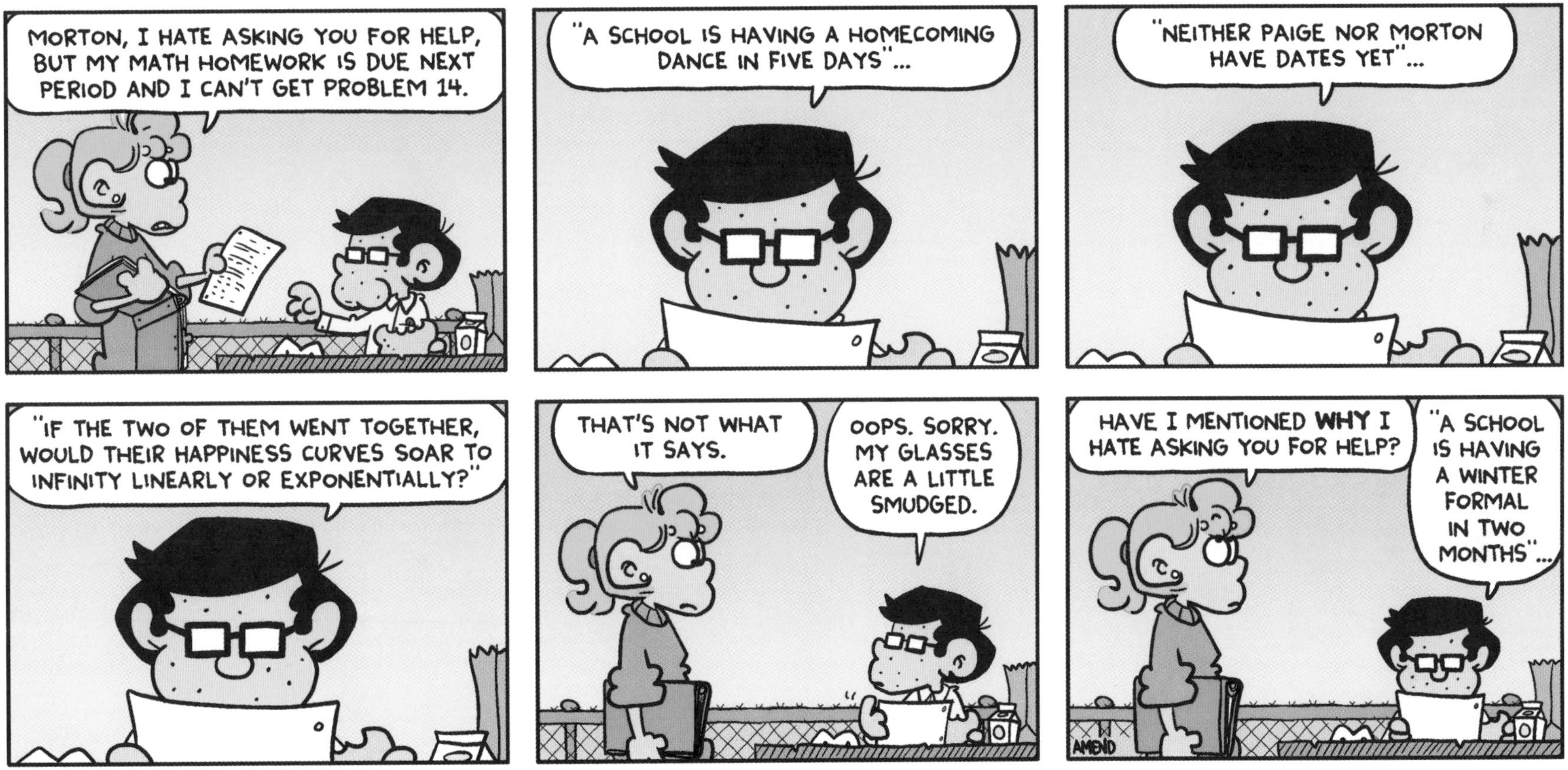
MORTON, I HATE ASKING YOU FOR HELP, BUT MY MATH HOMEWORK IS DUE NEXT PERIOD AND I CAN'T GET PROBLEM 14.
"A SCHOOL IS HAVING A HOMECOMING DANCE IN FIVE DAYS"...
"NEITHER PAIGE NOR MORTON HAVE DATES YET"...
"IF THE TWO OF THEM WENT TOGETHER, WOULD THEIR HAPPINESS CURVES SOAR TO INFINITY LINEARLY OR EXPONENTIALLY?"
THAT'S NOT WHAT IT SAYS.
OOPS. SORRY. MY GLASSES ARE A LITTLE SMUDGED.
HAVE I MENTIONED **WHY** I HATE ASKING YOU FOR HELP?
"A SCHOOL IS HAVING A WINTER FORMAL IN TWO MONTHS"...
AMEND

Try Hard

IS THAT THE NEW STARCRAFT EXPANSION?

"LEGACY OF THE VOID." YEAH.

MY PLAN IS TO PRACTICE NIGHT AND DAY AND GET REALLY, REALLY GOOD AT IT SO I CAN PLAY PROFESSIONALLY AND WIN BOATLOADS OF MONEY AT TOURNAMENTS.

I THOUGHT YOU WERE TRYING TO BE A "ROCKET LEAGUE" PRO.

THAT WAS BEFORE I REALIZED I'D NEVER BE GOOD ENOUGH AT THAT GAME.

AND BEFORE THAT WEREN'T YOU TRYING TO BE A "DOTA 2" PRO?

THAT WAS BEFORE I REALIZED I'D NEVER BE GOOD ENOUGH AT **THAT** GAME.

AND BEFORE THAT THERE WAS "LEAGUE OF LEGENDS" AND "COUNTER-STRIKE" AND "WORLD OF TANKS" AND WHAT WAS THAT FIRST GAME WHERE YOU WERE POSITIVELY DETERMINED TO GO PRO?

OH, YEAH, IT WAS THE **LAST** STARCRAFT EXPANSION.

LOOK, IF YOU'RE TRYING TO SAY SOMETHING, JUST SAY IT!

Culinary Art

Carved wood

Carved Stone

Carved ice

Carved turkey

Cyborg Monday

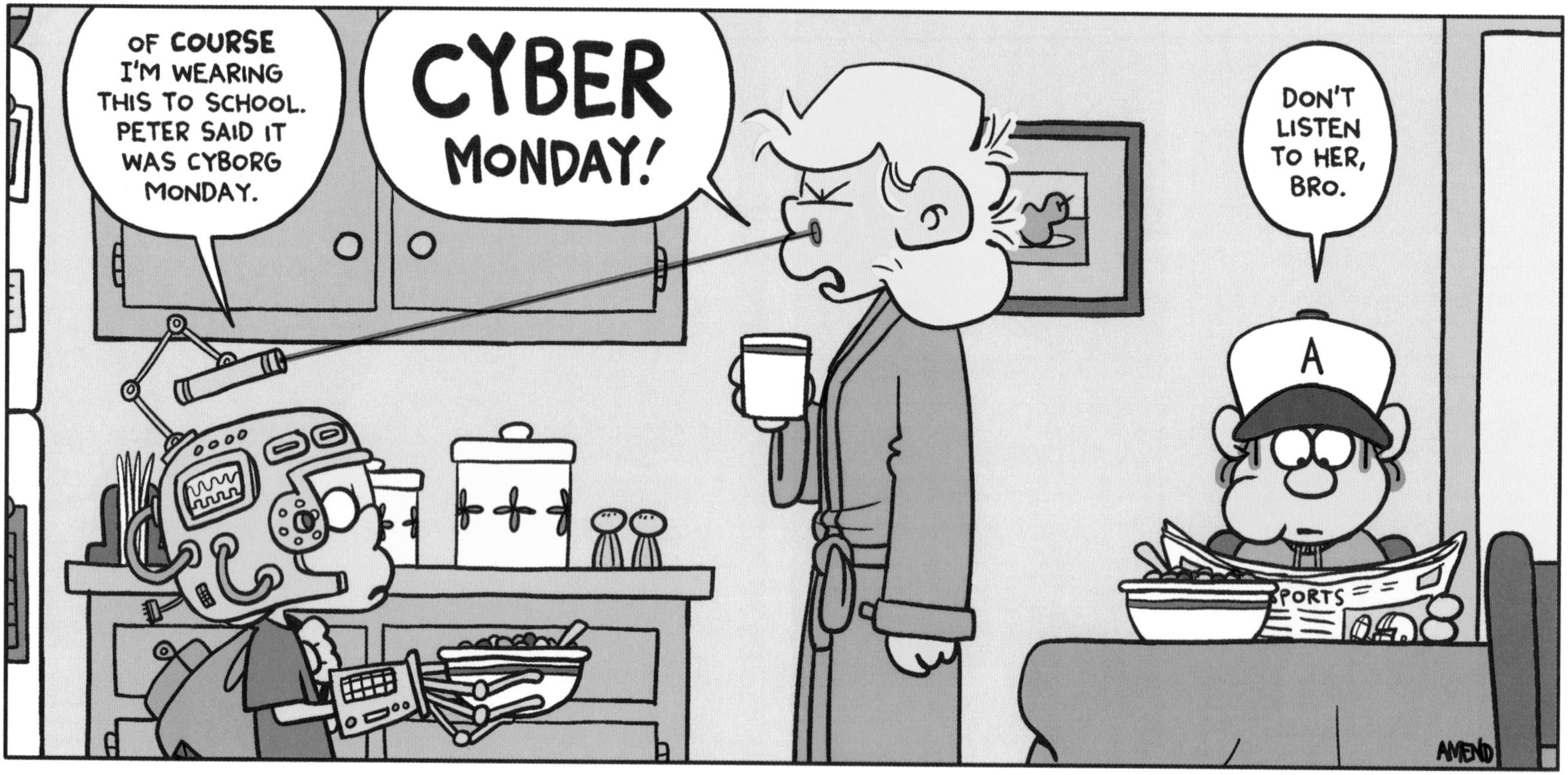
OF COURSE I'M WEARING THIS TO SCHOOL. PETER SAID IT WAS CYBORG MONDAY.
CYBER MONDAY!
DON'T LISTEN TO HER, BRO.
A
SPORTS
AMEND

Hot Stuff

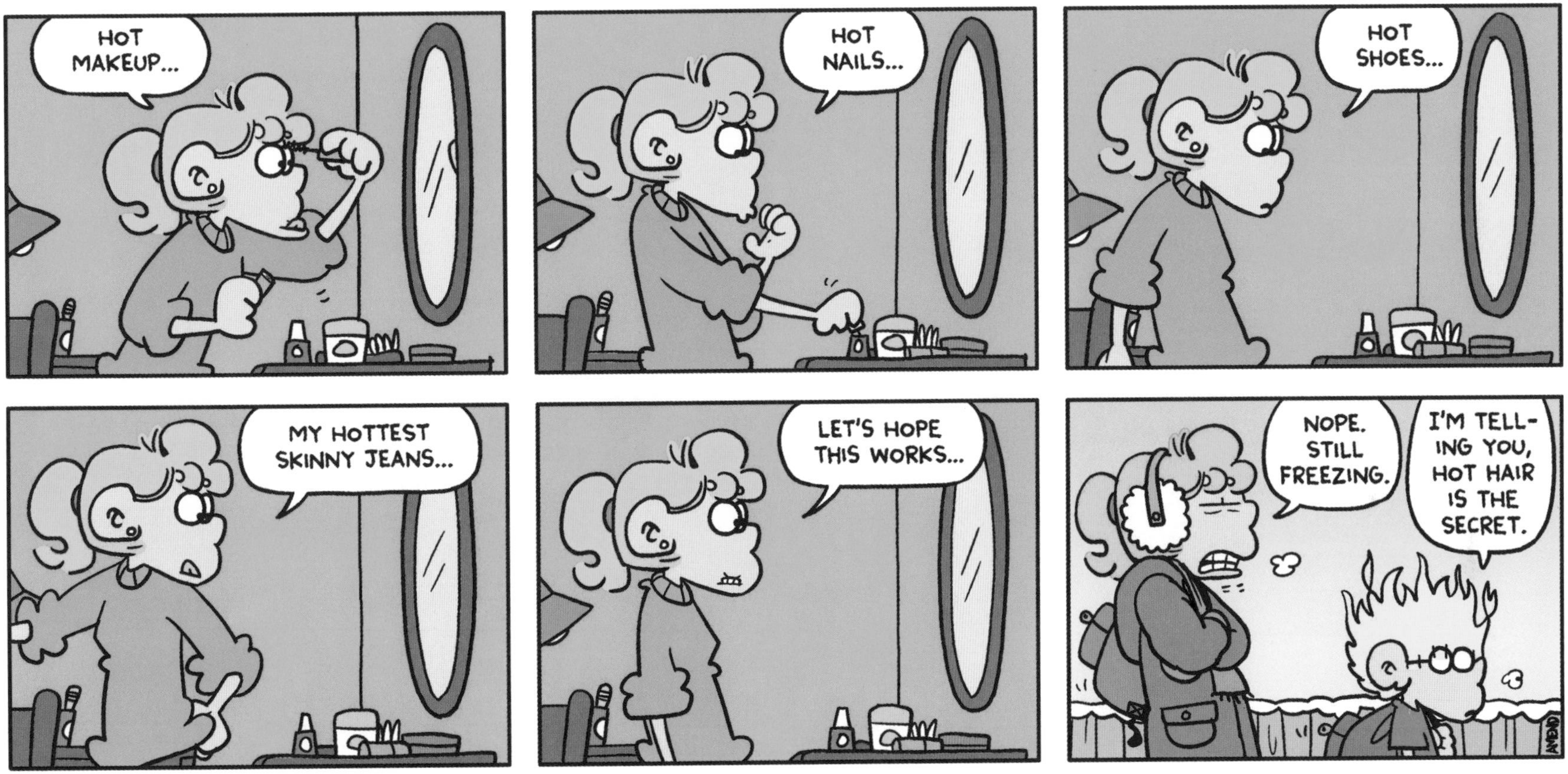

HOT MAKEUP...
HOT NAILS...
HOT SHOES...
MY HOTTEST SKINNY JEANS...
LET'S HOPE THIS WORKS...
NOPE. STILL FREEZING.
I'M TELL-ING YOU, HOT HAIR IS THE SECRET.

BB-Ache

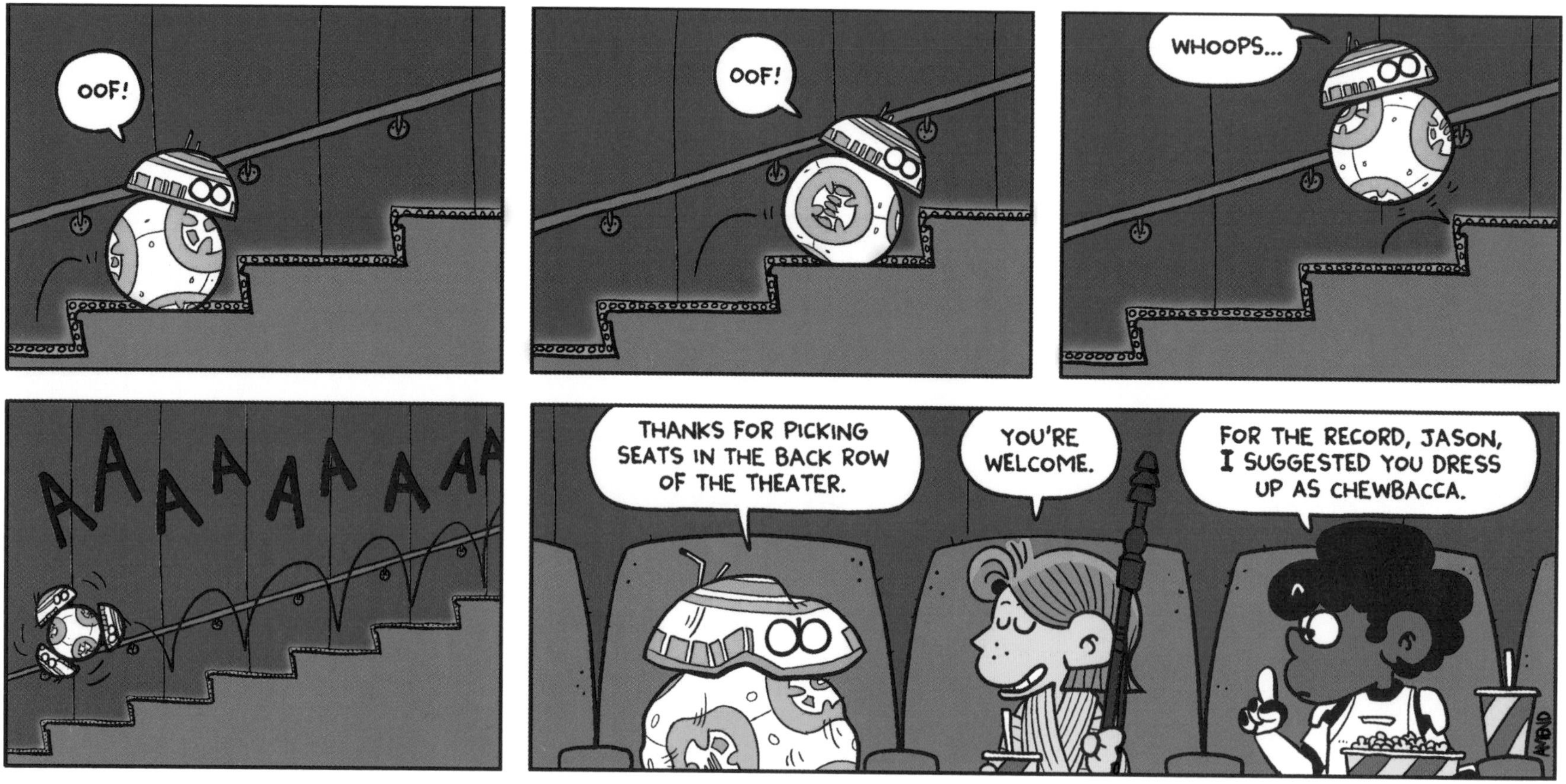
OOF!
OOF!
WHOOPS...
AAAAAAAAA
THANKS FOR PICKING SEATS IN THE BACK ROW OF THE THEATER.
YOU'RE WELCOME.
FOR THE RECORD, JASON, I SUGGESTED YOU DRESS UP AS CHEWBACCA.

Spicy

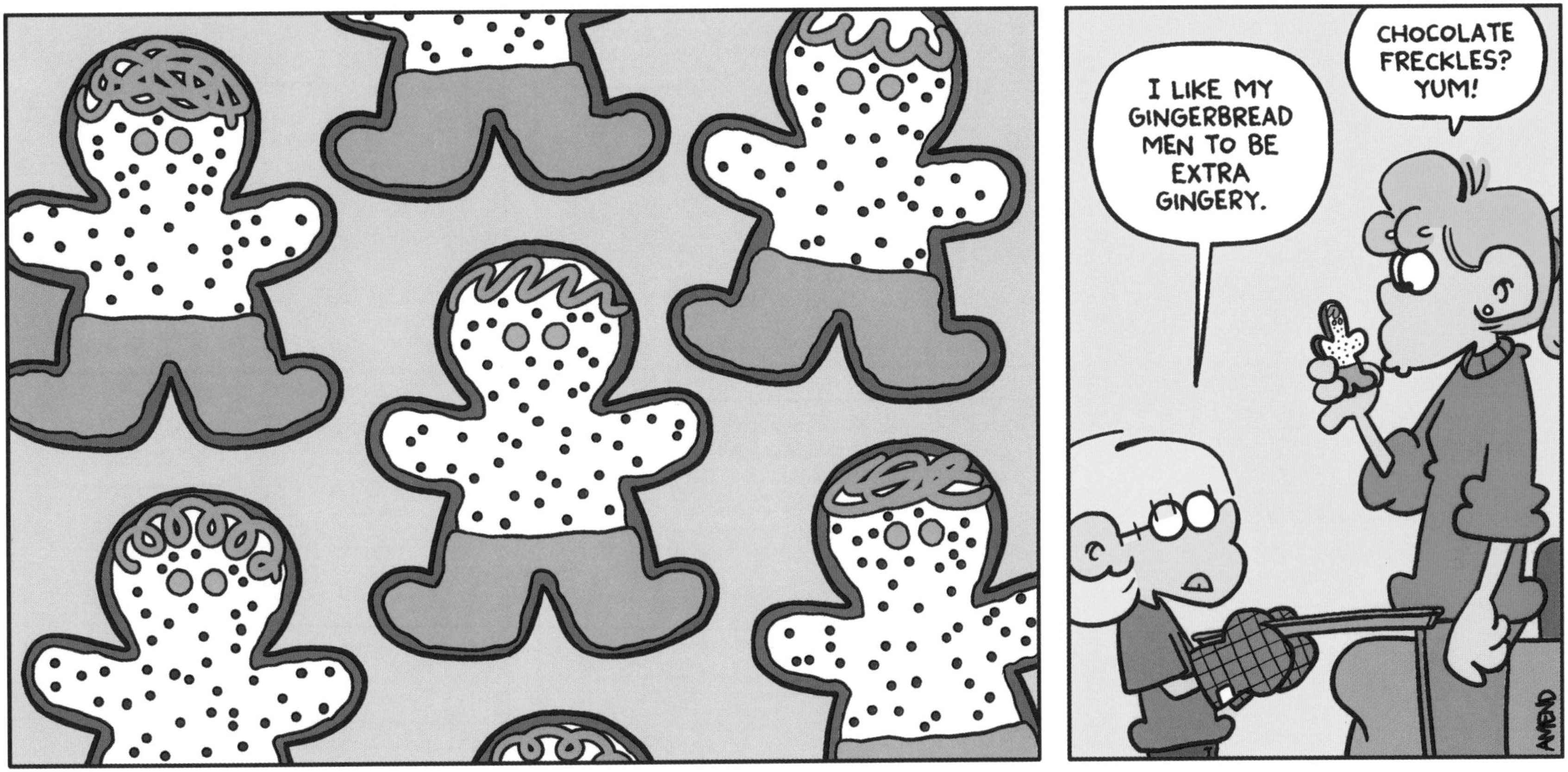
I LIKE MY GINGERBREAD MEN TO BE EXTRA GINGERY.
CHOCOLATE FRECKLES? YUM!
AMEND

TY Notes

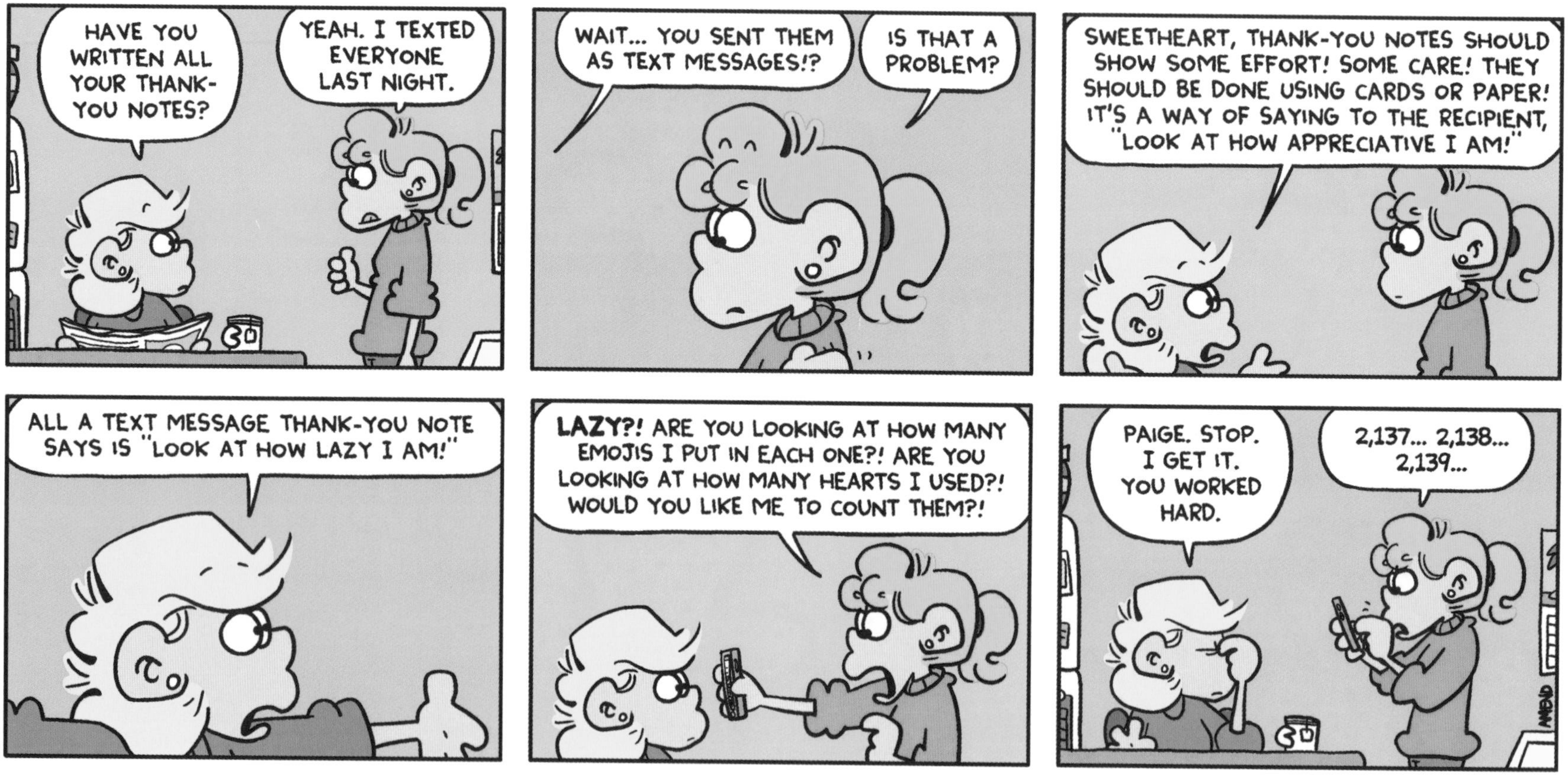
HAVE YOU WRITTEN ALL YOUR THANK-YOU NOTES?
YEAH. I TEXTED EVERYONE LAST NIGHT.
WAIT... YOU SENT THEM AS TEXT MESSAGES!?
IS THAT A PROBLEM?
SWEETHEART, THANK-YOU NOTES SHOULD SHOW SOME EFFORT! SOME CARE! THEY SHOULD BE DONE USING CARDS OR PAPER! IT'S A WAY OF SAYING TO THE RECIPIENT, "LOOK AT HOW APPRECIATIVE I AM!"
ALL A TEXT MESSAGE THANK-YOU NOTE SAYS IS "LOOK AT HOW LAZY I AM!"
LAZY?! ARE YOU LOOKING AT HOW MANY EMOJIS I PUT IN EACH ONE?! ARE YOU LOOKING AT HOW MANY HEARTS I USED?! WOULD YOU LIKE ME TO COUNT THEM?!
PAIGE. STOP. I GET IT. YOU WORKED HARD.
2,137... 2,138... 2,139...

A New Record

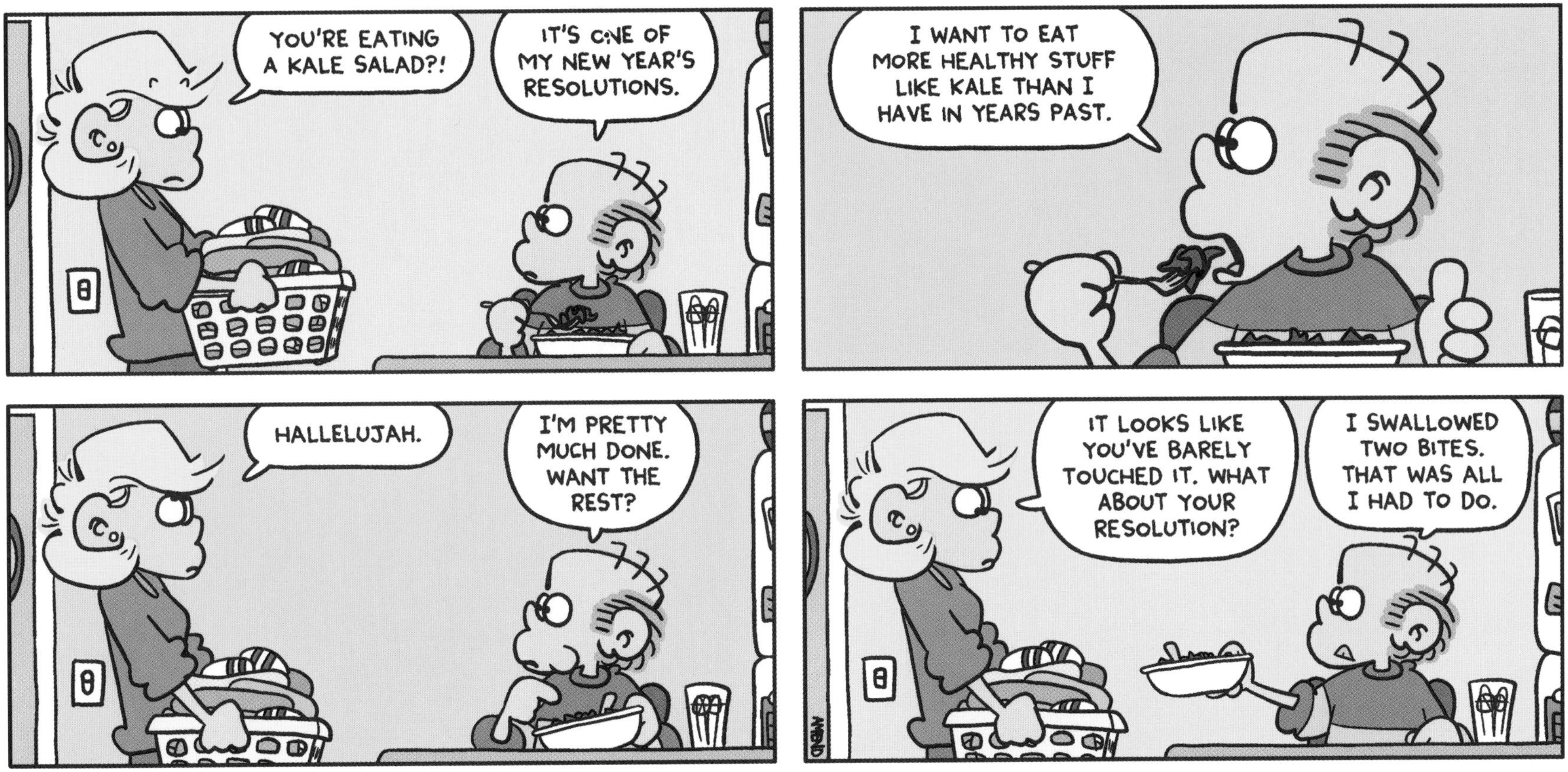
YOU'RE EATING A KALE SALAD?!
IT'S ONE OF MY NEW YEAR'S RESOLUTIONS.
I WANT TO EAT MORE HEALTHY STUFF LIKE KALE THAN I HAVE IN YEARS PAST.
HALLELUJAH.
I'M PRETTY MUCH DONE. WANT THE REST?
IT LOOKS LIKE YOU'VE BARELY TOUCHED IT. WHAT ABOUT YOUR RESOLUTION?
I SWALLOWED TWO BITES. THAT WAS ALL I HAD TO DO.

Alexander Colders

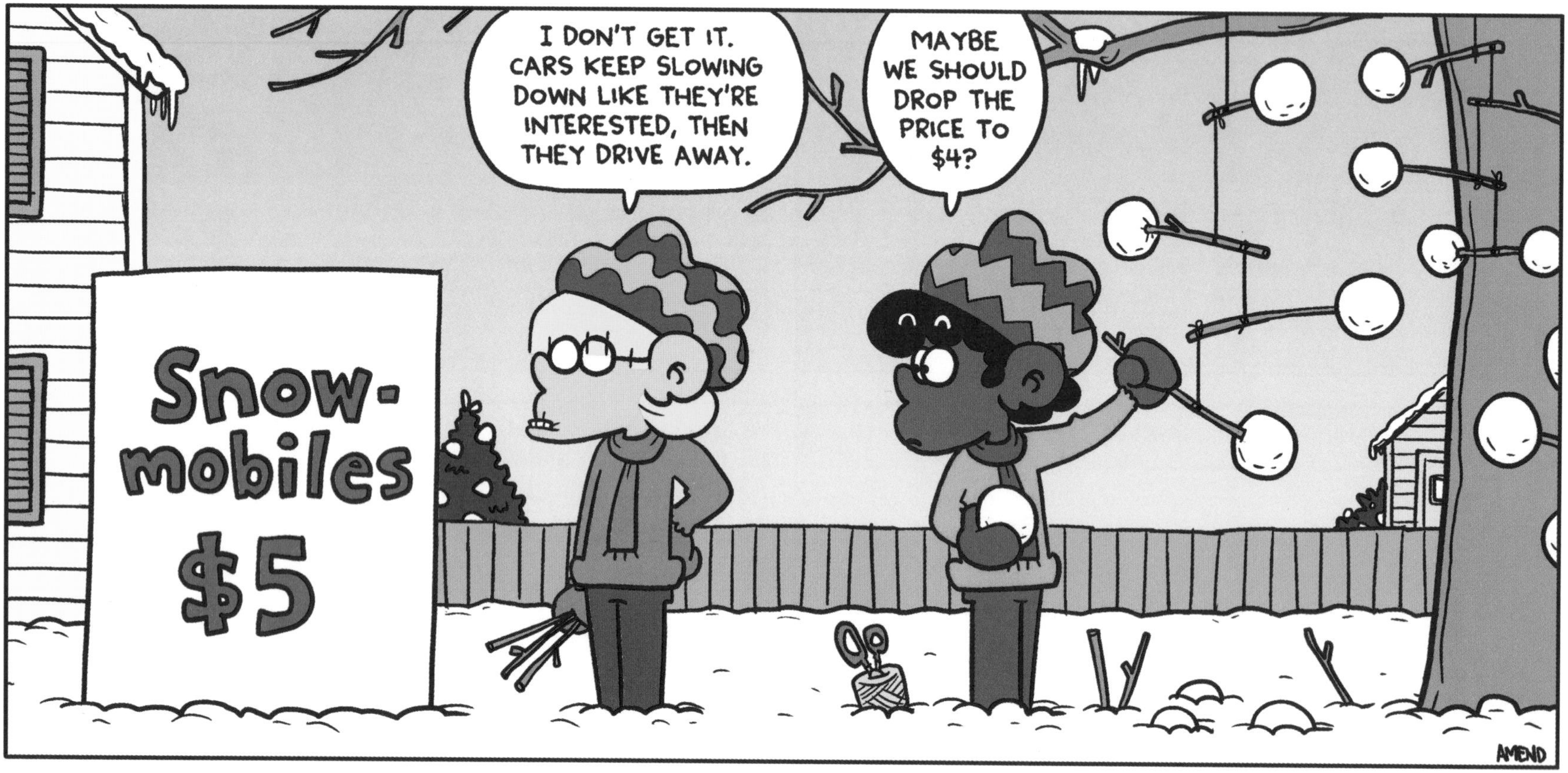
Snow-mobiles $5
I DON'T GET IT. CARS KEEP SLOWING DOWN LIKE THEY'RE INTERESTED, THEN THEY DRIVE AWAY.
MAYBE WE SHOULD DROP THE PRICE TO $4?
AMEND

Netflix and Chili

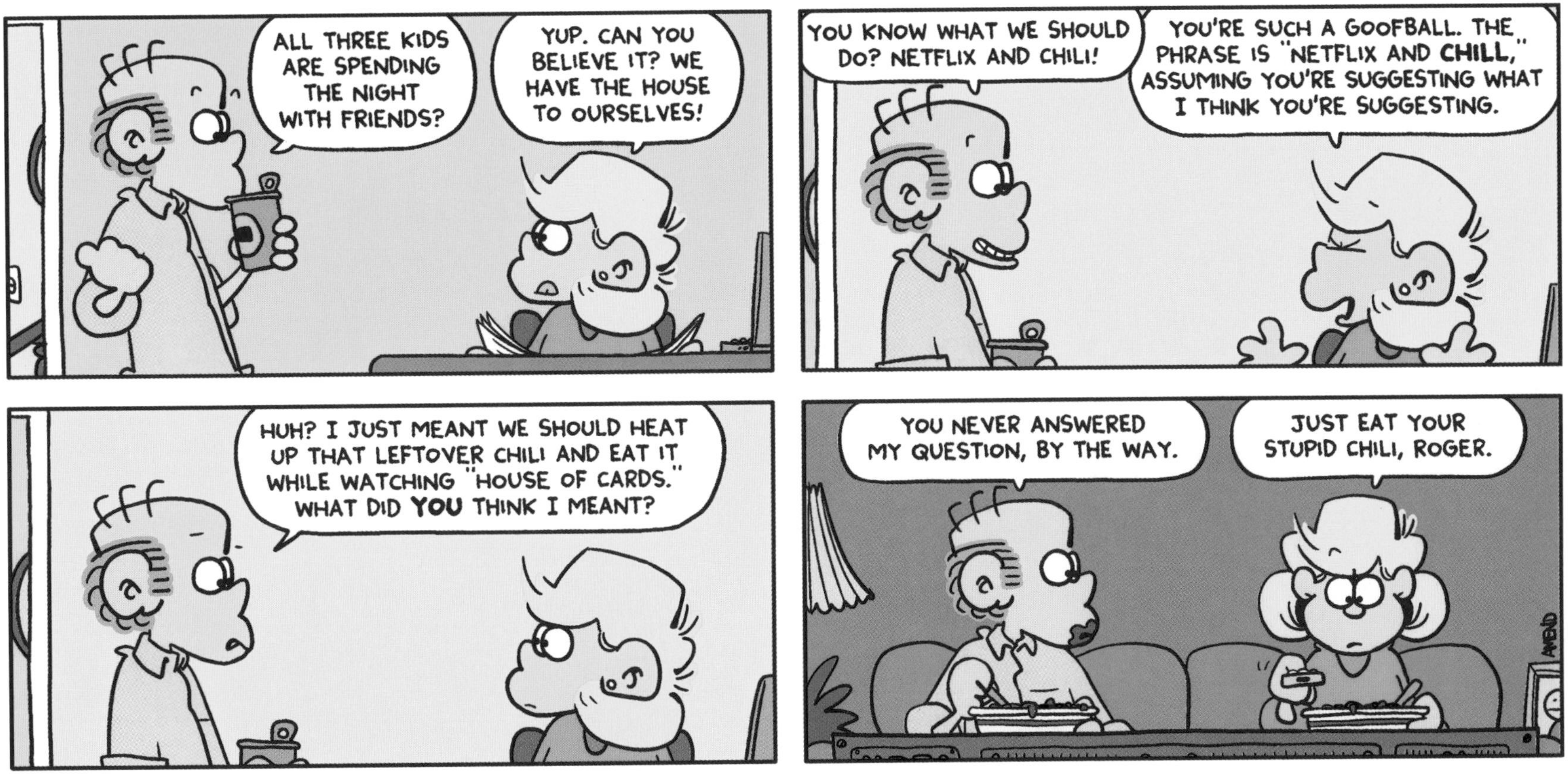
ALL THREE KIDS ARE SPENDING THE NIGHT WITH FRIENDS?
YUP. CAN YOU BELIEVE IT? WE HAVE THE HOUSE TO OURSELVES!
YOU KNOW WHAT WE SHOULD DO? NETFLIX AND CHILI!
YOU'RE SUCH A GOOFBALL. THE PHRASE IS "NETFLIX AND **CHILL**," ASSUMING YOU'RE SUGGESTING WHAT I THINK YOU'RE SUGGESTING.
HUH? I JUST MEANT WE SHOULD HEAT UP THAT LEFTOVER CHILI AND EAT IT WHILE WATCHING "HOUSE OF CARDS." WHAT DID **YOU** THINK I MEANT?
YOU NEVER ANSWERED MY QUESTION, BY THE WAY.
JUST EAT YOUR STUPID CHILI, ROGER.

Bit of a Stretch

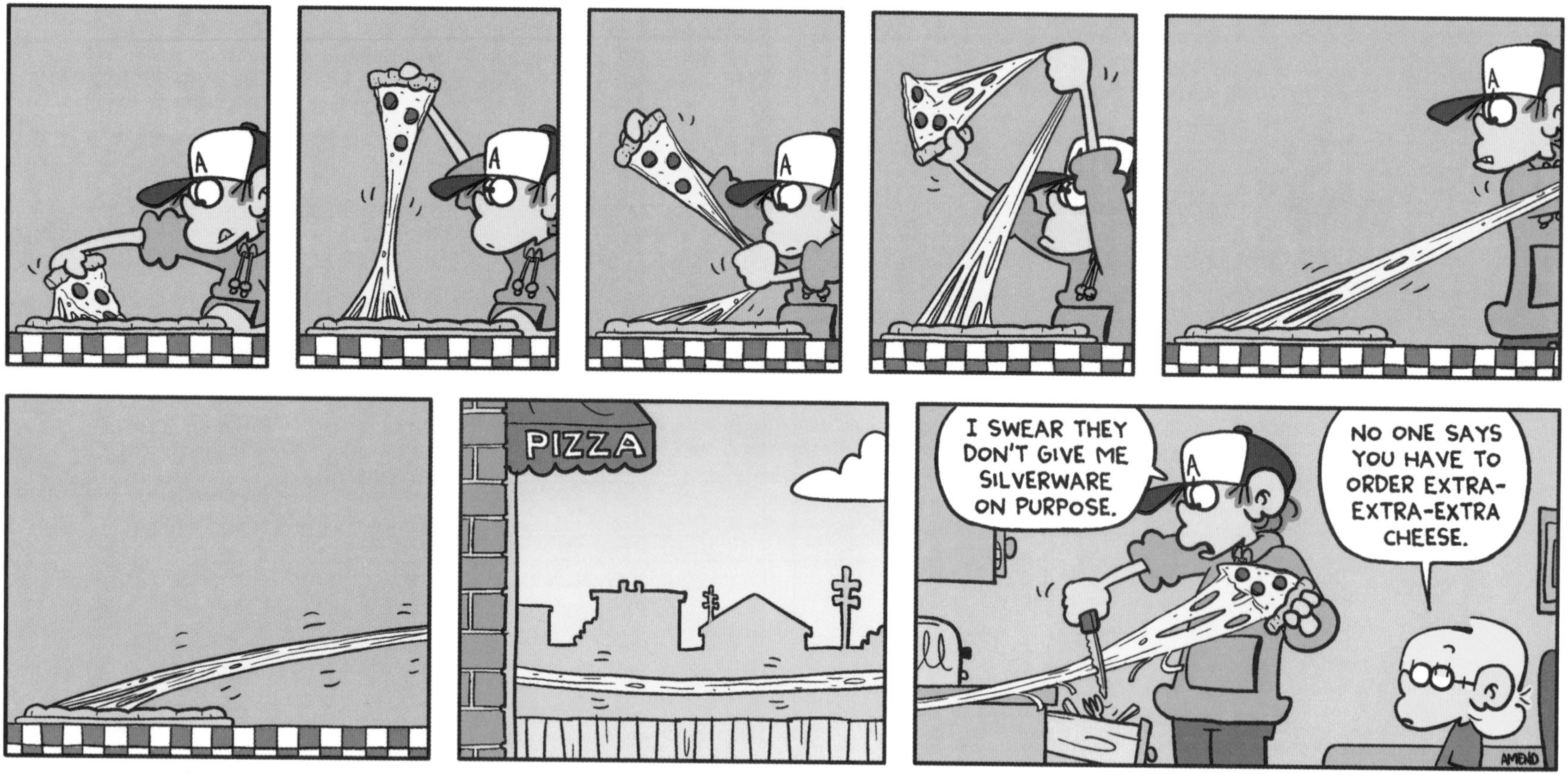
PIZZA
I SWEAR THEY DON'T GIVE ME SILVERWARE ON PURPOSE.
NO ONE SAYS YOU HAVE TO ORDER EXTRA-EXTRA-EXTRA CHEESE.
AMEND

The Asocial Network

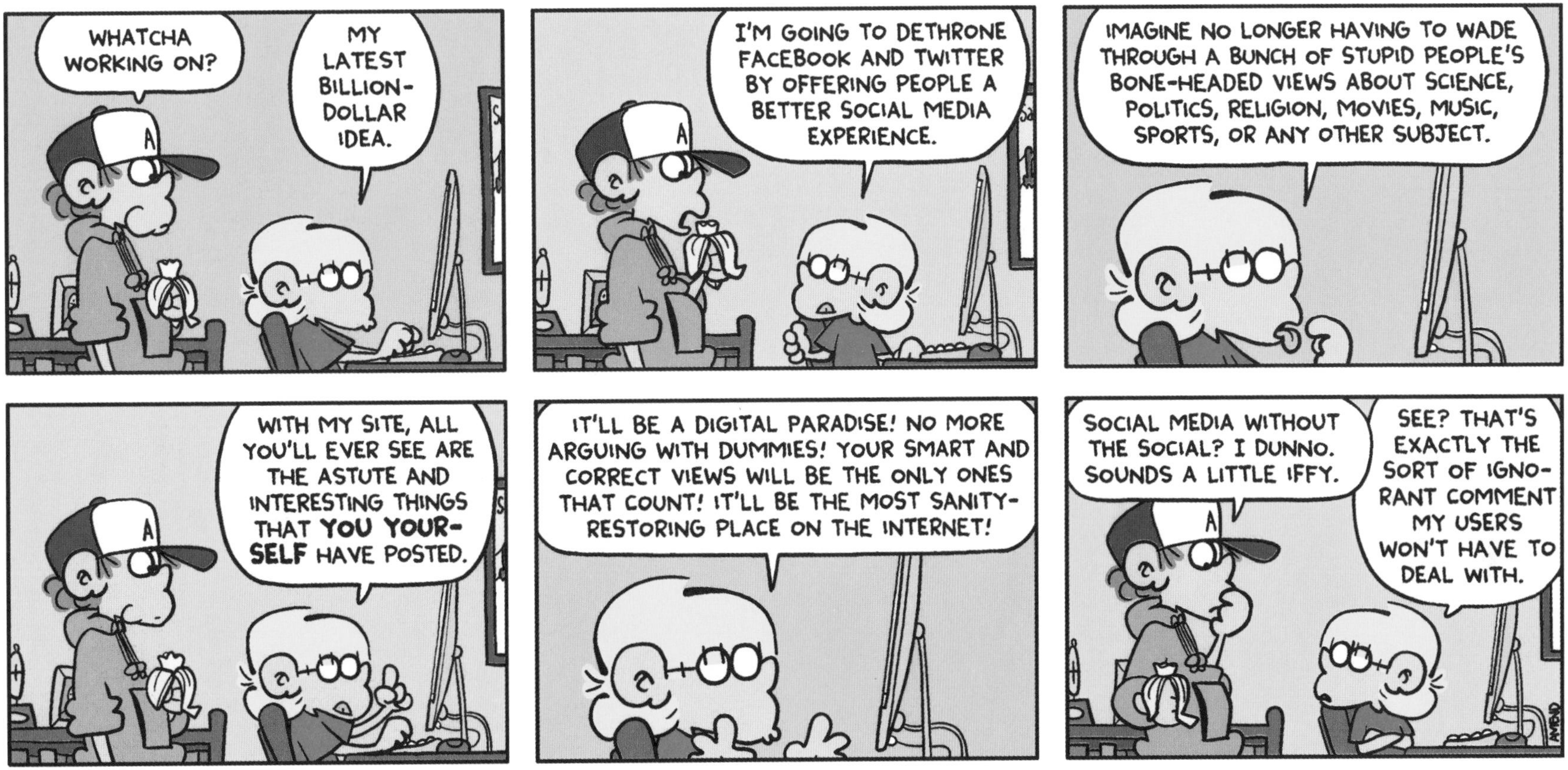

WHATCHA WORKING ON?
MY LATEST BILLION-DOLLAR IDEA.
I'M GOING TO DETHRONE FACEBOOK AND TWITTER BY OFFERING PEOPLE A BETTER SOCIAL MEDIA EXPERIENCE.
IMAGINE NO LONGER HAVING TO WADE THROUGH A BUNCH OF STUPID PEOPLE'S BONE-HEADED VIEWS ABOUT SCIENCE, POLITICS, RELIGION, MOVIES, MUSIC, SPORTS, OR ANY OTHER SUBJECT.
WITH MY SITE, ALL YOU'LL EVER SEE ARE THE ASTUTE AND INTERESTING THINGS THAT **YOU YOURSELF** HAVE POSTED.
IT'LL BE A DIGITAL PARADISE! NO MORE ARGUING WITH DUMMIES! YOUR SMART AND CORRECT VIEWS WILL BE THE ONLY ONES THAT COUNT! IT'LL BE THE MOST SANITY-RESTORING PLACE ON THE INTERNET!
SOCIAL MEDIA WITHOUT THE SOCIAL? I DUNNO. SOUNDS A LITTLE IFFY.
SEE? THAT'S EXACTLY THE SORT OF IGNORANT COMMENT MY USERS WON'T HAVE TO DEAL WITH.

Weird L

EXCITED FOR SUPER BOWL L?

ACTUALLY, THEY'RE SKIPPING THE ROMAN NUMERALS THIS YEAR. IT'S JUST PLAIN OL' "SUPER BOWL 50."

HOW COME?

WHO KNOWS. MAYBE THEY THOUGHT USING AN "L" ALL BY ITSELF WOULD BE CONFUSING OR WEIRD.

REALLY? IT DOESN'T SEEM ALL THAT WEIRD TO ME.

WELL, KEEP IN MIND YOU AND I MIGHT BE A TINY BIT NUMB TO NUMERIC WEIRDNESS.

EXCITED FOR SUPER BOWL $(7^2 + 1)$?

AMEND

Notice Me

THINK YOU'RE WEARING ENOUGH PERFUME??

MAN, I HOPE SO.

IT'S VALENTINE'S DAY. EVERY KID AT SCHOOL IS GOING TO BE VYING FOR SUITORS.

I FIGURE JOB ONE IS TO GET NOTICED. BOYS AREN'T GOING TO DECLARE THEIR LOVE FOR ME IF THEY DON'T KNOW I EXIST.

HENCE MY "NOTICE ME" OUTFIT CHOICE, MY "NOTICE ME" GLITTERY EYE SHADOW, AND MY "NOTICE ME" SCULPTABLE HAIR PASTE.

PAIGE, IF I WERE YOU, I'D JUST RELAX AND NOT TRY TO FORCE THINGS.

YOU AND I OPERATE DIFFERENTLY, MOTHER.

BELIEVE ME, I'M AWARE OF THAT.

OH, I ALSO HAVE THIS "NOTICE ME" AIR HORN.

Food Science

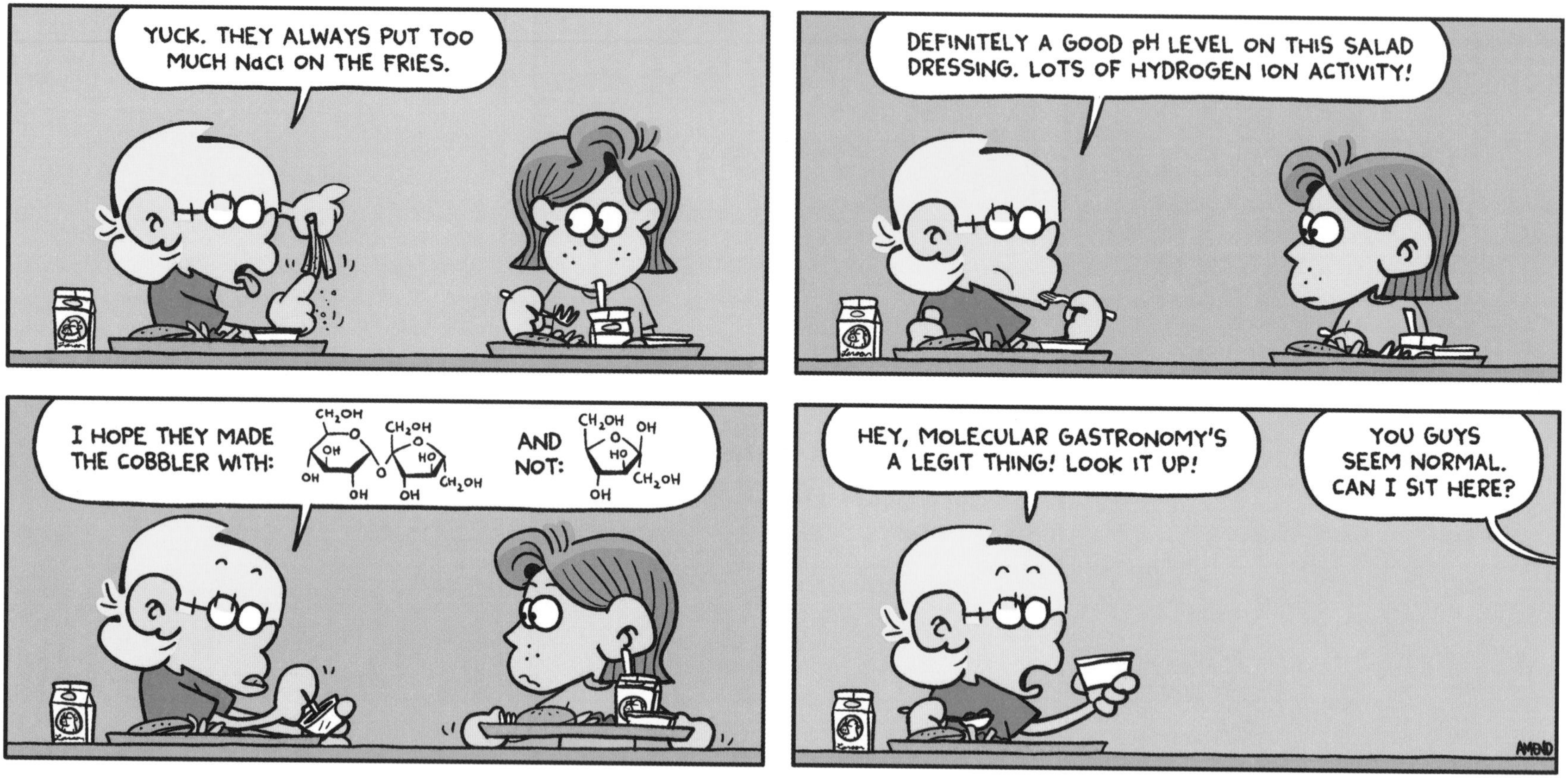
YUCK. THEY ALWAYS PUT TOO MUCH NaCl ON THE FRIES.
DEFINITELY A GOOD pH LEVEL ON THIS SALAD DRESSING. LOTS OF HYDROGEN ION ACTIVITY!
I HOPE THEY MADE THE COBBLER WITH:
AND NOT:
HEY, MOLECULAR GASTRONOMY'S A LEGIT THING! LOOK IT UP!
YOU GUYS SEEM NORMAL. CAN I SIT HERE?
AMEND

Peter Fox Presents

A Peter Fox Production

Of a Peter Fox Essay

"'Animal Farm' as Political Allegory"

Written by Peter Fox

Typed by Peter Fox

Starring the Characters of 'Animal Farm'

A Book by George Orwell

Published by Signet Classics

Assigned by Ms. Christopher

The Greatest and Kindest Teacher Ever

SO AT WHAT POINT DO YOU ACTUALLY WRITE THE ESSAY?

DEPENDS. ANY IDEA WHAT "ALLEGORY" MEANS?

$password

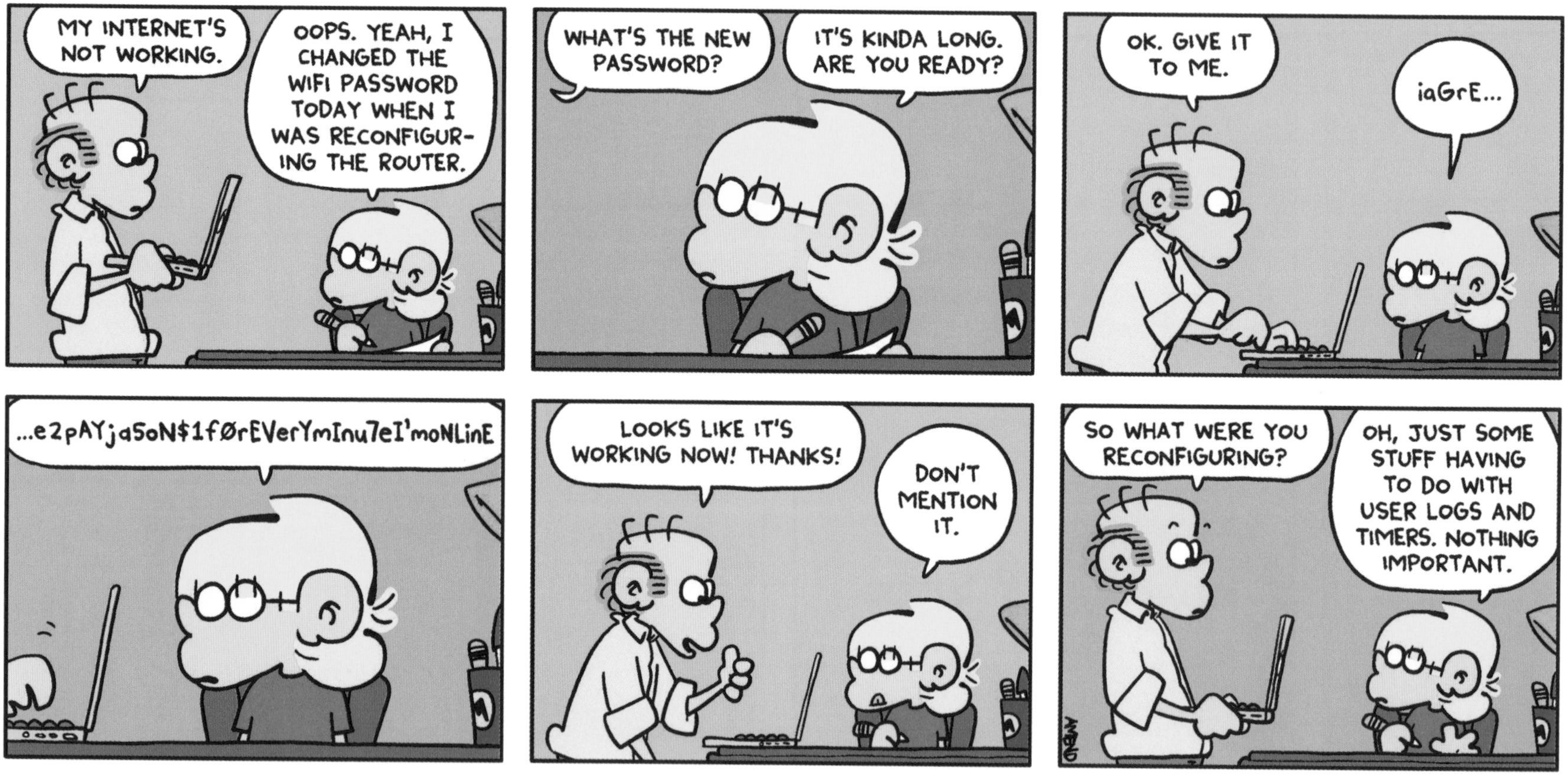
MY INTERNET'S NOT WORKING.
OOPS. YEAH, I CHANGED THE WIFI PASSWORD TODAY WHEN I WAS RECONFIGURING THE ROUTER.
WHAT'S THE NEW PASSWORD?
IT'S KINDA LONG. ARE YOU READY?
OK. GIVE IT TO ME.
iaGrE...
...e2pAYja5oN$1fØrEVerYmInu7eI'moNLinE
LOOKS LIKE IT'S WORKING NOW! THANKS!
DON'T MENTION IT.
SO WHAT WERE YOU RECONFIGURING?
OH, JUST SOME STUFF HAVING TO DO WITH USER LOGS AND TIMERS. NOTHING IMPORTANT.

Tournamental

ROGER FOX, YOU CORRECTLY PREDICTED THE WINNER OF EVERY MATCHUP IN THIS YEAR'S NCAA MEN'S BASKETBALL TOURNAMENT! HOW'S IT FEEL?

IT FEELS GOOD, ROGER. I JUST FILLED OUT MY BRACKET ONE GAME AT A TIME, TURNED IT IN, AND THE TEAMS DID THE REST. WHAT CAN I SAY?

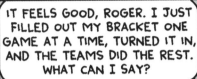

NATURALLY YOU CRUSHED EVERYONE IN YOUR OFFICE'S BETTING POOL! ANY PLANS FOR SPENDING YOUR BIG WINNINGS?

WELL, AS YOU KNOW I'M NOT THE MATERIALISTIC SORT, BUT I DO THINK A NEW CAR MIGHT BE IN ORDER. MAYBE A TESLA. OR A FERRARI. OR BOTH.

HEH, YOU'LL CERTAINLY NEED A FAST CAR WITH ALL THE WOMEN WHO'LL BE CHASING AFTER YOU ONCE WORD OF THIS FEAT GETS OUT, MR. ULTRAPERFECTION!

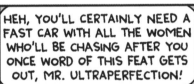

MR. **WHAT**??

UH...

YOU MIGHT WANT TO INVEST IN A MORE SOUNDPROOF BATHROOM FIRST.

GOOD CALL, ROGER. AS ALWAYS.

Good News

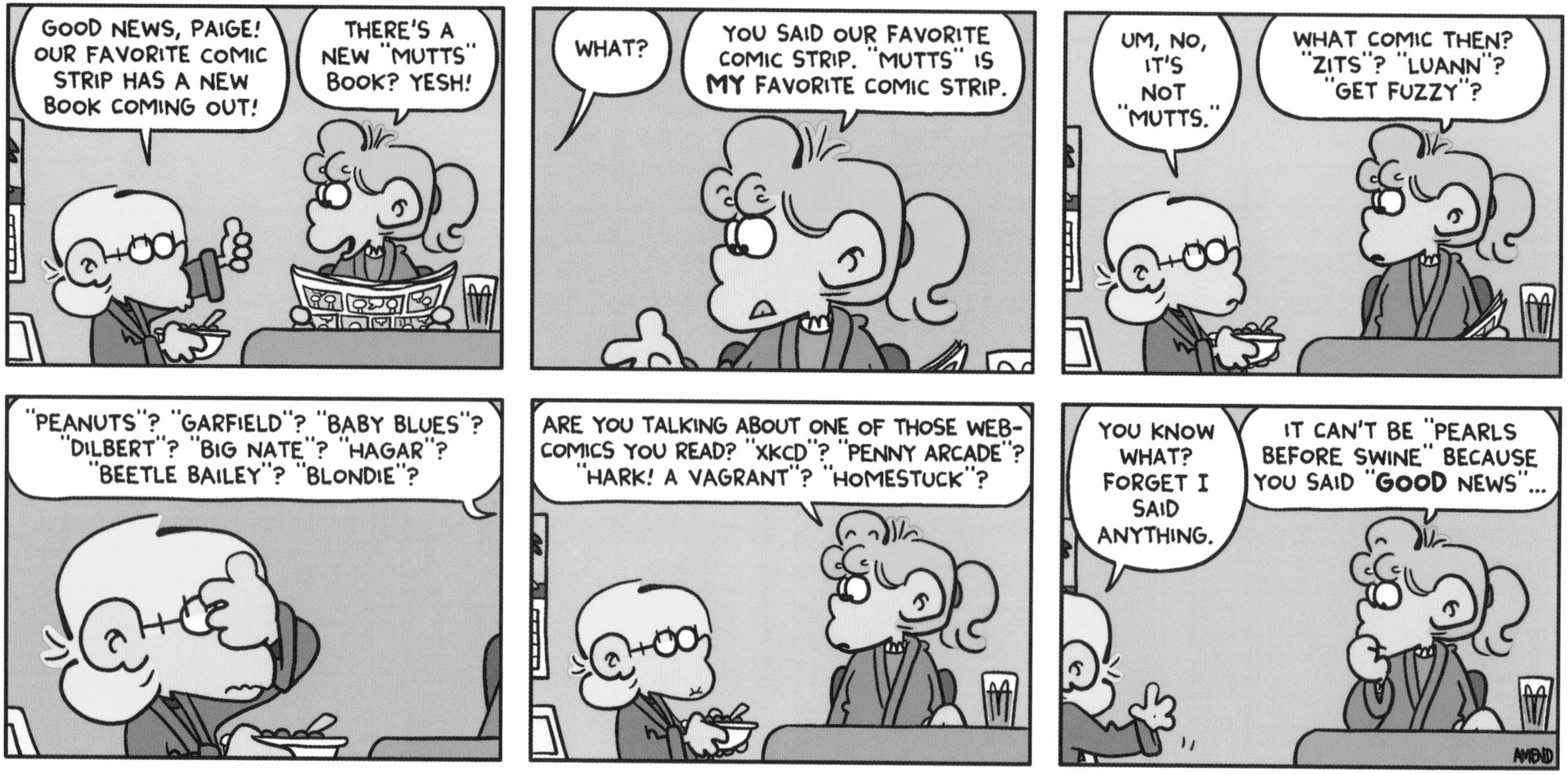

GOOD NEWS, PAIGE! OUR FAVORITE COMIC STRIP HAS A NEW BOOK COMING OUT!
THERE'S A NEW "MUTTS" BOOK? YESH!
WHAT?
YOU SAID OUR FAVORITE COMIC STRIP. "MUTTS" IS **MY** FAVORITE COMIC STRIP.
UM, NO, IT'S NOT "MUTTS."
WHAT COMIC THEN? "ZITS"? "LUANN"? "GET FUZZY"?
"PEANUTS"? "GARFIELD"? "BABY BLUES"? "DILBERT"? "BIG NATE"? "HAGAR"? "BEETLE BAILEY"? "BLONDIE"?
ARE YOU TALKING ABOUT ONE OF THOSE WEB-COMICS YOU READ? "XKCD"? "PENNY ARCADE"? "HARK! A VAGRANT"? "HOMESTUCK"?
YOU KNOW WHAT? FORGET I SAID ANYTHING.
IT CAN'T BE "PEARLS BEFORE SWINE" BECAUSE YOU SAID "**GOOD** NEWS"...
AMEND

Easter Piggies

FRUIT... CHEESE... SALAD... BREAD...

SEAFOOD... PASTA... SOUP... VEGGIES...

EGGS... SAUSAGE... BACON... POTATOES...

ROAST BEEF... HAM... TURKEY... SALMON...

CAKE... PIE... TARTS... CHOCOLATE MOUSSE...

MAYBE A LITTLE MORE BACON...

GUYS, WHEN THEY SAY "ALL YOU CAN EAT," IT'S NOT A REQUIREMENT.

SAYS YOU.

IT'S OK FOR ME TO TAKE THE WHOLE SHRIMP BOWL, RIGHT?

Force Outs

CAN YOU IMAGINE HOW DOMINATING A JEDI OR SITH WOULD BE AS A MAJOR LEAGUE BASEBALL PITCHER?

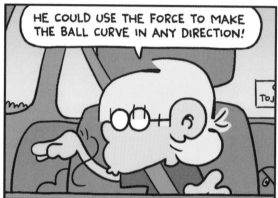

HE COULD USE THE FORCE TO MAKE THE BALL CURVE IN ANY DIRECTION!

HE COULD USE HIS MIND TRICKS ON THE UMPIRES SO EVERY PITCH WOULD BE CALLED A STRIKE!

IN CLOSE GAMES HE COULD MAKE THE OTHER TEAM CHOKE. LITERALLY.

THE ONLY PROBLEM IS HIS LIGHTSABER BAT WOULD CUT THE BALL IN TWO. HE'D NEVER GET A HIT.

IF HE PITCHED IN THE AMERICAN LEAGUE HE WOULDN'T HAVE TO BAT.

A PERFECT SOLUTION! WE SHOULD HAVE THESE DISCUSSIONS MORE OFTEN!

WE DIDN'T HAVE THIS DISCUSSION. AND IF YOU TELL ANYONE WE DID...

Don't Drop Me

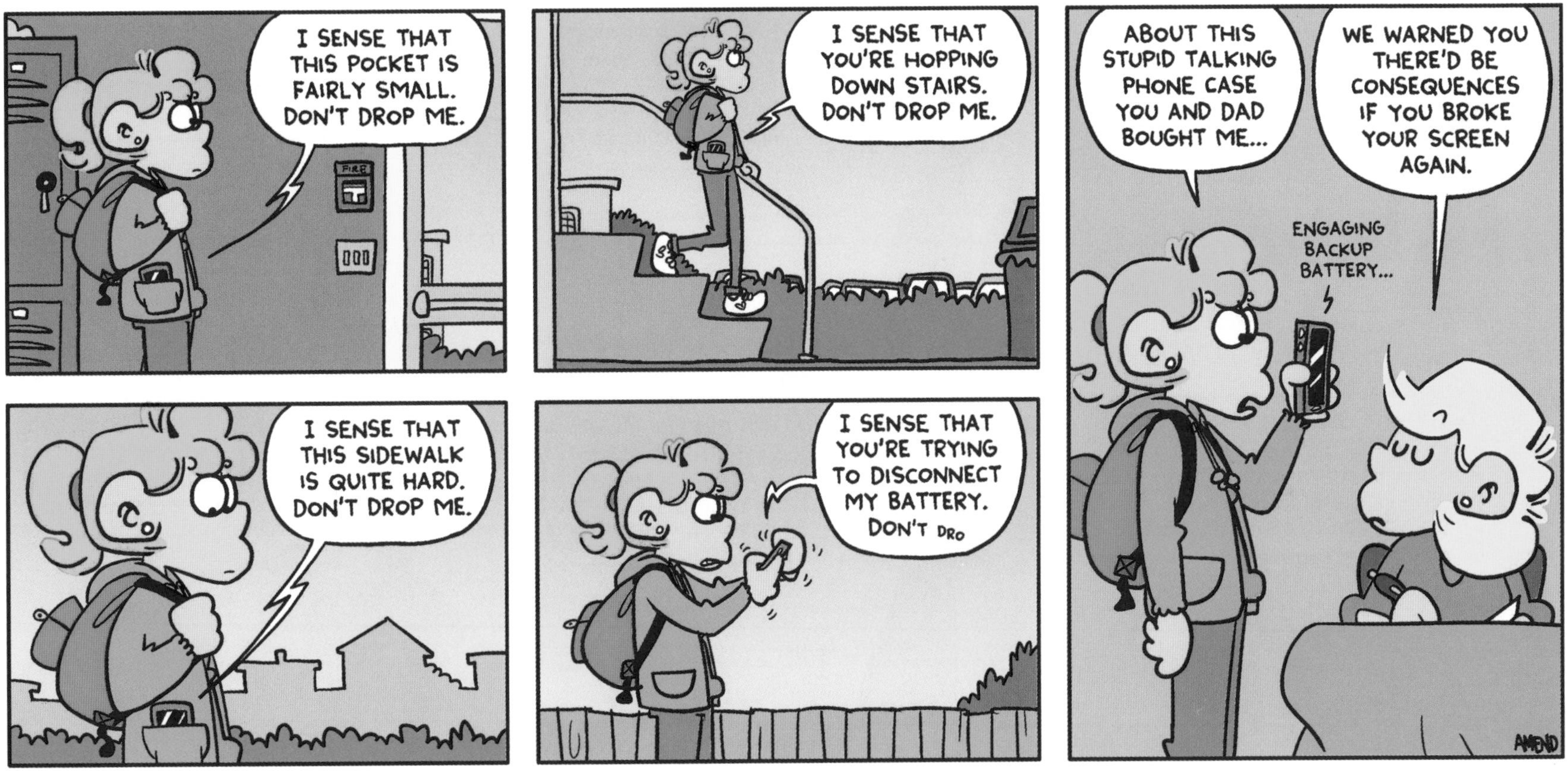

I SENSE THAT THIS POCKET IS FAIRLY SMALL. DON'T DROP ME.
I SENSE THAT YOU'RE HOPPING DOWN STAIRS. DON'T DROP ME.
I SENSE THAT THIS SIDEWALK IS QUITE HARD. DON'T DROP ME.
I SENSE THAT YOU'RE TRYING TO DISCONNECT MY BATTERY. DON'T DRO
ABOUT THIS STUPID TALKING PHONE CASE YOU AND DAD BOUGHT ME...
WE WARNED YOU THERE'D BE CONSEQUENCES IF YOU BROKE YOUR SCREEN AGAIN.
ENGAGING BACKUP BATTERY...
AMEND

Raining WHAT?!

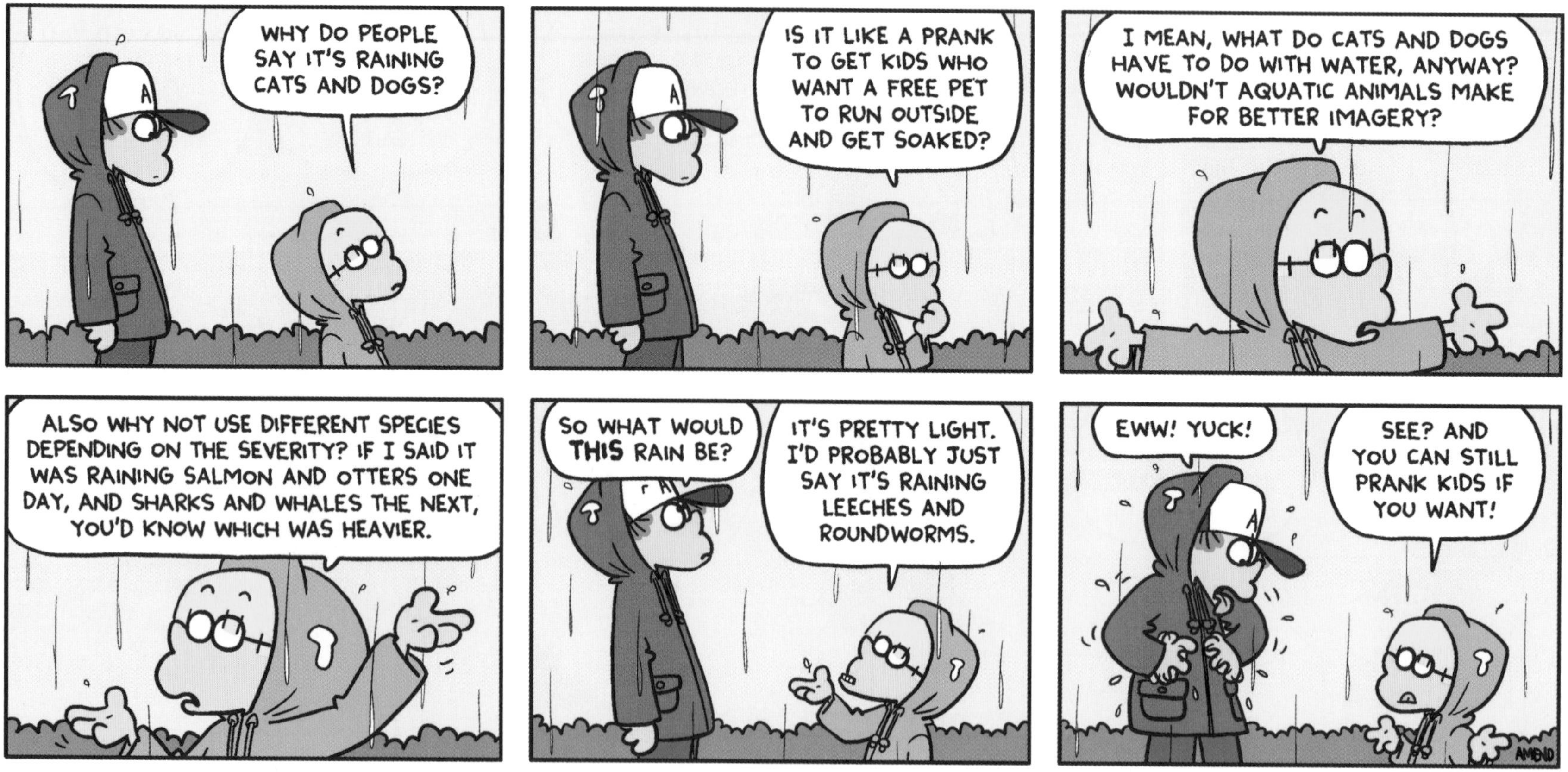
WHY DO PEOPLE SAY IT'S RAINING CATS AND DOGS?
IS IT LIKE A PRANK TO GET KIDS WHO WANT A FREE PET TO RUN OUTSIDE AND GET SOAKED?
I MEAN, WHAT DO CATS AND DOGS HAVE TO DO WITH WATER, ANYWAY? WOULDN'T AQUATIC ANIMALS MAKE FOR BETTER IMAGERY?
ALSO WHY NOT USE DIFFERENT SPECIES DEPENDING ON THE SEVERITY? IF I SAID IT WAS RAINING SALMON AND OTTERS ONE DAY, AND SHARKS AND WHALES THE NEXT, YOU'D KNOW WHICH WAS HEAVIER.
SO WHAT WOULD THIS RAIN BE?
IT'S PRETTY LIGHT. I'D PROBABLY JUST SAY IT'S RAINING LEECHES AND ROUNDWORMS.
EWW! YUCK!
SEE? AND YOU CAN STILL PRANK KIDS IF YOU WANT!
AMEND

Tonight's Watch

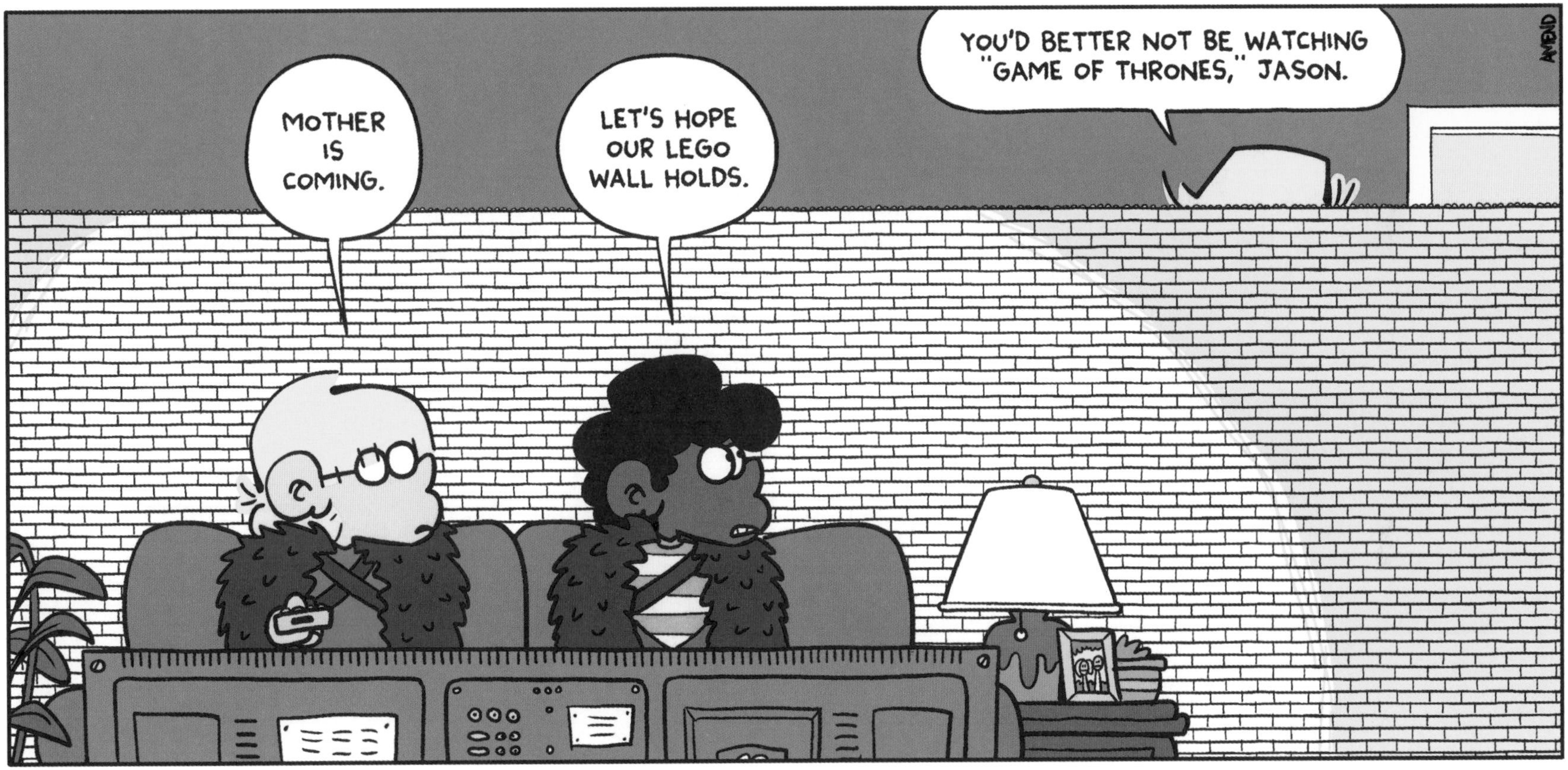
MOTHER IS COMING.
LET'S HOPE OUR LEGO WALL HOLDS.
YOU'D BETTER NOT BE WATCHING "GAME OF THRONES," JASON.
AMEND

Show Off and Tell

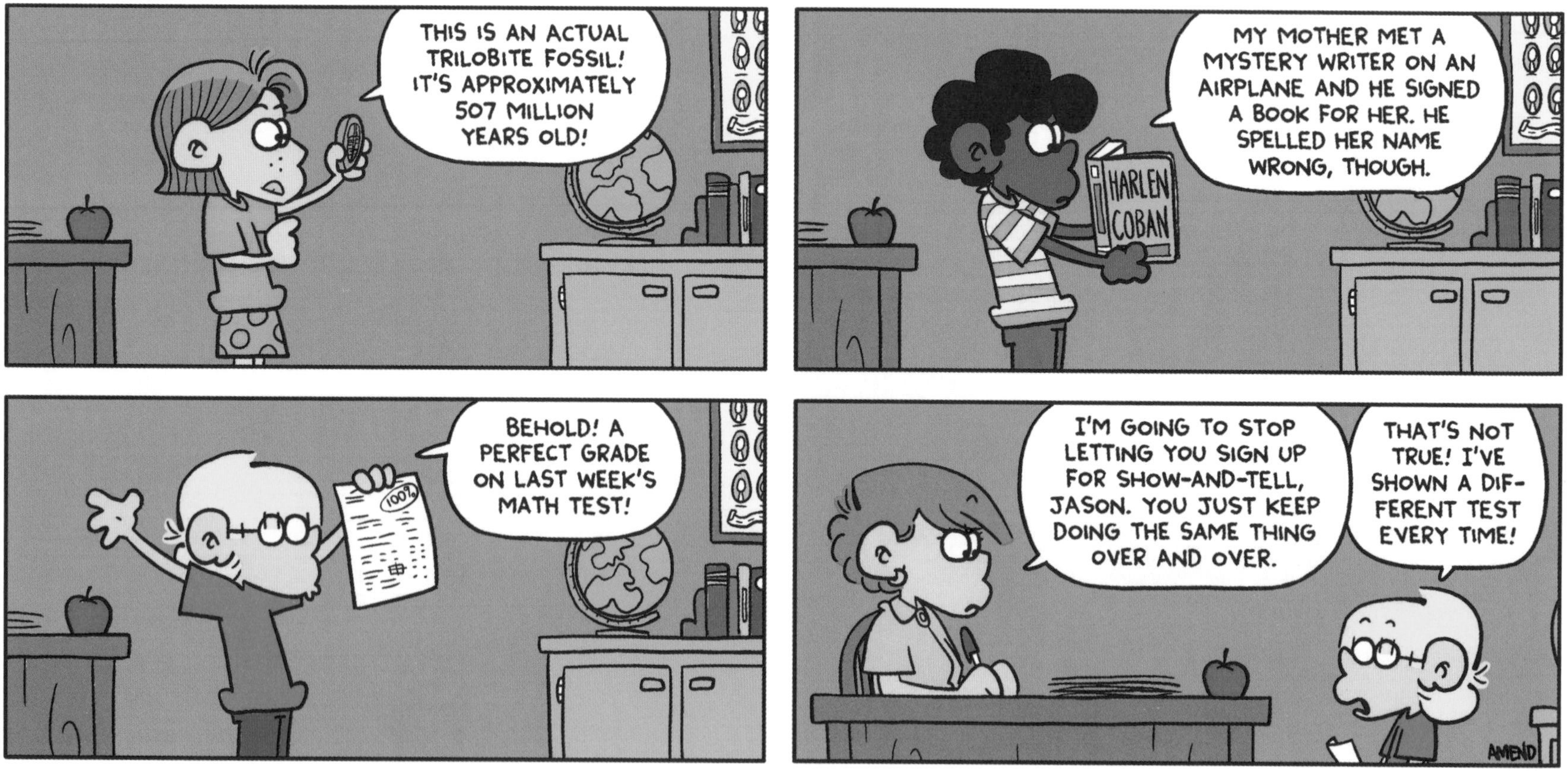
THIS IS AN ACTUAL TRILOBITE FOSSIL! IT'S APPROXIMATELY 507 MILLION YEARS OLD!
MY MOTHER MET A MYSTERY WRITER ON AN AIRPLANE AND HE SIGNED A BOOK FOR HER. HE SPELLED HER NAME WRONG, THOUGH.
HARLEN COBAN
BEHOLD! A PERFECT GRADE ON LAST WEEK'S MATH TEST!
100%
I'M GOING TO STOP LETTING YOU SIGN UP FOR SHOW-AND-TELL, JASON. YOU JUST KEEP DOING THE SAME THING OVER AND OVER.
THAT'S NOT TRUE! I'VE SHOWN A DIF-FERENT TEST EVERY TIME!
AMEND

Starstruck

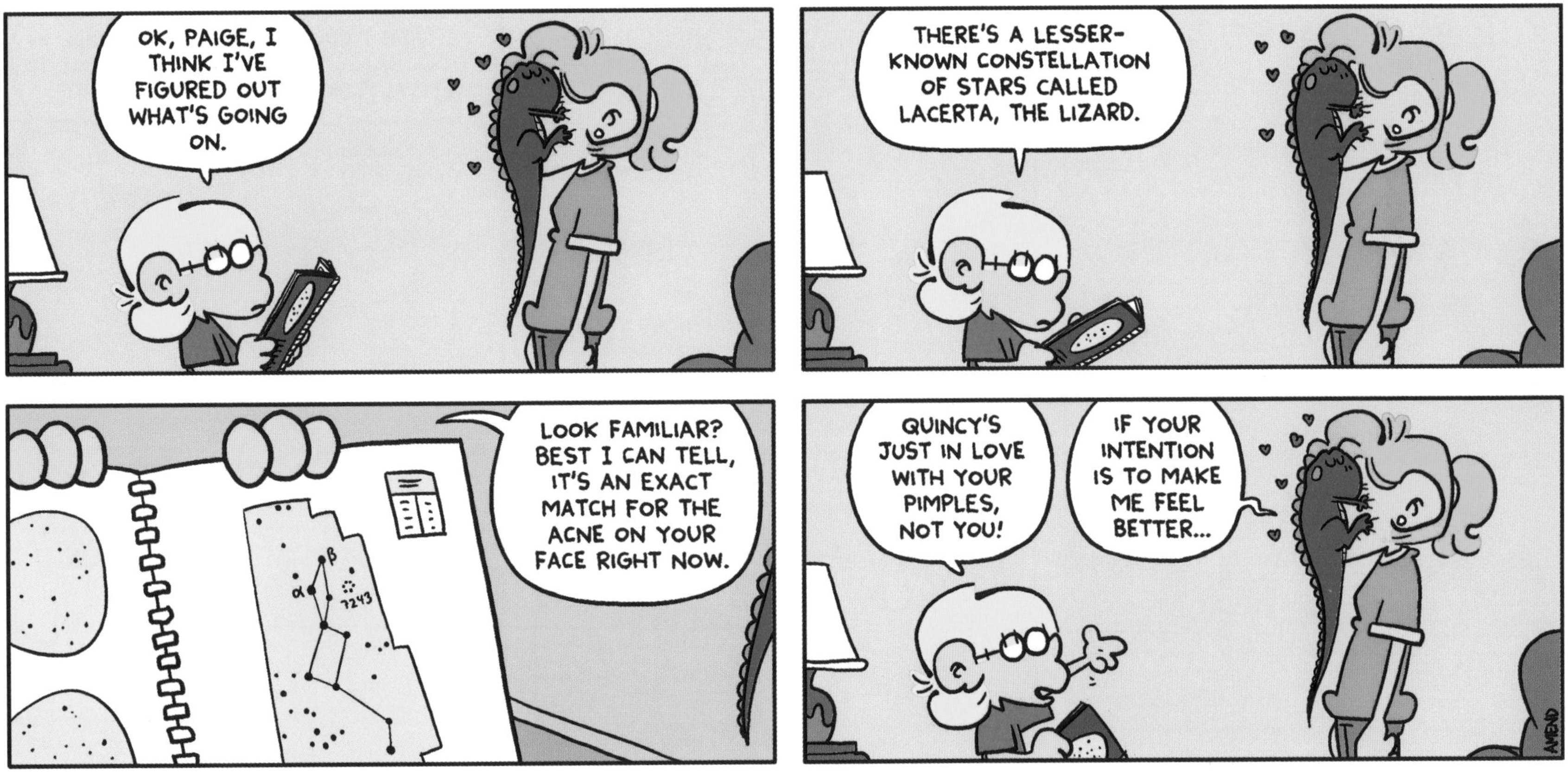
OK, PAIGE, I THINK I'VE FIGURED OUT WHAT'S GOING ON.
THERE'S A LESSER-KNOWN CONSTELLATION OF STARS CALLED LACERTA, THE LIZARD.
LOOK FAMILIAR? BEST I CAN TELL, IT'S AN EXACT MATCH FOR THE ACNE ON YOUR FACE RIGHT NOW.
QUINCY'S JUST IN LOVE WITH YOUR PIMPLES, NOT YOU!
IF YOUR INTENTION IS TO MAKE ME FEEL BETTER...

Holed It

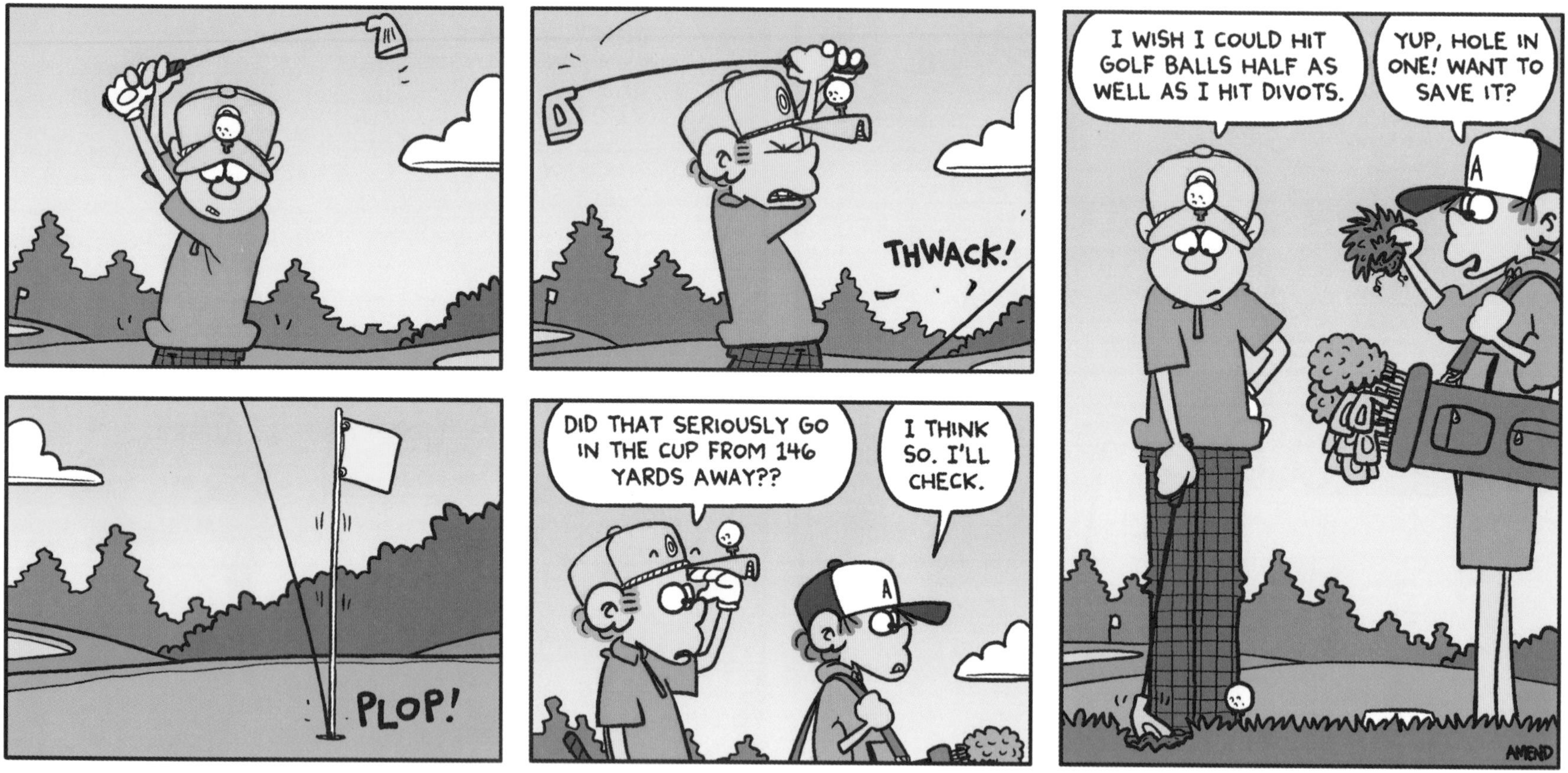

THWACK!
PLOP!
DID THAT SERIOUSLY GO IN THE CUP FROM 146 YARDS AWAY??
I THINK SO. I'LL CHECK.
I WISH I COULD HIT GOLF BALLS HALF AS WELL AS I HIT DIVOTS.
YUP, HOLE IN ONE! WANT TO SAVE IT?
AMEND

Motivational Tools

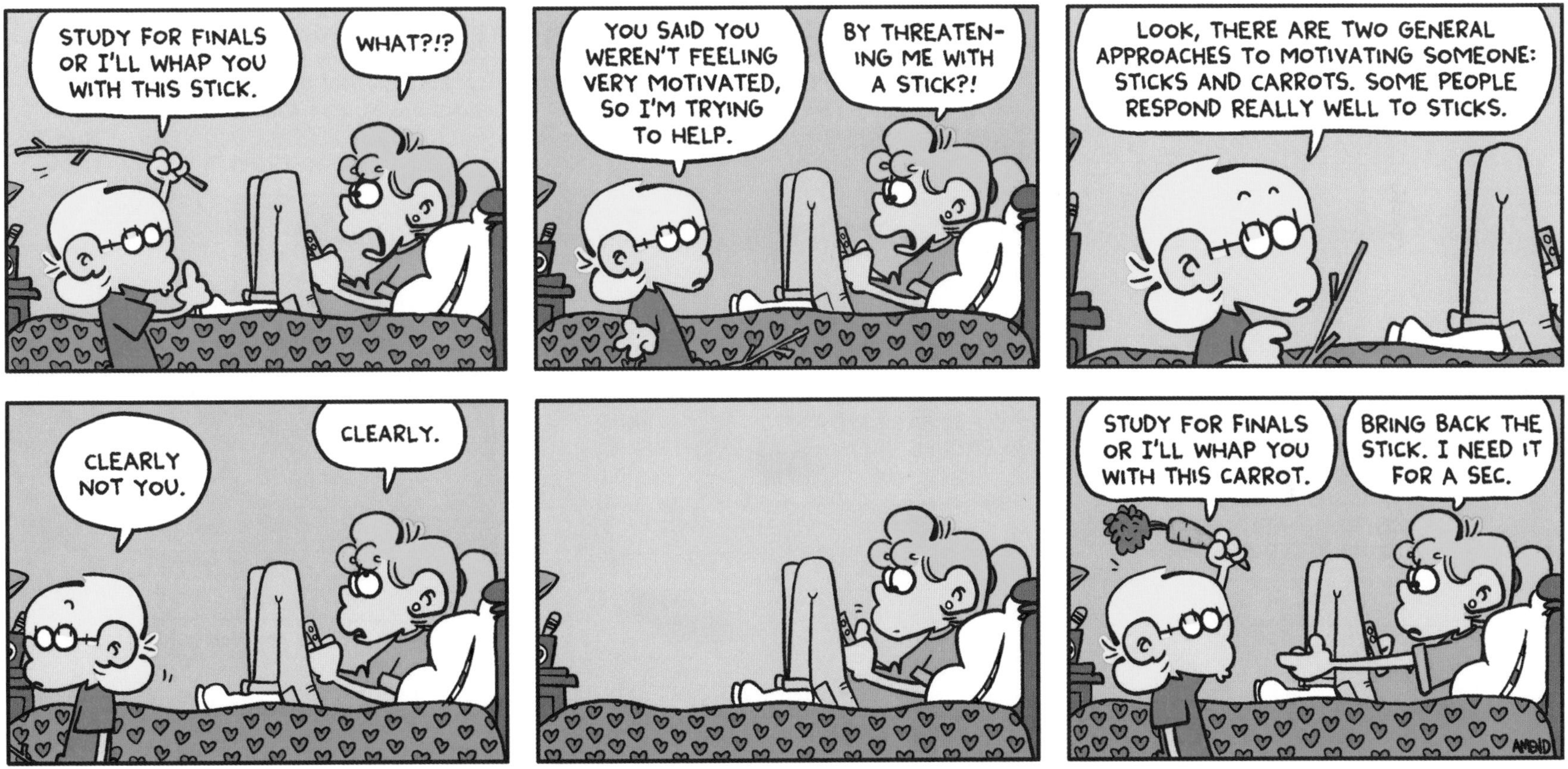
STUDY FOR FINALS OR I'LL WHAP YOU WITH THIS STICK.
WHAT?!?
YOU SAID YOU WEREN'T FEELING VERY MOTIVATED, SO I'M TRYING TO HELP.
BY THREATENING ME WITH A STICK?!
LOOK, THERE ARE TWO GENERAL APPROACHES TO MOTIVATING SOMEONE: STICKS AND CARROTS. SOME PEOPLE RESPOND REALLY WELL TO STICKS.
CLEARLY NOT YOU.
CLEARLY.
STUDY FOR FINALS OR I'LL WHAP YOU WITH THIS CARROT.
BRING BACK THE STICK. I NEED IT FOR A SEC.
AMEND

College Dreams

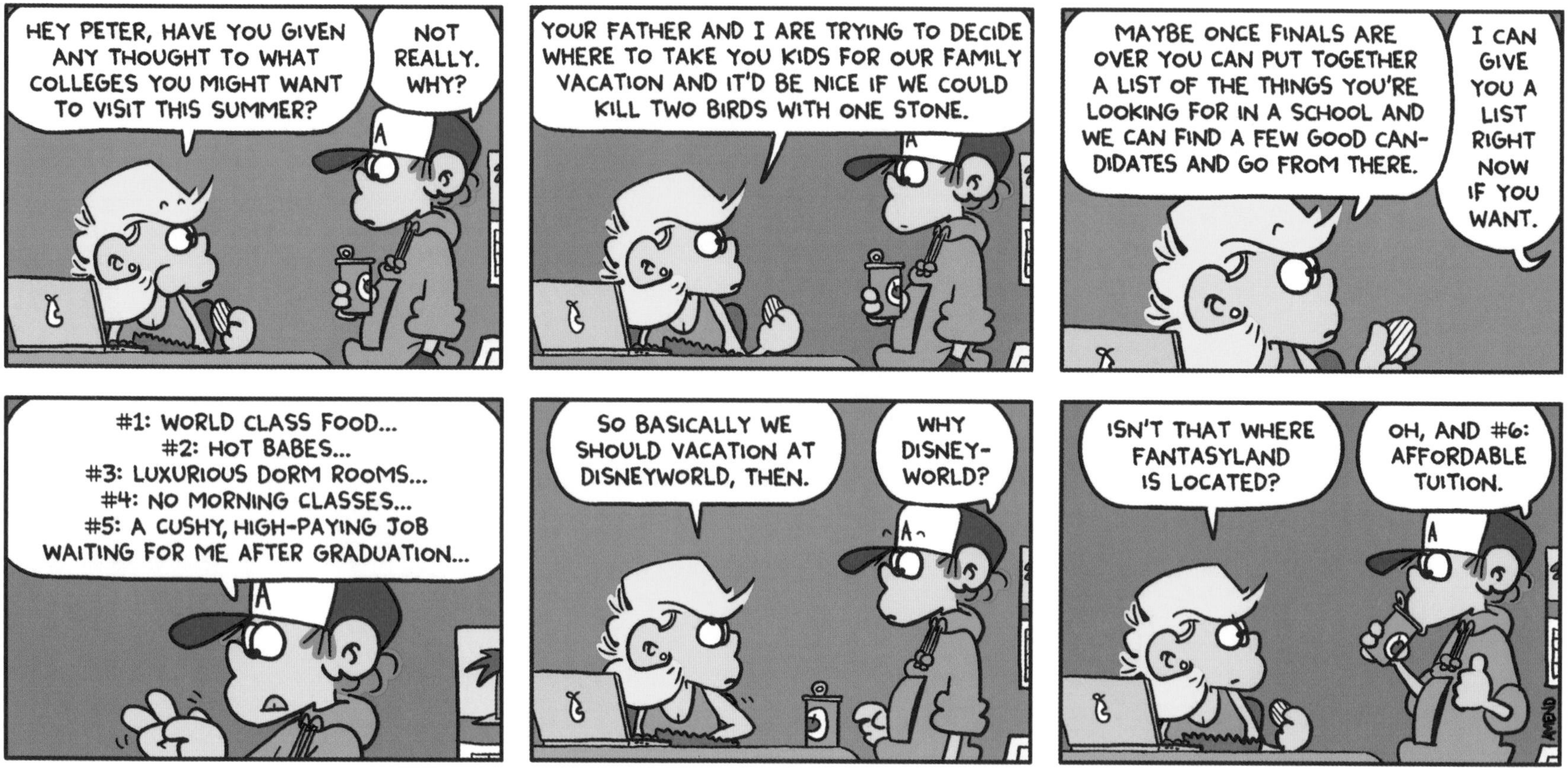
HEY PETER, HAVE YOU GIVEN ANY THOUGHT TO WHAT COLLEGES YOU MIGHT WANT TO VISIT THIS SUMMER?
NOT REALLY. WHY?
YOUR FATHER AND I ARE TRYING TO DECIDE WHERE TO TAKE YOU KIDS FOR OUR FAMILY VACATION AND IT'D BE NICE IF WE COULD KILL TWO BIRDS WITH ONE STONE.
MAYBE ONCE FINALS ARE OVER YOU CAN PUT TOGETHER A LIST OF THE THINGS YOU'RE LOOKING FOR IN A SCHOOL AND WE CAN FIND A FEW GOOD CANDIDATES AND GO FROM THERE.
I CAN GIVE YOU A LIST RIGHT NOW IF YOU WANT.
#1: WORLD CLASS FOOD... #2: HOT BABES... #3: LUXURIOUS DORM ROOMS... #4: NO MORNING CLASSES... #5: A CUSHY, HIGH-PAYING JOB WAITING FOR ME AFTER GRADUATION...
SO BASICALLY WE SHOULD VACATION AT DISNEYWORLD, THEN.
WHY DISNEYWORLD?
ISN'T THAT WHERE FANTASYLAND IS LOCATED?
OH, AND #6: AFFORDABLE TUITION.
AMEND

Theater Rep

CAN WE BUY TICKETS AHEAD OF TIME FOR THE "WARCRAFT" MOVIE?

DEPENDS. ARE YOU REVERED WITH THE PAVILIONPLEX MOVIE THEATER FACTION? IT'S A PREREQUISITE FOR ADVANCE TICKET SALES.

UM, NO. HOW DO WE DO THAT?

MY ASSOCIATE HERE HAS A REPEATABLE QUEST THAT REWARDS 25 REPUTATION POINTS FOR EVERY 10 PIECES OF POPCORN YOU PICK UP OFF THE FLOOR. TO GO FROM NEUTRAL TO REVERED, YOU'LL NEED TO GATHER 8,400 PIECES.

AND IF YOU'RE INTO BRAGGING RIGHTS, AN ADDITIONAL 8,400 PIECES WILL GET YOU TO EXALTED, WHICH EARNS YOU THE TITLE "BUTTERY FINGERS." NOT A LOT OF KIDS HAVE GOTTEN THAT YET.

I'LL GIVE YOU CREDIT... THE FLOORS HAVE NEVER BEEN CLEANER.

AND YOU SAID DOING THIS WOULD BE CRUEL. JUST LOOK AT THOSE SMILES!

WOOHOO! THERE'S LIKE SIX OR SEVEN BEHIND THIS TRASH CAN!

NICE!

Jerky Boys

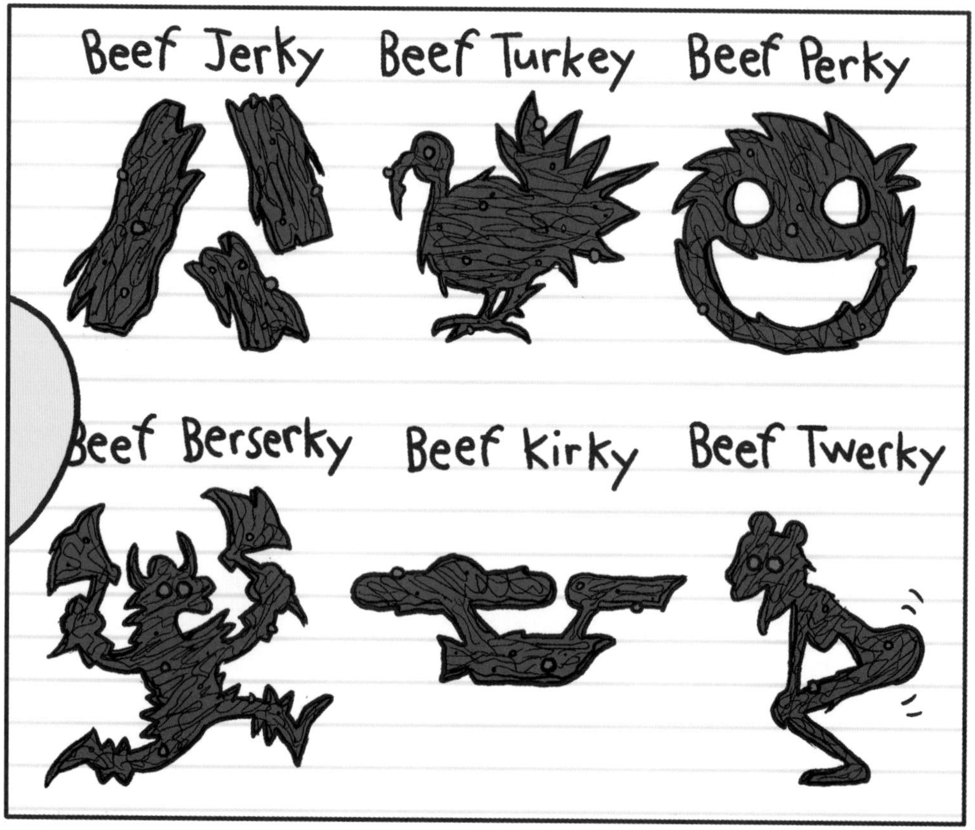
Beef Jerky
Beef Turkey
Beef Perky
Beef Berserky
Beef Kirky
Beef Twerky

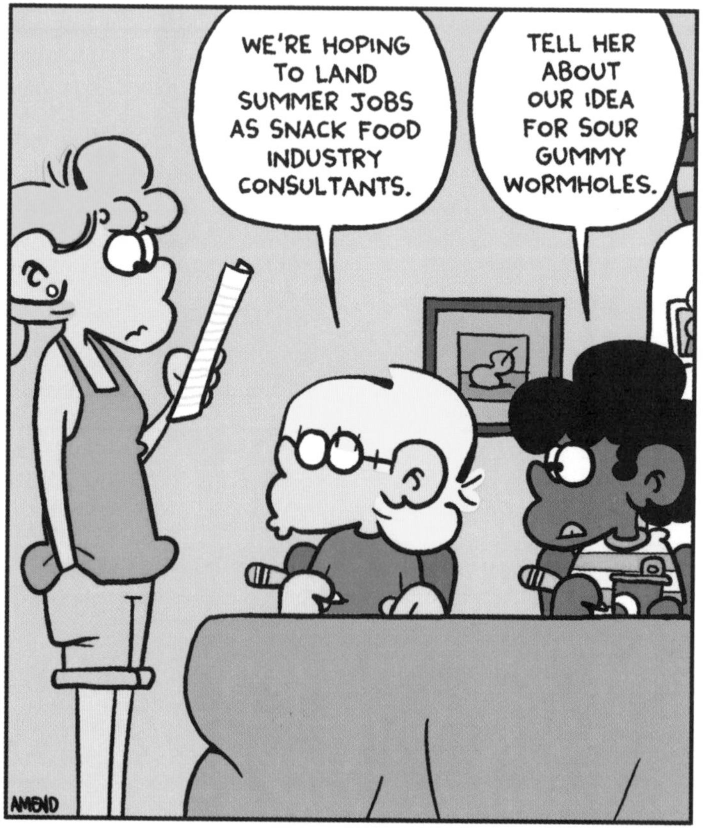
WE'RE HOPING TO LAND SUMMER JOBS AS SNACK FOOD INDUSTRY CONSULTANTS.
TELL HER ABOUT OUR IDEA FOR SOUR GUMMY WORMHOLES.
AMEND

Yard Clippings

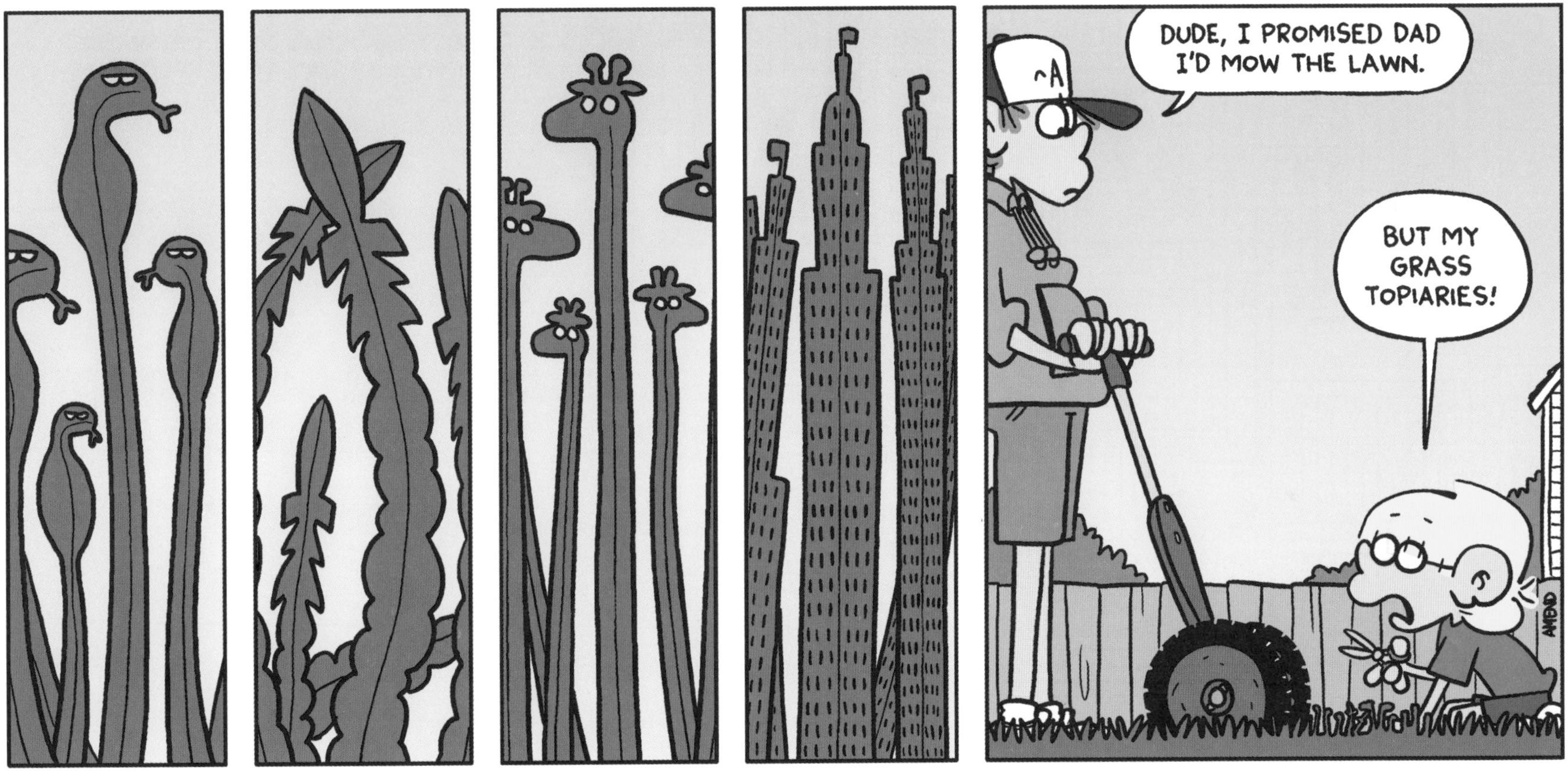
DUDE, I PROMISED DAD I'D MOW THE LAWN.
BUT MY GRASS TOPIARIES!

Exhausteen

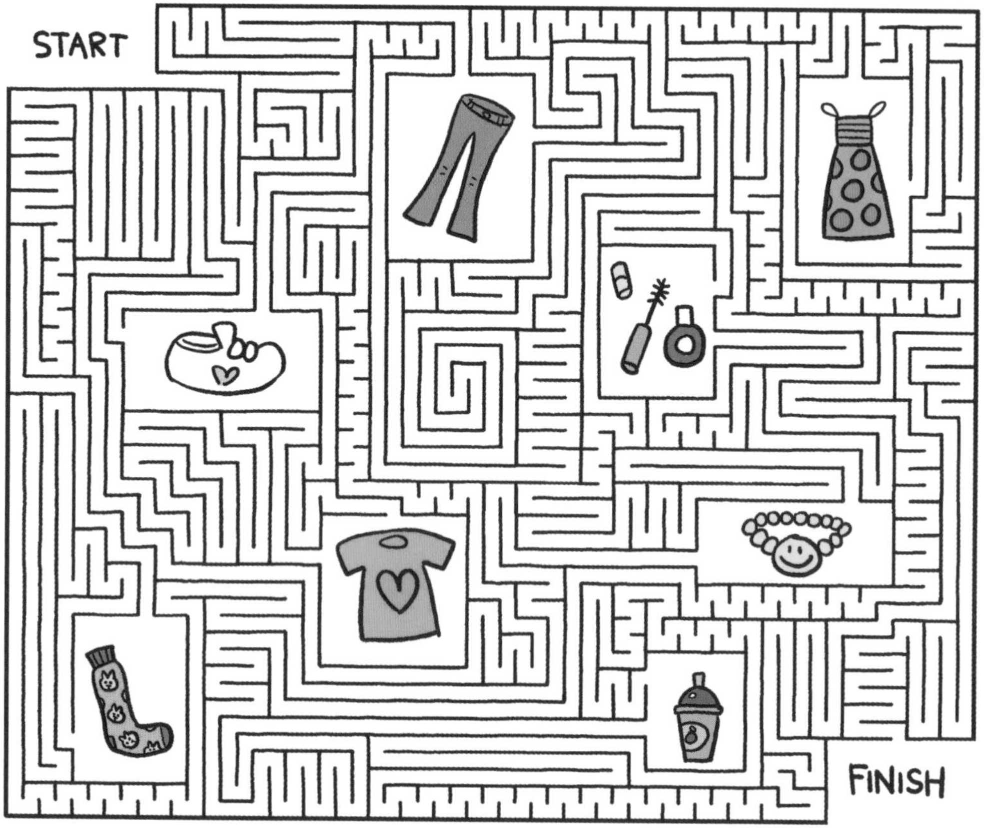
START
FINISH

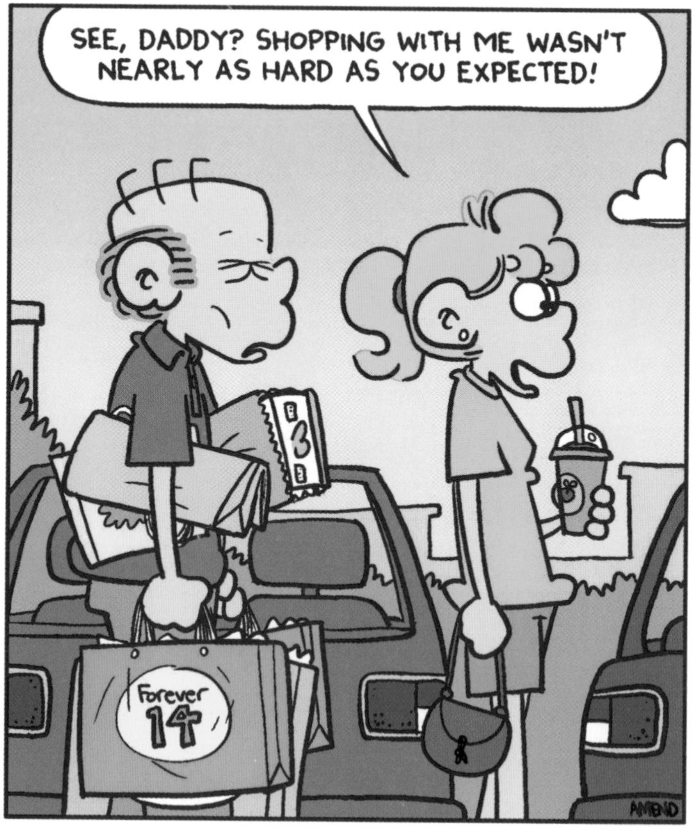
SEE, DADDY? SHOPPING WITH ME WASN'T NEARLY AS HARD AS YOU EXPECTED!
Forever 14
AMEND

Competitive Eating

HAVE YOU SEEN PETER AND JASON?

THEY'RE OUT BACK HAVING A HOT DOG EATING CONTEST.

REALLY? THAT DOESN'T SOUND VERY FAIR. PETER CAN OUT-EAT A HIPPO.

IT'S NOT A CONTEST TO SEE WHO CAN EAT THE MOST.

WHAT SORT OF CONTEST IS IT, THEN?

FIRST ONE TO BARF LOSES.

AND YOU HAVE TO SWALLOW AN ENTIRE BITE.

GUYS, C'MON! THEY AREN'T **THAT** BURNT!

First One's Free

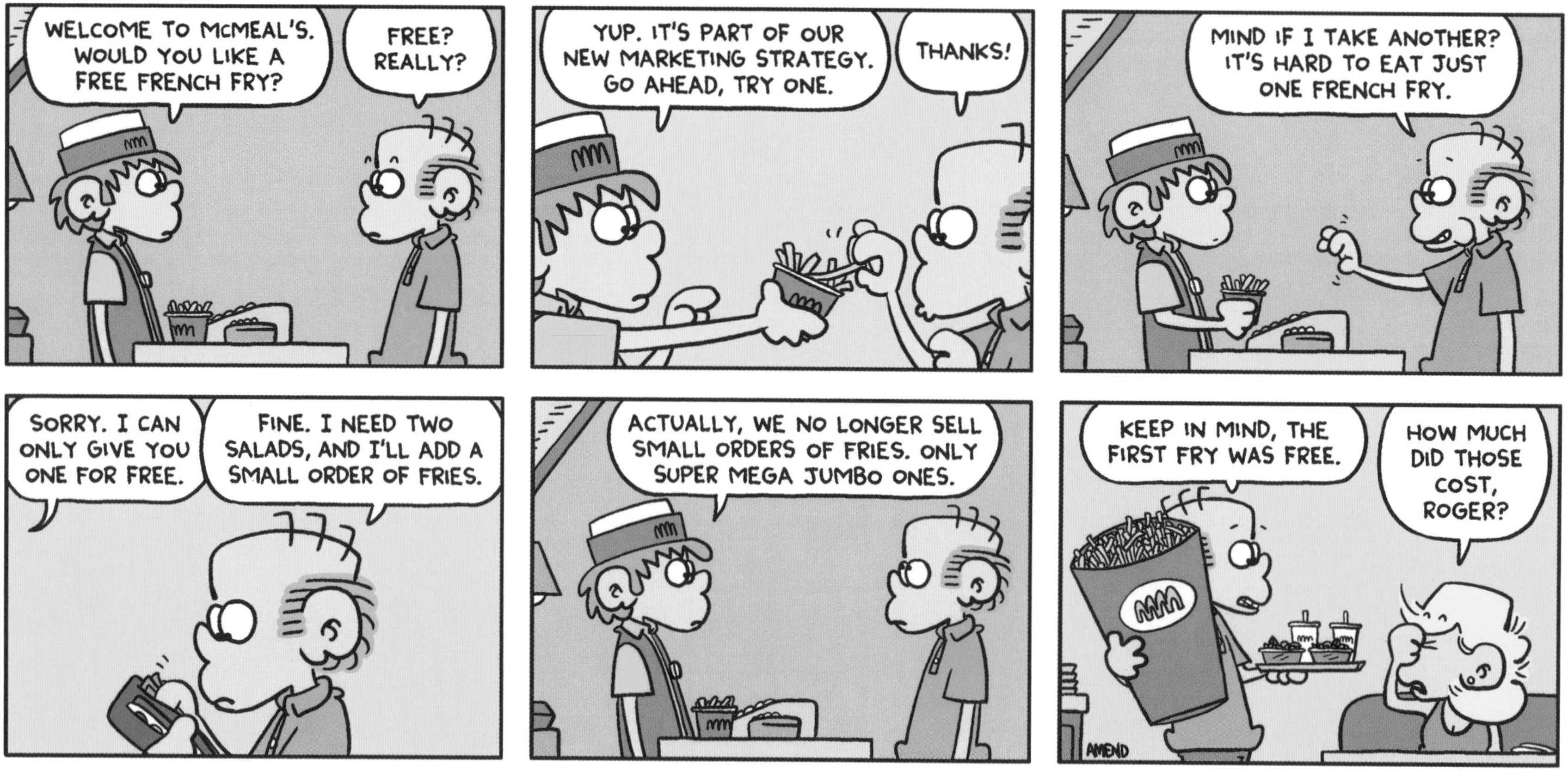
WELCOME TO MCMEAL'S. WOULD YOU LIKE A FREE FRENCH FRY?
FREE? REALLY?
YUP. IT'S PART OF OUR NEW MARKETING STRATEGY. GO AHEAD, TRY ONE.
THANKS!
MIND IF I TAKE ANOTHER? IT'S HARD TO EAT JUST ONE FRENCH FRY.
SORRY. I CAN ONLY GIVE YOU ONE FOR FREE.
FINE. I NEED TWO SALADS, AND I'LL ADD A SMALL ORDER OF FRIES.
ACTUALLY, WE NO LONGER SELL SMALL ORDERS OF FRIES. ONLY SUPER MEGA JUMBO ONES.
KEEP IN MIND, THE FIRST FRY WAS FREE.
HOW MUCH DID THOSE COST, ROGER?
AMEND

Dental Crygene

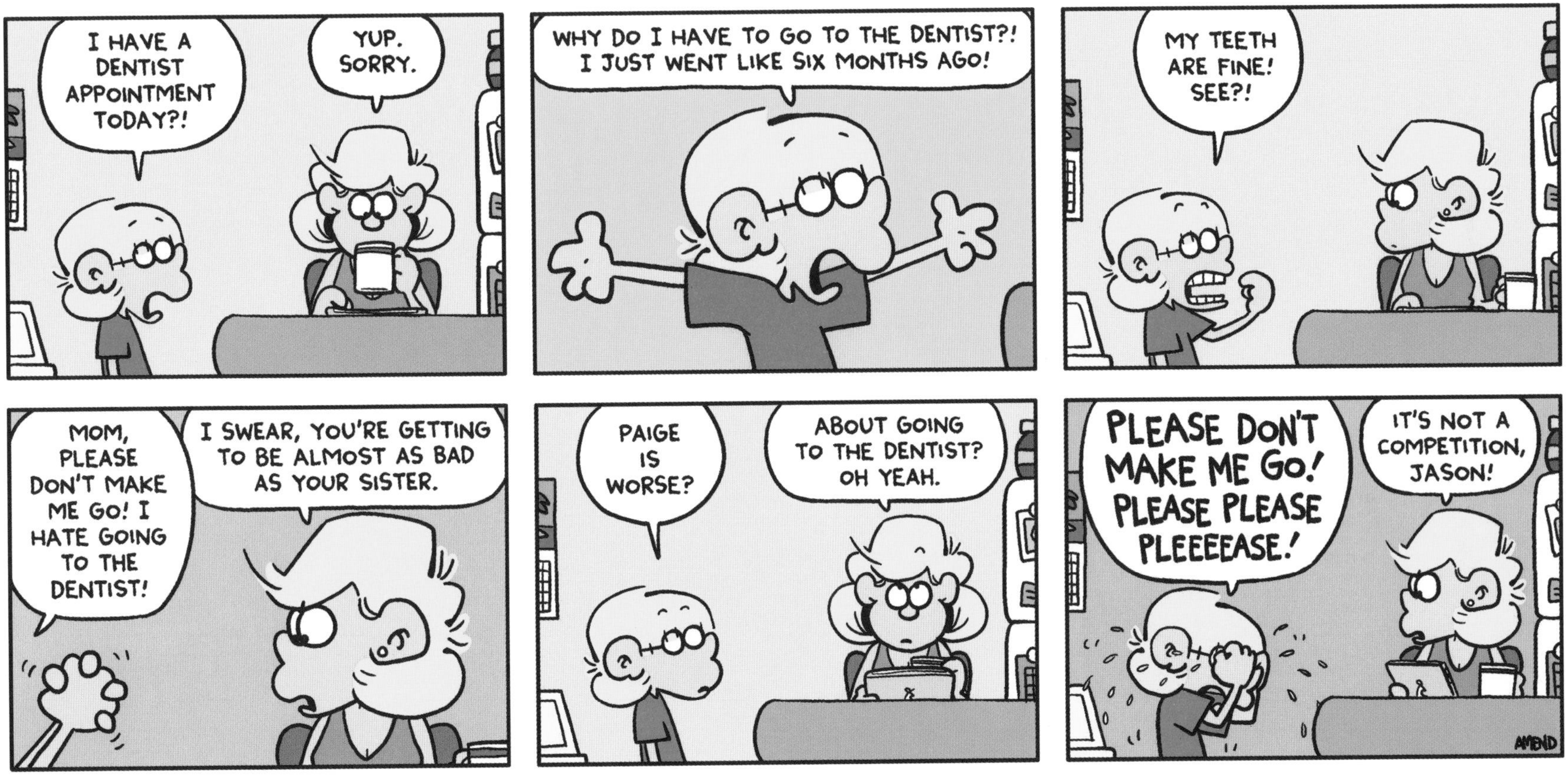
I HAVE A DENTIST APPOINTMENT TODAY?!
YUP. SORRY.
WHY DO I HAVE TO GO TO THE DENTIST?! I JUST WENT LIKE SIX MONTHS AGO!
MY TEETH ARE FINE! SEE?!
MOM, PLEASE DON'T MAKE ME GO! I HATE GOING TO THE DENTIST!
I SWEAR, YOU'RE GETTING TO BE ALMOST AS BAD AS YOUR SISTER.
PAIGE IS WORSE?
ABOUT GOING TO THE DENTIST? OH YEAH.
PLEASE DON'T MAKE ME GO! PLEASE PLEASE PLEEEEASE!
IT'S NOT A COMPETITION, JASON!
AMEND

Summer Is Here

SLURRRP

SLURRRRRP!

MY HAIR ISN'T RED, I'M NOT A PRIESTESS, AND IT'S CALLED BLUEBERRY SYRUP.

JON SNOWCONE LIVES AGAIN!

UH OH...

EXCUSE ME, RED PRIESTESS? I HAVE ADDITIONAL NEED OF YOUR MAGIC!

Experi-mental

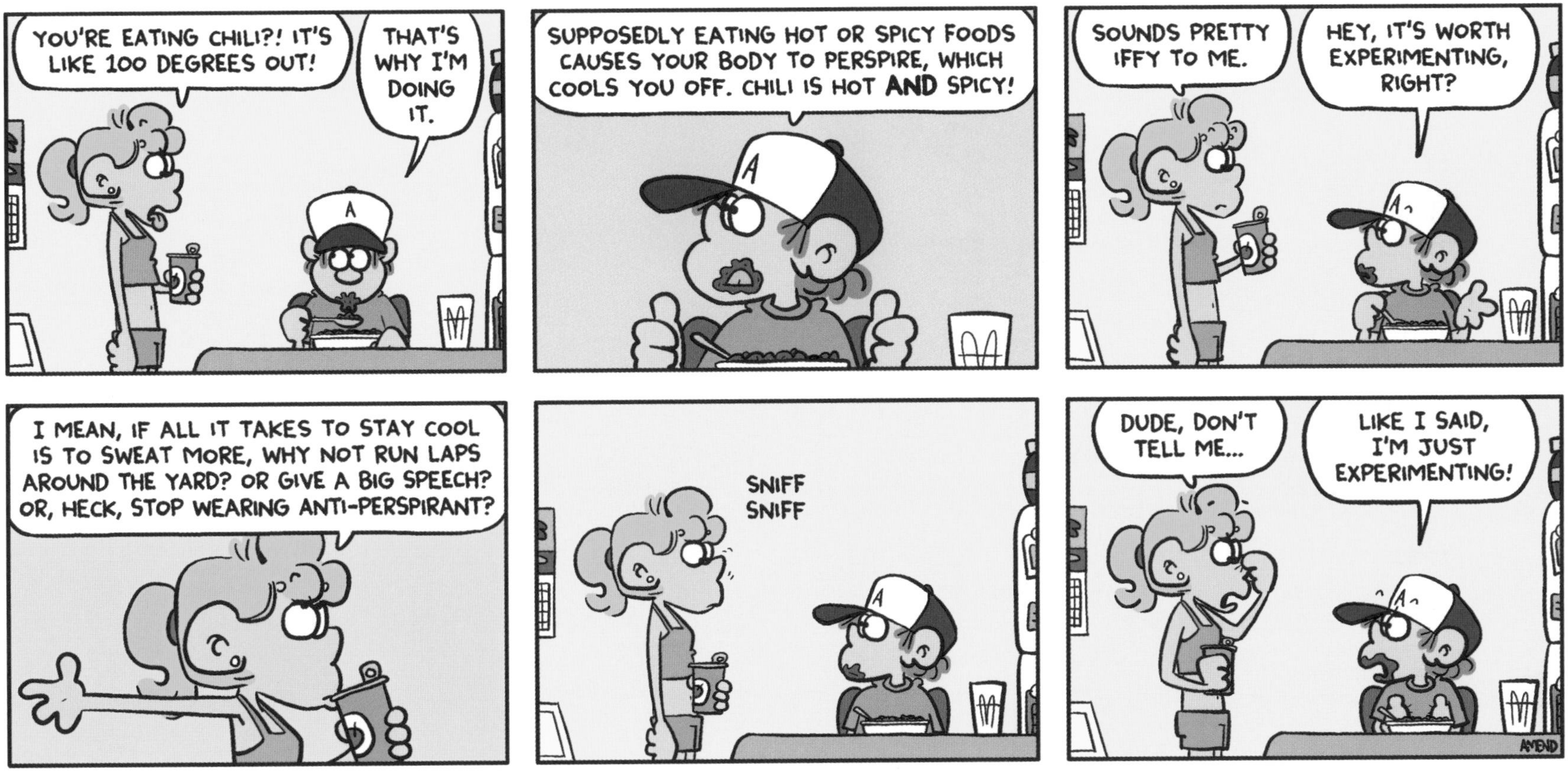
YOU'RE EATING CHILI?! IT'S LIKE 100 DEGREES OUT!
THAT'S WHY I'M DOING IT.
SUPPOSEDLY EATING HOT OR SPICY FOODS CAUSES YOUR BODY TO PERSPIRE, WHICH COOLS YOU OFF. CHILI IS HOT AND SPICY!
SOUNDS PRETTY IFFY TO ME.
HEY, IT'S WORTH EXPERIMENTING, RIGHT?
I MEAN, IF ALL IT TAKES TO STAY COOL IS TO SWEAT MORE, WHY NOT RUN LAPS AROUND THE YARD? OR GIVE A BIG SPEECH? OR, HECK, STOP WEARING ANTI-PERSPIRANT?
SNIFF SNIFF
DUDE, DON'T TELL ME...
LIKE I SAID, I'M JUST EXPERIMENTING!
AMEND

Shore Thing

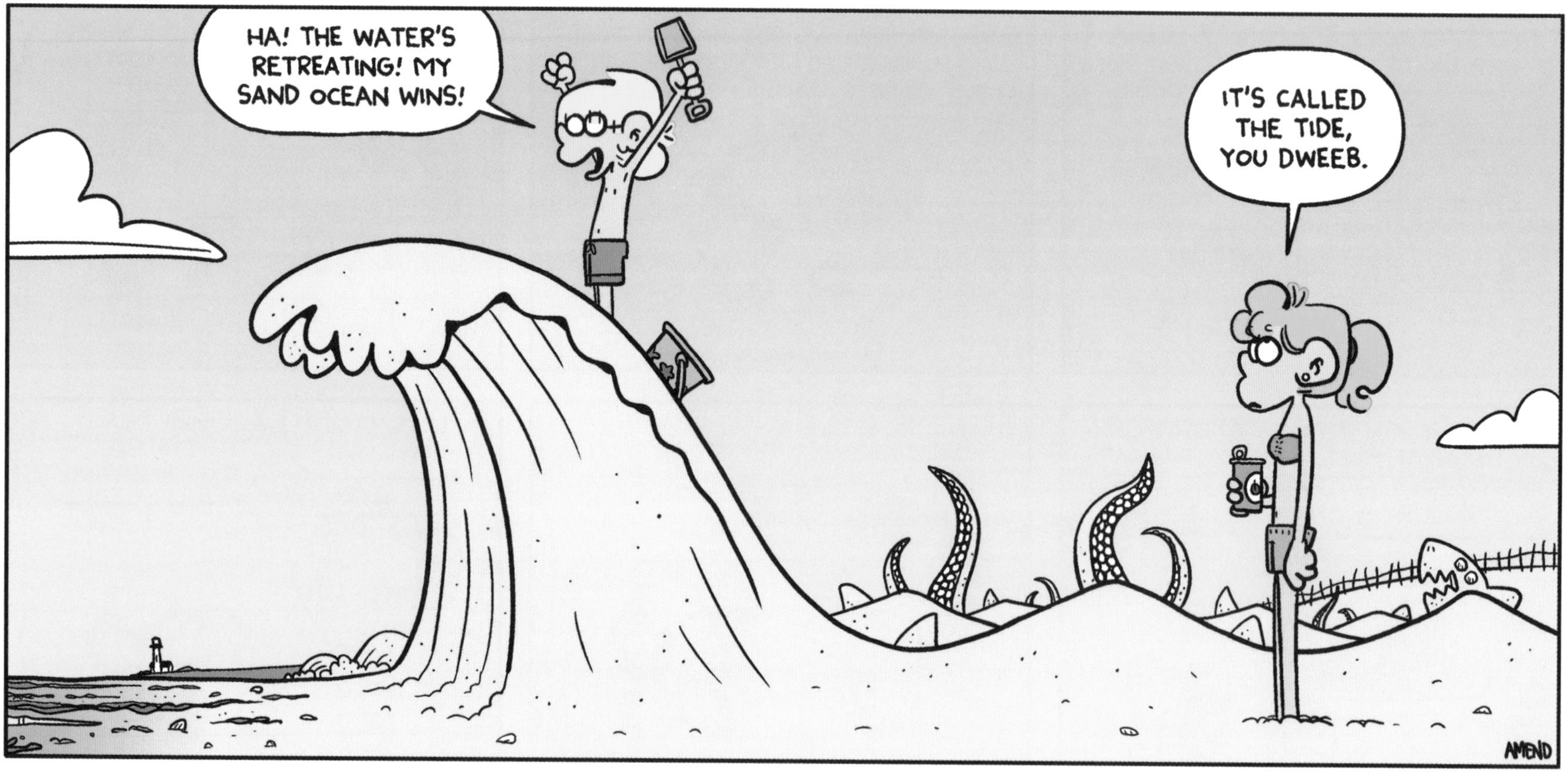
HA! THE WATER'S RETREATING! MY SAND OCEAN WINS!
IT'S CALLED THE TIDE, YOU DWEEB.
AMEND

Stretching the Truth

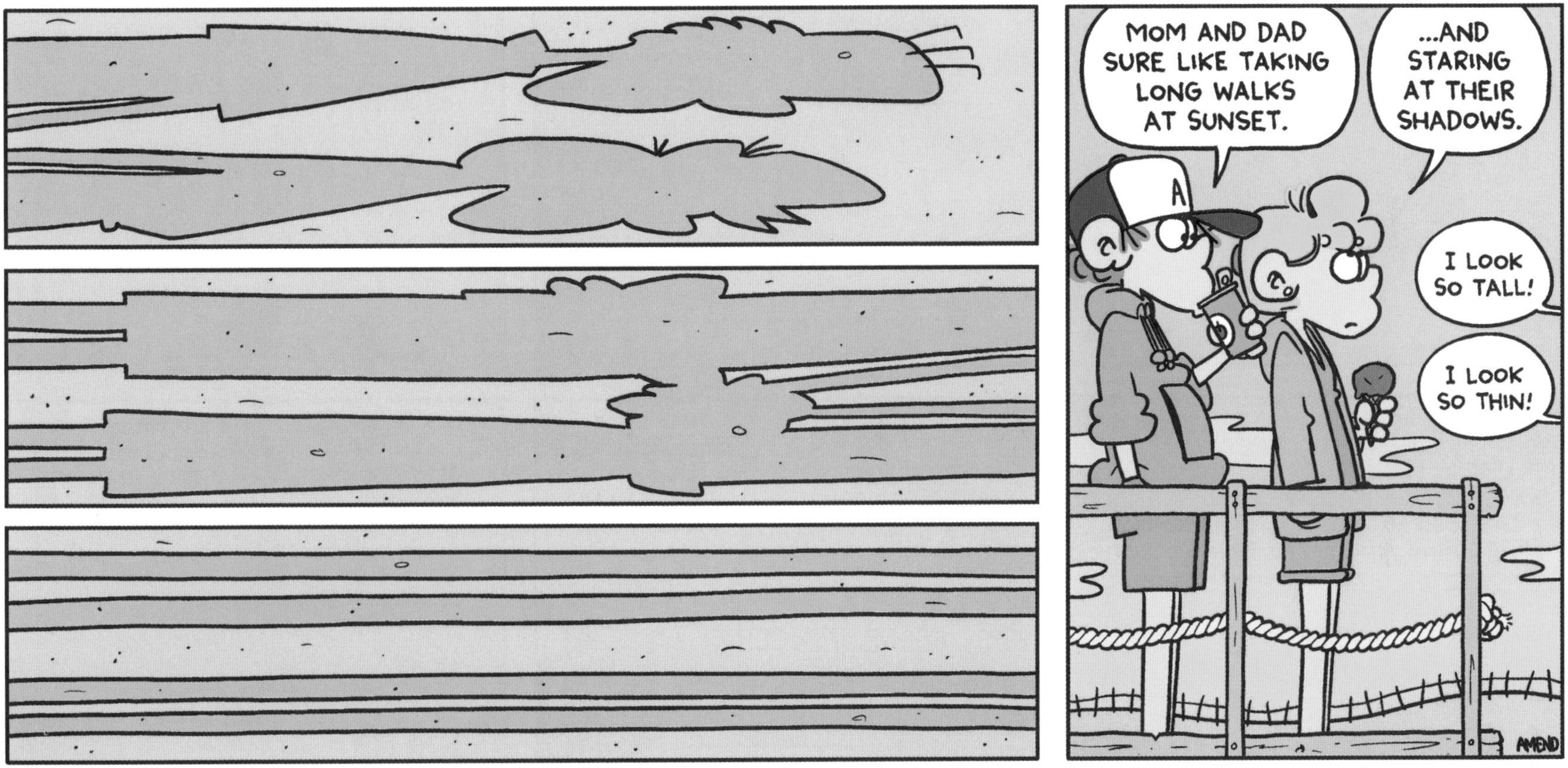
MOM AND DAD SURE LIKE TAKING LONG WALKS AT SUNSET.
...AND STARING AT THEIR SHADOWS.
I LOOK SO TALL!
I LOOK SO THIN!
AMEND

Back-to-School Haircut

SO WHAT ARE WE DOING TODAY?

MY MOM SAYS I NEED A BACK-TO-SCHOOL HAIRCUT.

SO BASICALLY A TRIM?

IS THAT WHAT A BACK-TO-SCHOOL HAIRCUT IS?

USUALLY.

DANG. I WAS HOPING IT MEANT SOMETHING MORE INTERESTING.

LIKE MAYBE YOU'D GIVE ME DUAL MOHAWKS TO FORM A BIG ROMAN NUMERAL "V" SINCE I'LL BE IN FIFTH GRADE. OR YOU'D SHAVE SOME SORT OF MESSAGE ONTO THE BACK OF MY HEAD LIKE "I ♡ HOMEWORK." OR, I DUNNO, YOU MIGHT EVEN DO BOTH!

IS THAT YOUR MOM SITTING OVER THERE?

THE LADY GLARING AT ME RIGHT NOW WITH NO DISCERNABLE SENSE OF HUMOR? YEAH.

LET'S GO WITH A TRIM.

MAYBE YOU COULD JUST SAY YOUR SCISSORS SLIPPED?

Pokémon Woe

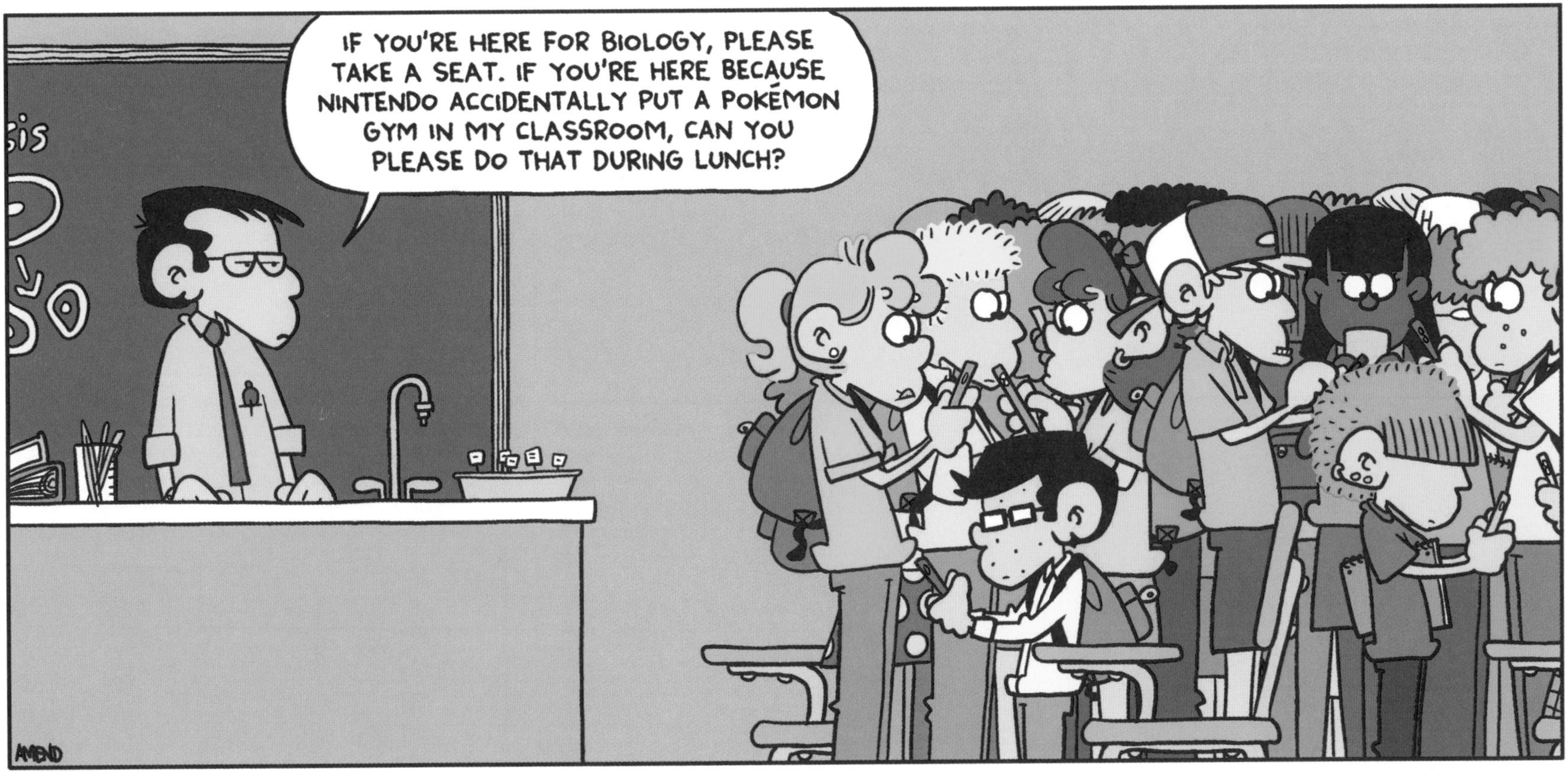
IF YOU'RE HERE FOR BIOLOGY, PLEASE TAKE A SEAT. IF YOU'RE HERE BECAUSE NINTENDO ACCIDENTALLY PUT A POKÉMON GYM IN MY CLASSROOM, CAN YOU PLEASE DO THAT DURING LUNCH?
AMEND

Emushies

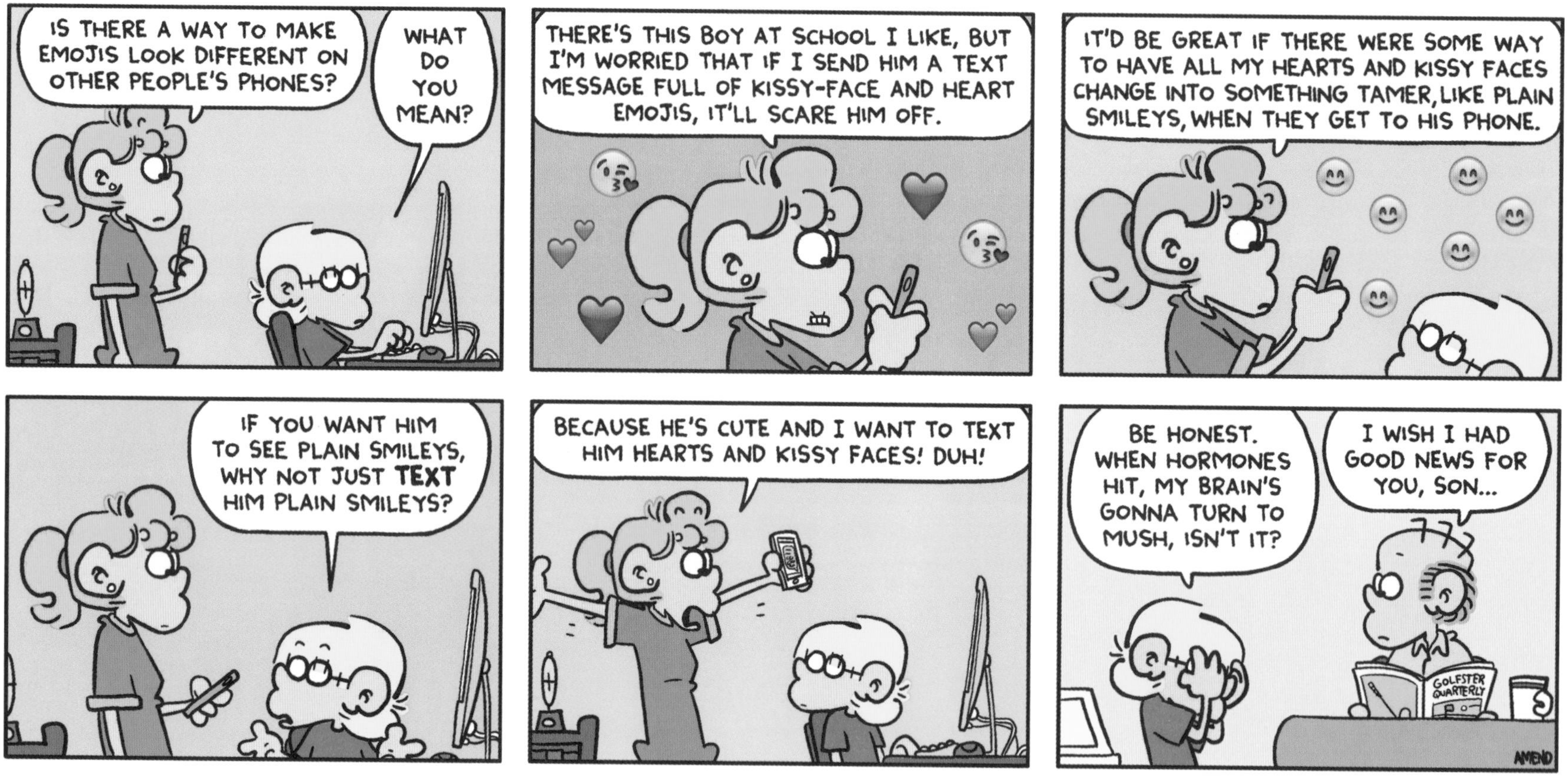
IS THERE A WAY TO MAKE EMOJIS LOOK DIFFERENT ON OTHER PEOPLE'S PHONES?
WHAT DO YOU MEAN?
THERE'S THIS BOY AT SCHOOL I LIKE, BUT I'M WORRIED THAT IF I SEND HIM A TEXT MESSAGE FULL OF KISSY-FACE AND HEART EMOJIS, IT'LL SCARE HIM OFF.
IT'D BE GREAT IF THERE WERE SOME WAY TO HAVE ALL MY HEARTS AND KISSY FACES CHANGE INTO SOMETHING TAMER, LIKE PLAIN SMILEYS, WHEN THEY GET TO HIS PHONE.
IF YOU WANT HIM TO SEE PLAIN SMILEYS, WHY NOT JUST **TEXT** HIM PLAIN SMILEYS?
BECAUSE HE'S CUTE AND I WANT TO TEXT HIM HEARTS AND KISSY FACES! DUH!
BE HONEST. WHEN HORMONES HIT, MY BRAIN'S GONNA TURN TO MUSH, ISN'T IT?
I WISH I HAD GOOD NEWS FOR YOU, SON...
GOLFSTER QUARTERLY
AMEND

Pizza Math

A round cheese pizza is sliced into eighths.

A round pepperoni pizza is sliced into fifths.

And a round mushroom pizza is sliced into sevenths.

How many degrees will the interior angles of each slice be?

I'M PRETTY SURE "DEPENDS ON THE OVEN TEMPERATURE" ISN'T THE RIGHT ANSWER.

YOUR FRIEND STEVE WORKS AT A PIZZA PLACE. CAN YOU CALL HIM?

Assuming the Worst

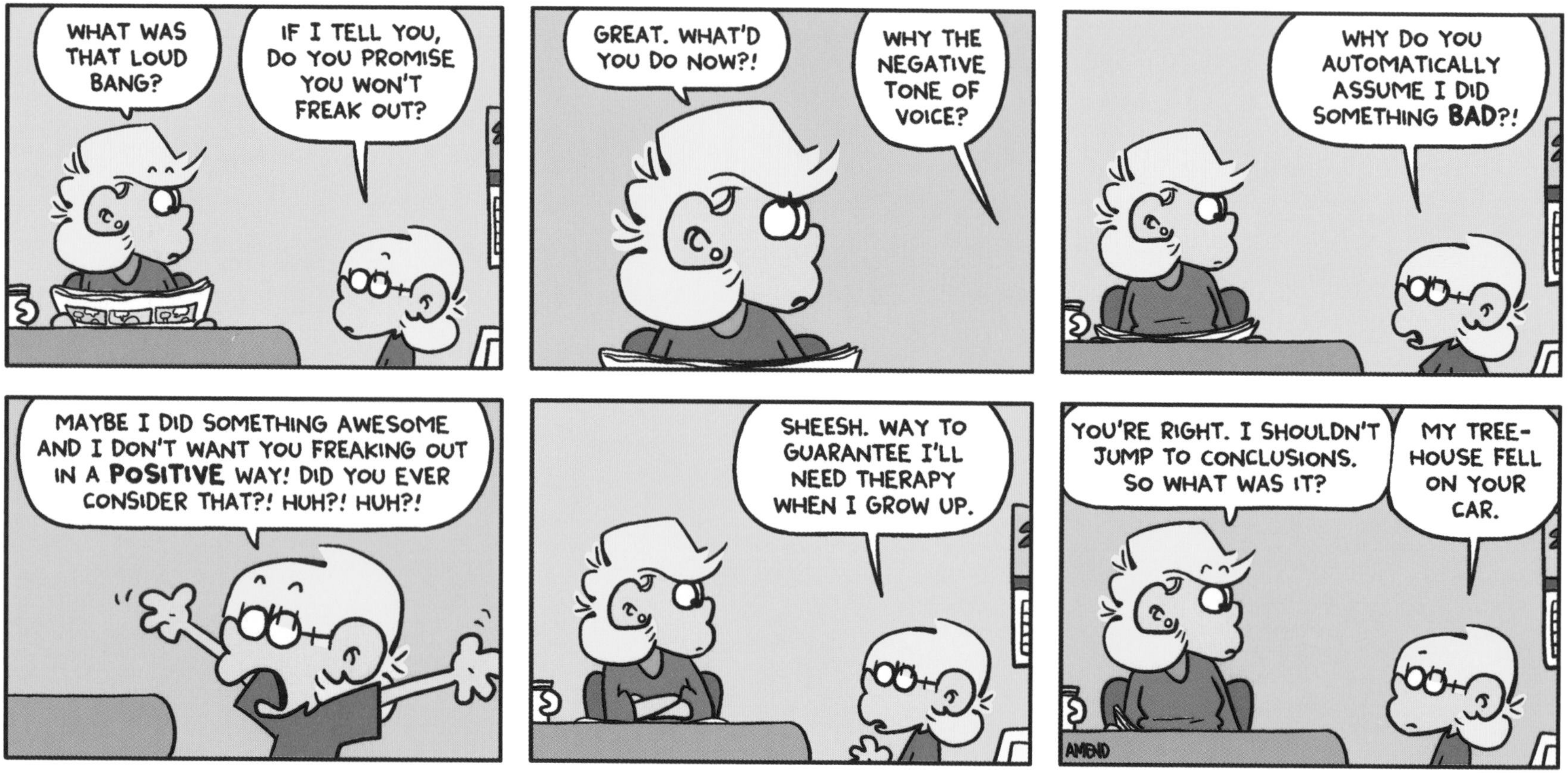
WHAT WAS THAT LOUD BANG?
IF I TELL YOU, DO YOU PROMISE YOU WON'T FREAK OUT?
GREAT. WHAT'D YOU DO NOW?!
WHY THE NEGATIVE TONE OF VOICE?
WHY DO YOU AUTOMATICALLY ASSUME I DID SOMETHING **BAD**?!
MAYBE I DID SOMETHING AWESOME AND I DON'T WANT YOU FREAKING OUT IN A **POSITIVE** WAY! DID YOU EVER CONSIDER THAT?! HUH?! HUH?!
SHEESH. WAY TO GUARANTEE I'LL NEED THERAPY WHEN I GROW UP.
YOU'RE RIGHT. I SHOULDN'T JUMP TO CONCLUSIONS. SO WHAT WAS IT?
MY TREE-HOUSE FELL ON YOUR CAR.
AMEND

Mmm! Pasta!

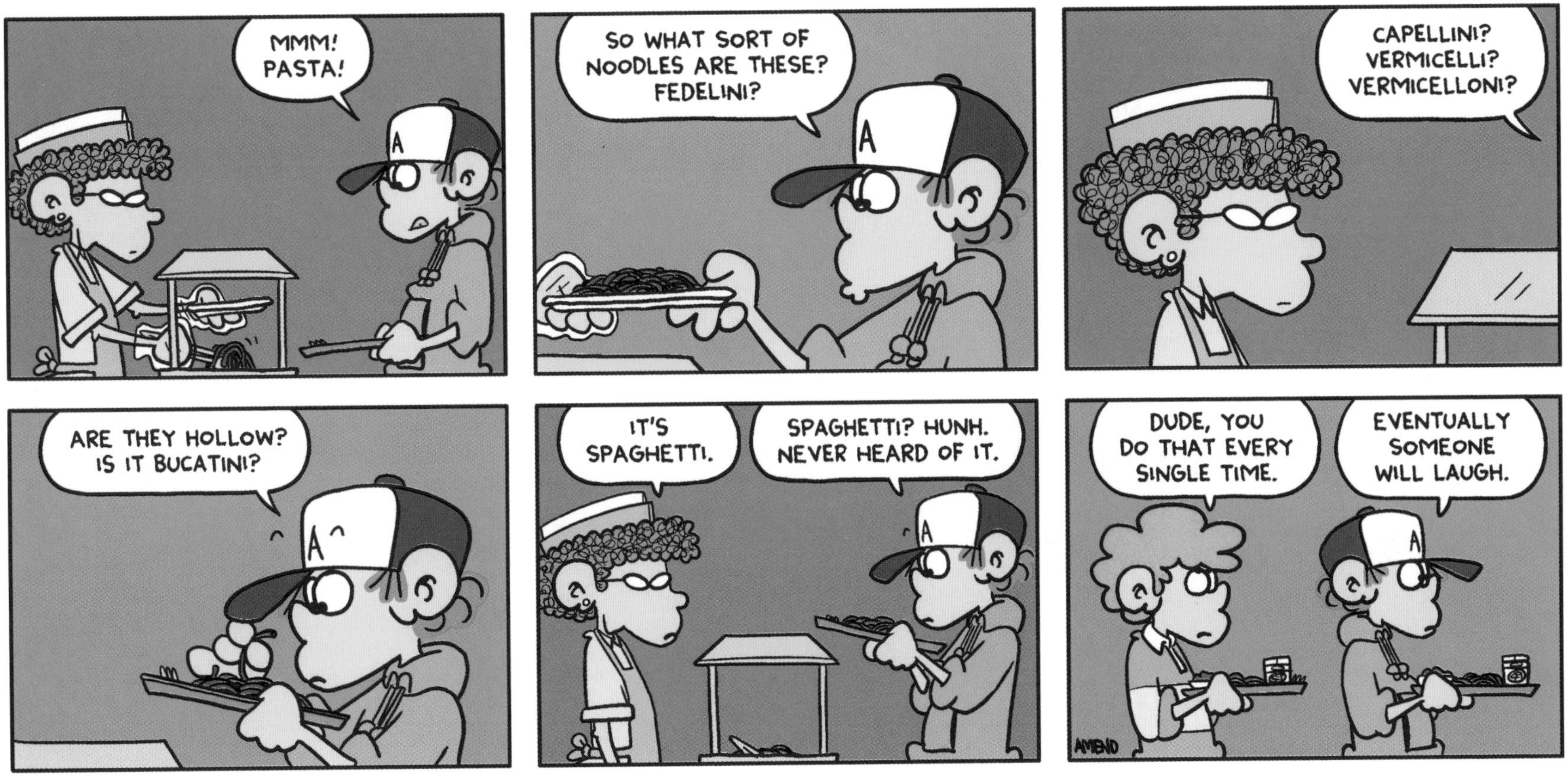
MMM! PASTA!
SO WHAT SORT OF NOODLES ARE THESE? FEDELINI?
CAPELLINI? VERMICELLI? VERMICELLONI?
ARE THEY HOLLOW? IS IT BUCATINI?
IT'S SPAGHETTI.
SPAGHETTI? HUNH. NEVER HEARD OF IT.
DUDE, YOU DO THAT EVERY SINGLE TIME.
EVENTUALLY SOMEONE WILL LAUGH.
AMEND

Hamiltonian

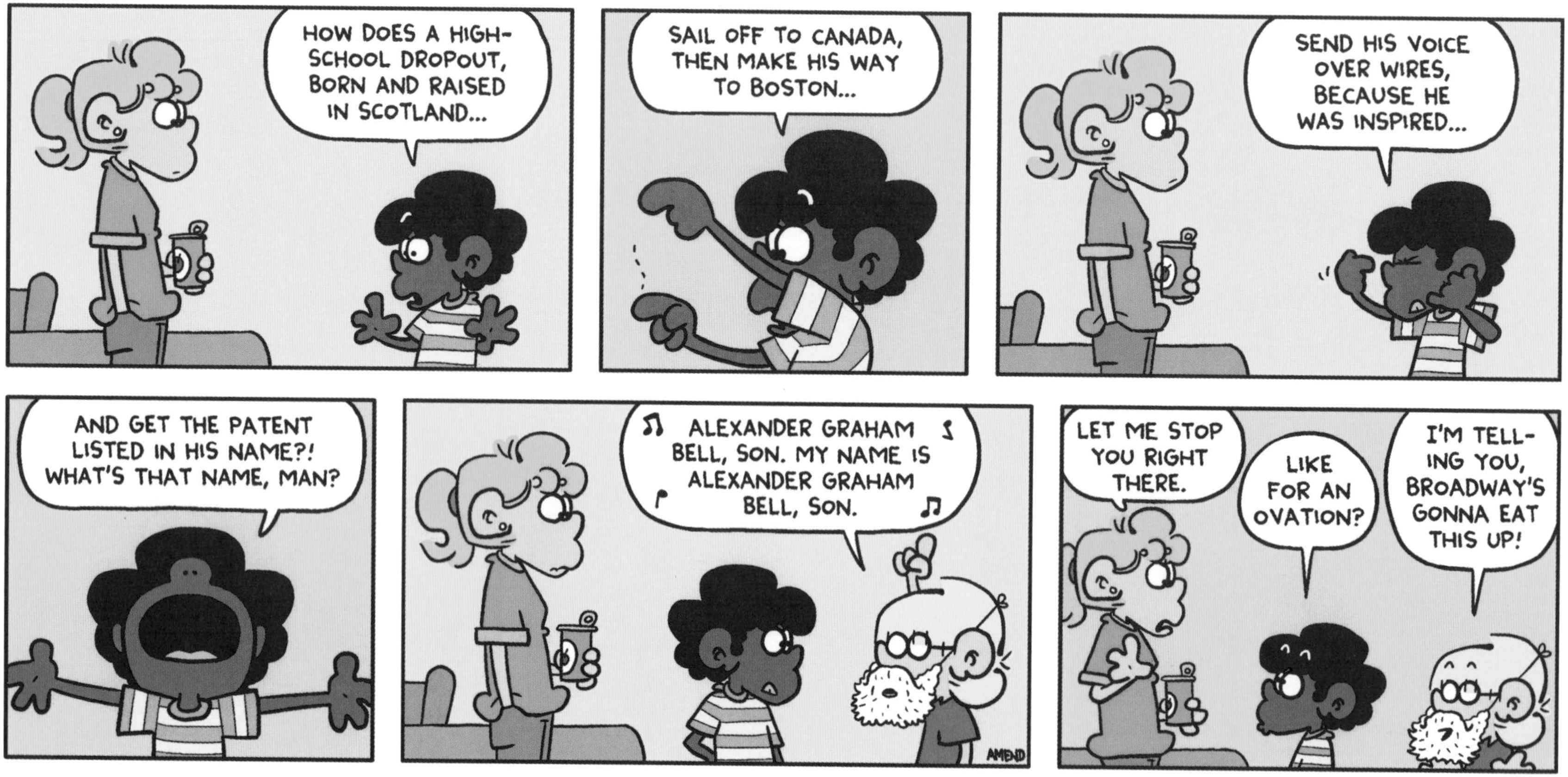
HOW DOES A HIGH-SCHOOL DROPOUT, BORN AND RAISED IN SCOTLAND...
SAIL OFF TO CANADA, THEN MAKE HIS WAY TO BOSTON...
SEND HIS VOICE OVER WIRES, BECAUSE HE WAS INSPIRED...
AND GET THE PATENT LISTED IN HIS NAME?! WHAT'S THAT NAME, MAN?
ALEXANDER GRAHAM BELL, SON. MY NAME IS ALEXANDER GRAHAM BELL, SON.
LET ME STOP YOU RIGHT THERE.
LIKE FOR AN OVATION?
I'M TELL-ING YOU, BROADWAY'S GONNA EAT THIS UP!
AMEND

Puzzling

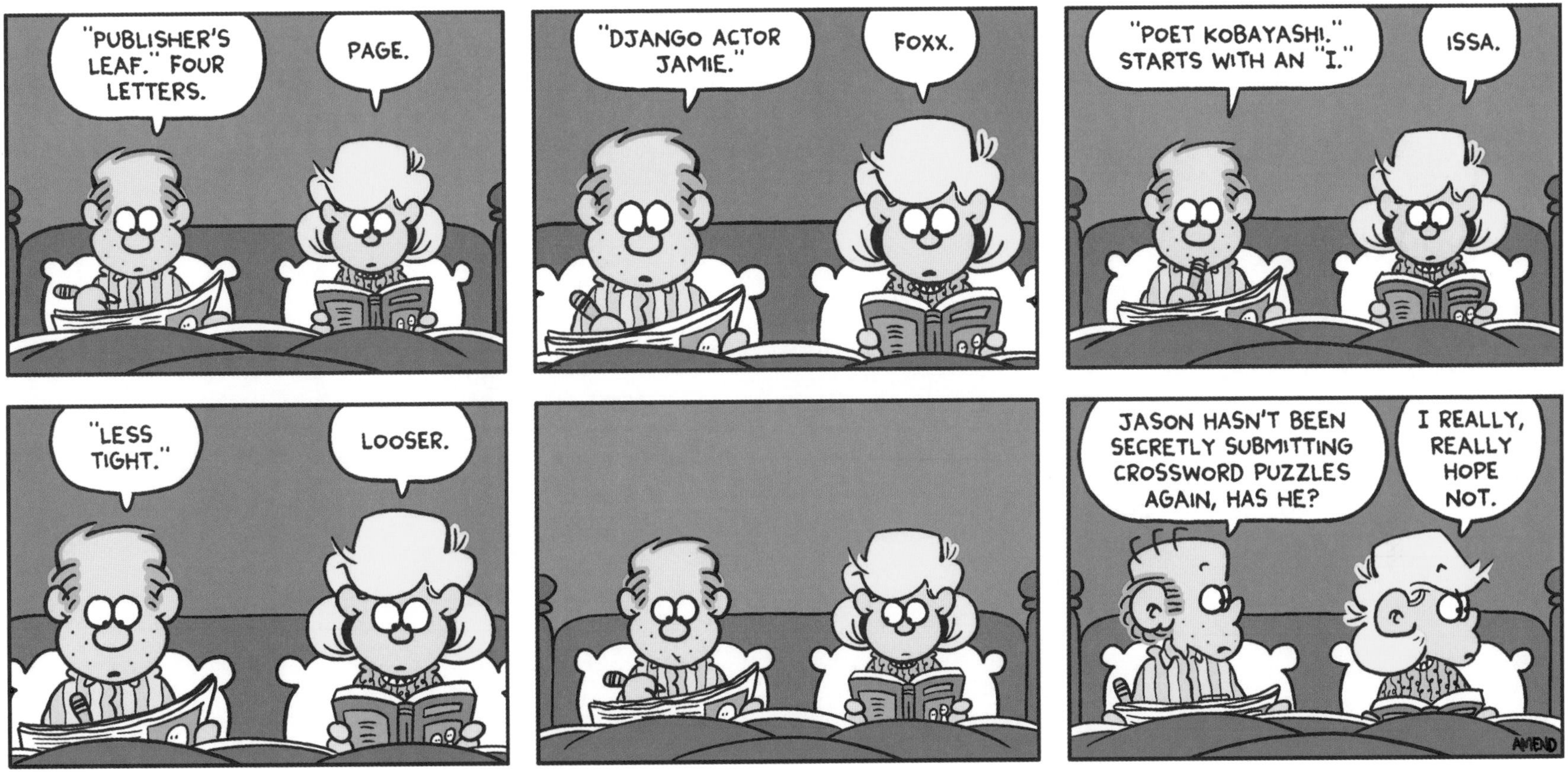

"PUBLISHER'S LEAF." FOUR LETTERS.
PAGE.
"DJANGO ACTOR JAMIE."
FOXX.
"POET KOBAYASHI." STARTS WITH AN "I."
ISSA.
"LESS TIGHT."
LOOSER.
JASON HASN'T BEEN SECRETLY SUBMITTING CROSSWORD PUZZLES AGAIN, HAS HE?
I REALLY, REALLY HOPE NOT.
AMEND

Spice Spice Baby

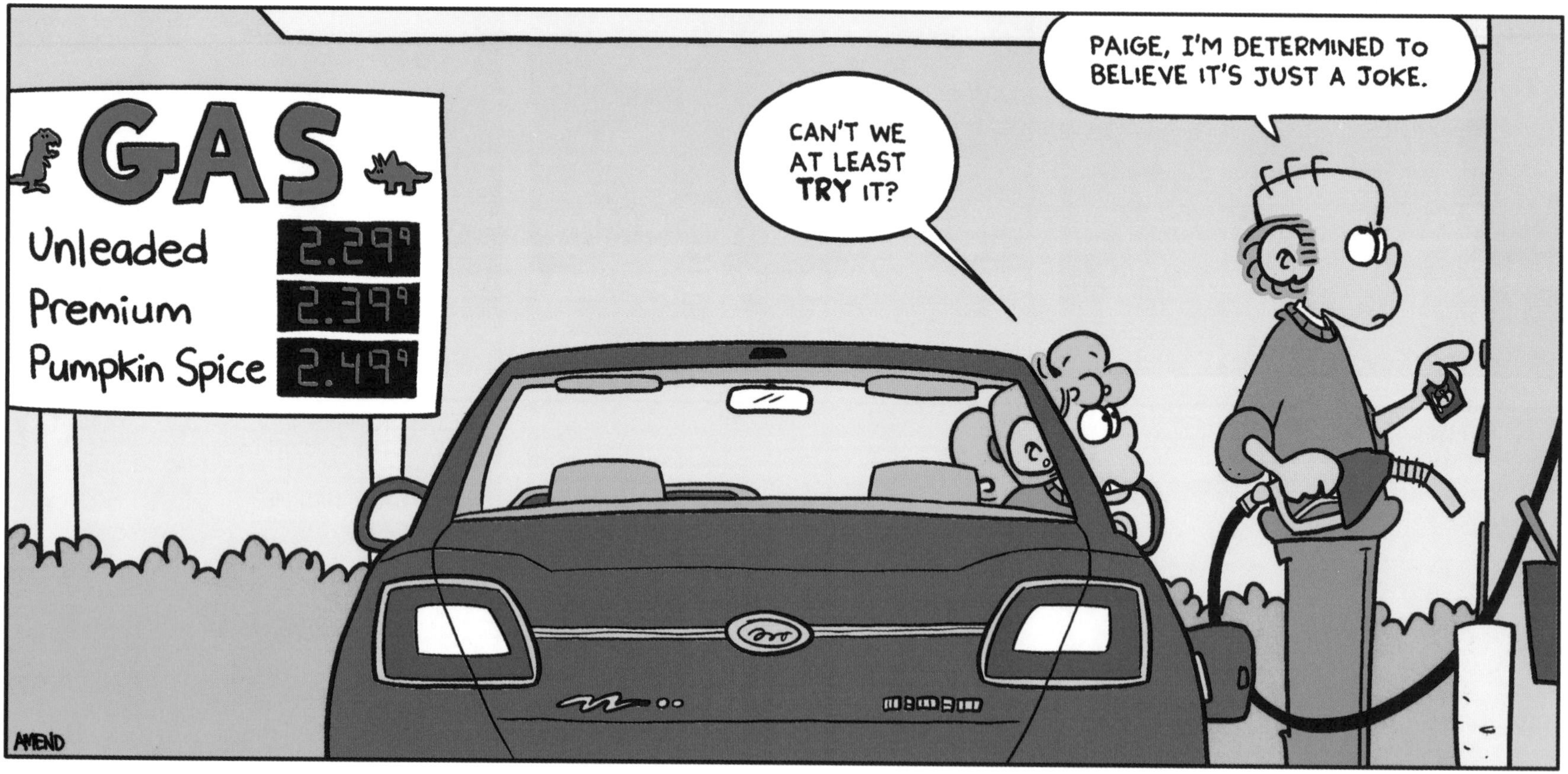
GAS
Unleaded 2.29⁹
Premium 2.39⁹
Pumpkin Spice 2.49⁹
CAN'T WE AT LEAST **TRY** IT?
PAIGE, I'M DETERMINED TO BELIEVE IT'S JUST A JOKE.
AMEND

Kickin' It

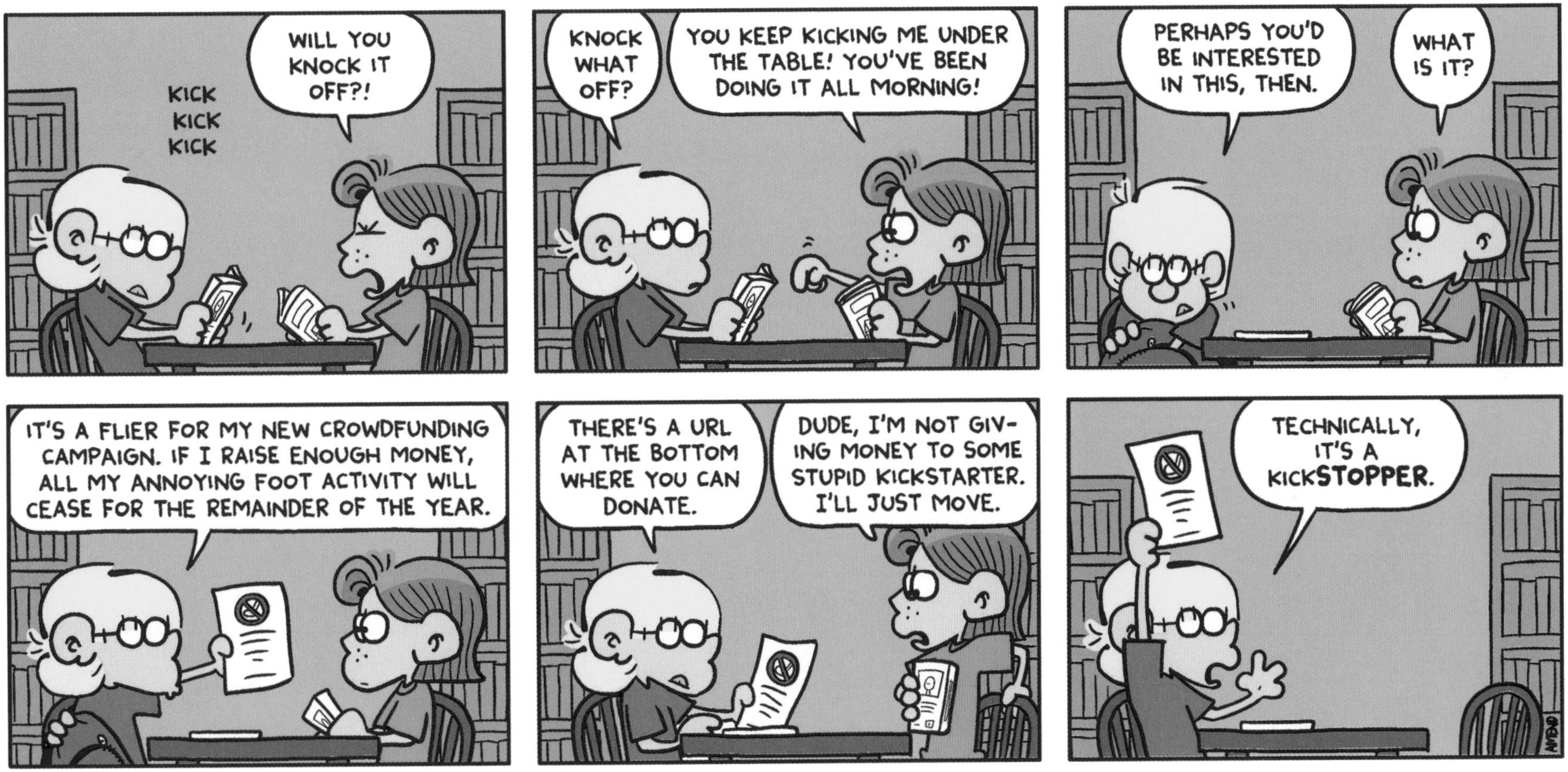
WILL YOU KNOCK IT OFF?!
KICK KICK KICK
KNOCK WHAT OFF?
YOU KEEP KICKING ME UNDER THE TABLE! YOU'VE BEEN DOING IT ALL MORNING!
PERHAPS YOU'D BE INTERESTED IN THIS, THEN.
WHAT IS IT?
IT'S A FLIER FOR MY NEW CROWDFUNDING CAMPAIGN. IF I RAISE ENOUGH MONEY, ALL MY ANNOYING FOOT ACTIVITY WILL CEASE FOR THE REMAINDER OF THE YEAR.
THERE'S A URL AT THE BOTTOM WHERE YOU CAN DONATE.
DUDE, I'M NOT GIVING MONEY TO SOME STUPID KICKSTARTER. I'LL JUST MOVE.
TECHNICALLY, IT'S A KICK**STOPPER**.

Trig or Treat

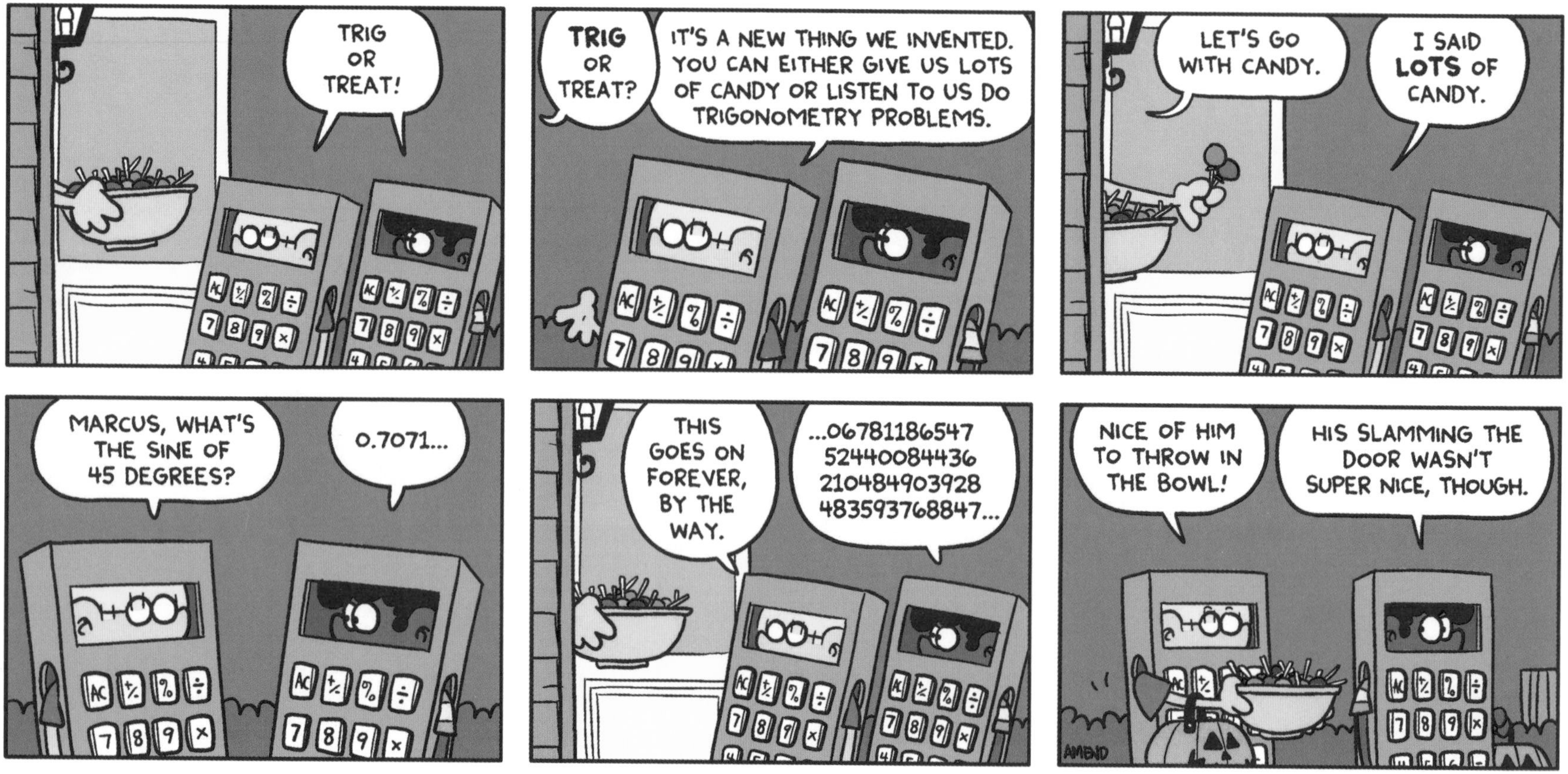
TRIG OR TREAT!
TRIG OR TREAT?
IT'S A NEW THING WE INVENTED. YOU CAN EITHER GIVE US LOTS OF CANDY OR LISTEN TO US DO TRIGONOMETRY PROBLEMS.
LET'S GO WITH CANDY.
I SAID LOTS OF CANDY.
MARCUS, WHAT'S THE SINE OF 45 DEGREES?
0.7071...
THIS GOES ON FOREVER, BY THE WAY.
...06781186547 52440084436 210484903928 483593768847...
NICE OF HIM TO THROW IN THE BOWL!
HIS SLAMMING THE DOOR WASN'T SUPER NICE, THOUGH.
AMEND

Dorkahontas

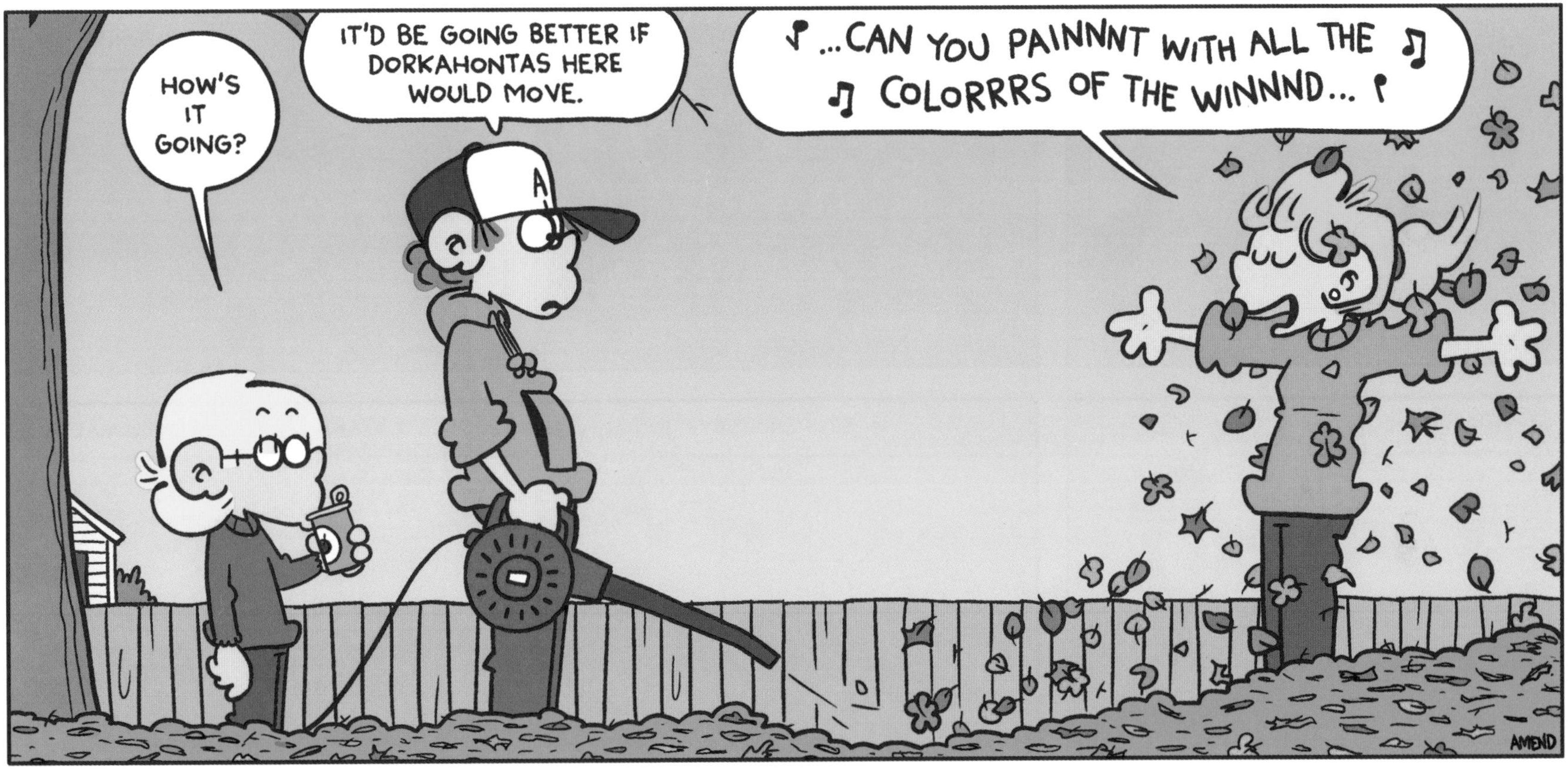
HOW'S IT GOING?
IT'D BE GOING BETTER IF DORKAHONTAS HERE WOULD MOVE.
♪ ...CAN YOU PAINNNT WITH ALL THE ♫ ♫ COLORRRS OF THE WINNND... ♪
AMEND

Awesom Grades

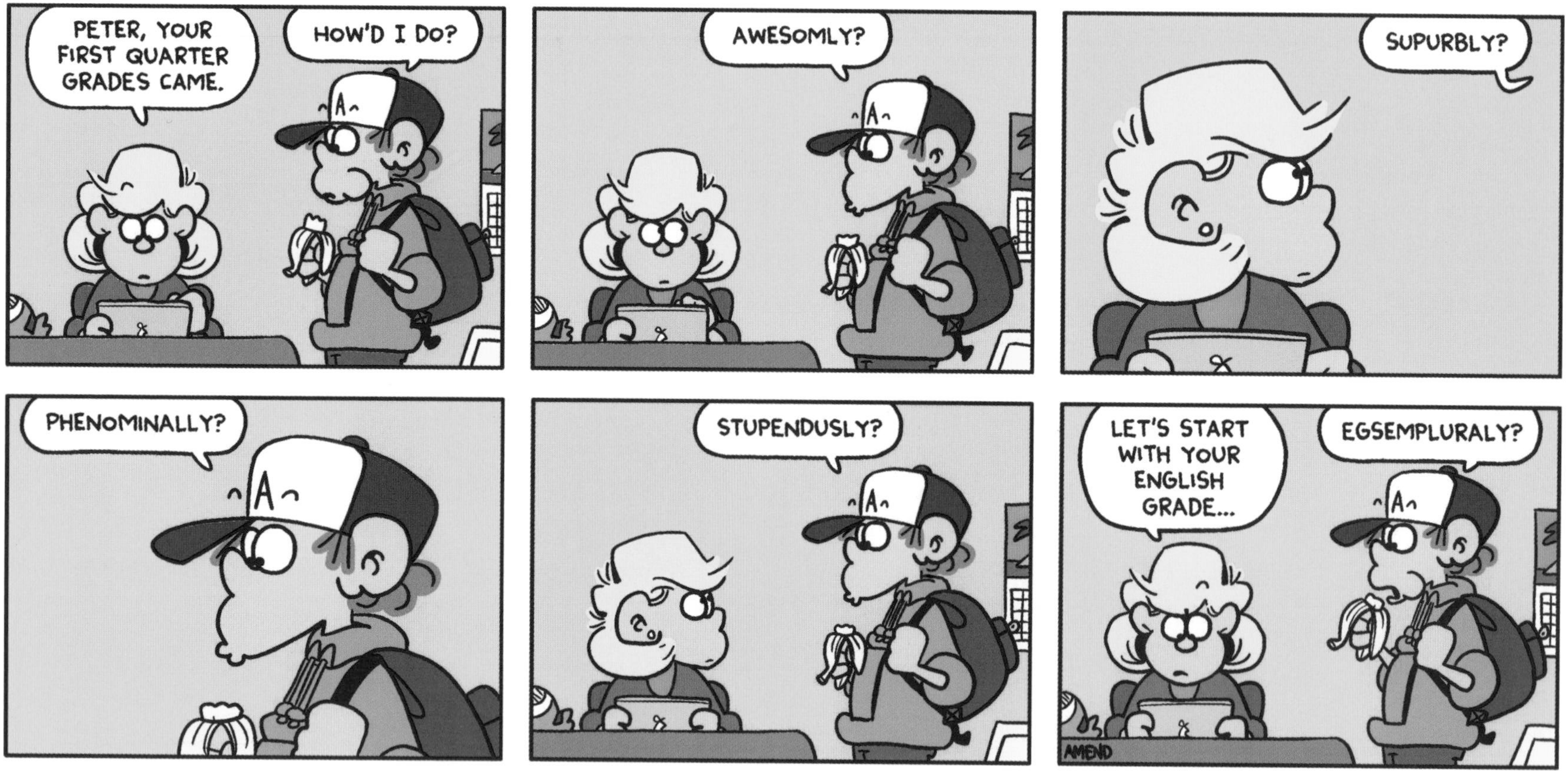

PETER, YOUR FIRST QUARTER GRADES CAME.
HOW'D I DO?
AWESOMLY?
SUPURBLY?
PHENOMINALLY?
STUPENDUSLY?
LET'S START WITH YOUR ENGLISH GRADE...
EGSEMPLURALY?
AMEND

Handmade

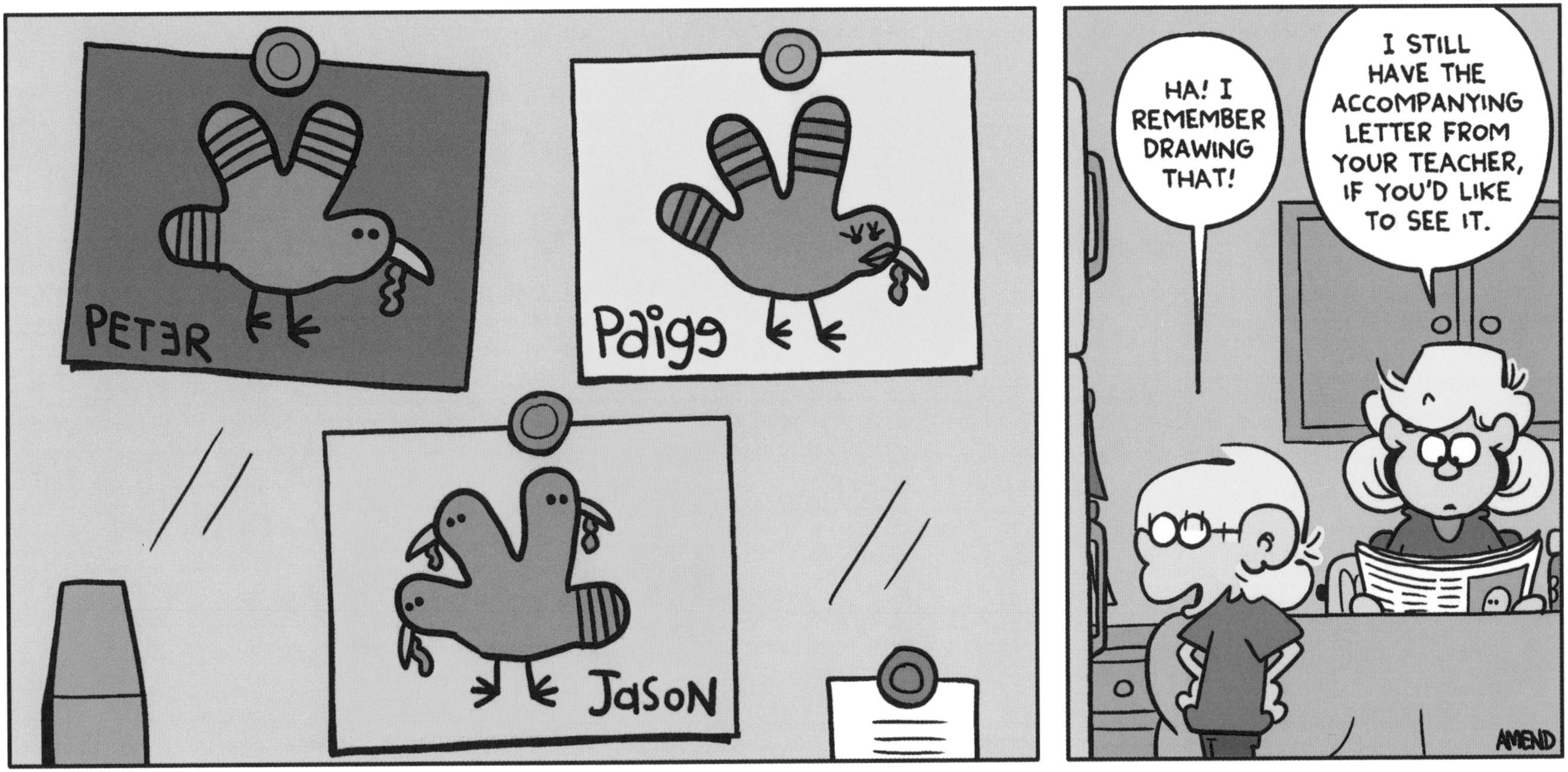
PETER
Paige
JASON
HA! I REMEMBER DRAWING THAT!
I STILL HAVE THE ACCOMPANYING LETTER FROM YOUR TEACHER, IF YOU'D LIKE TO SEE IT.
AMEND

Super Rope Bros

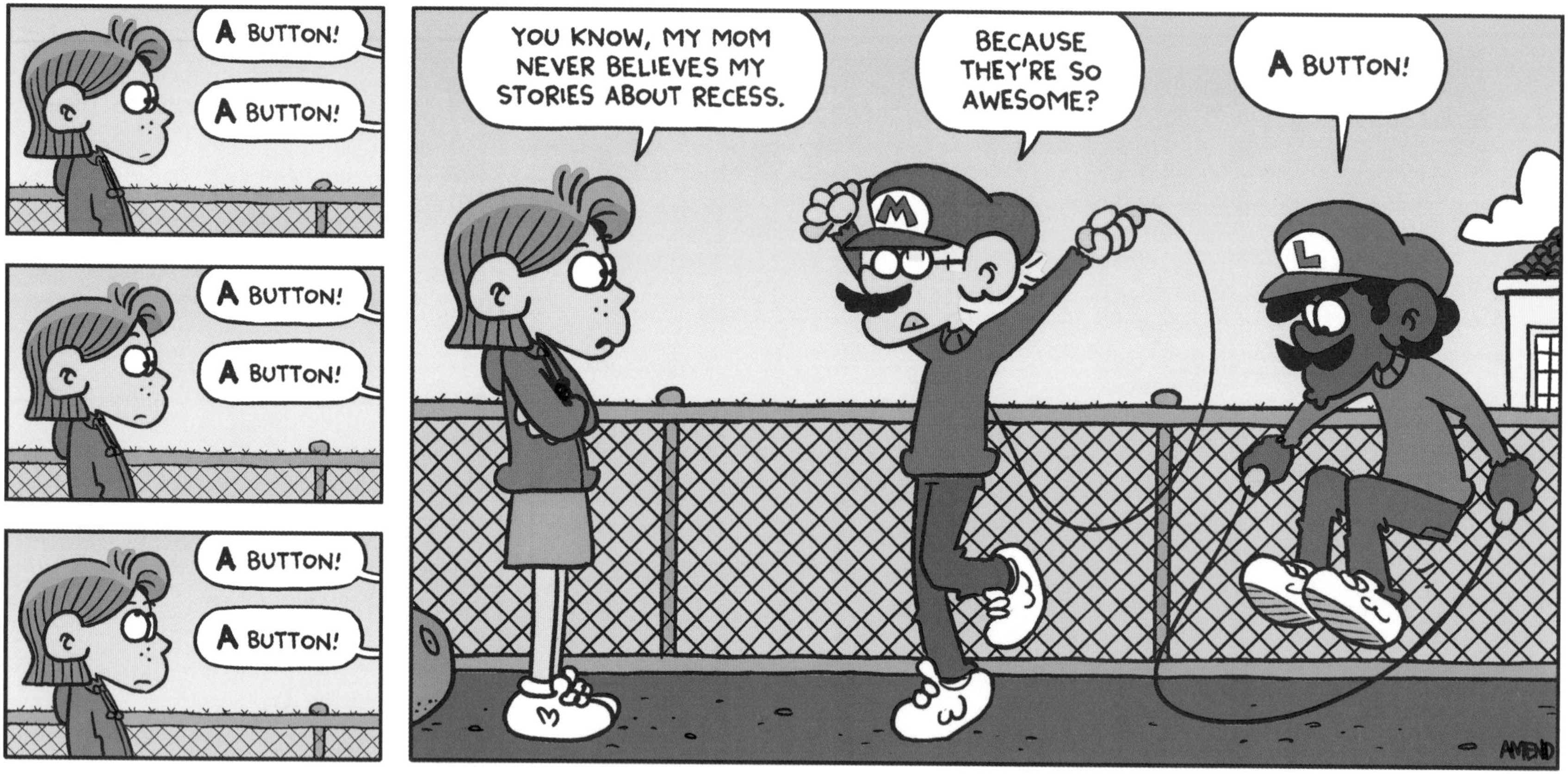
A BUTTON!
A BUTTON!
A BUTTON!
A BUTTON!
A BUTTON!
A BUTTON!
YOU KNOW, MY MOM NEVER BELIEVES MY STORIES ABOUT RECESS.
BECAUSE THEY'RE SO AWESOME?
A BUTTON!
AMEND

Pressuring the QB

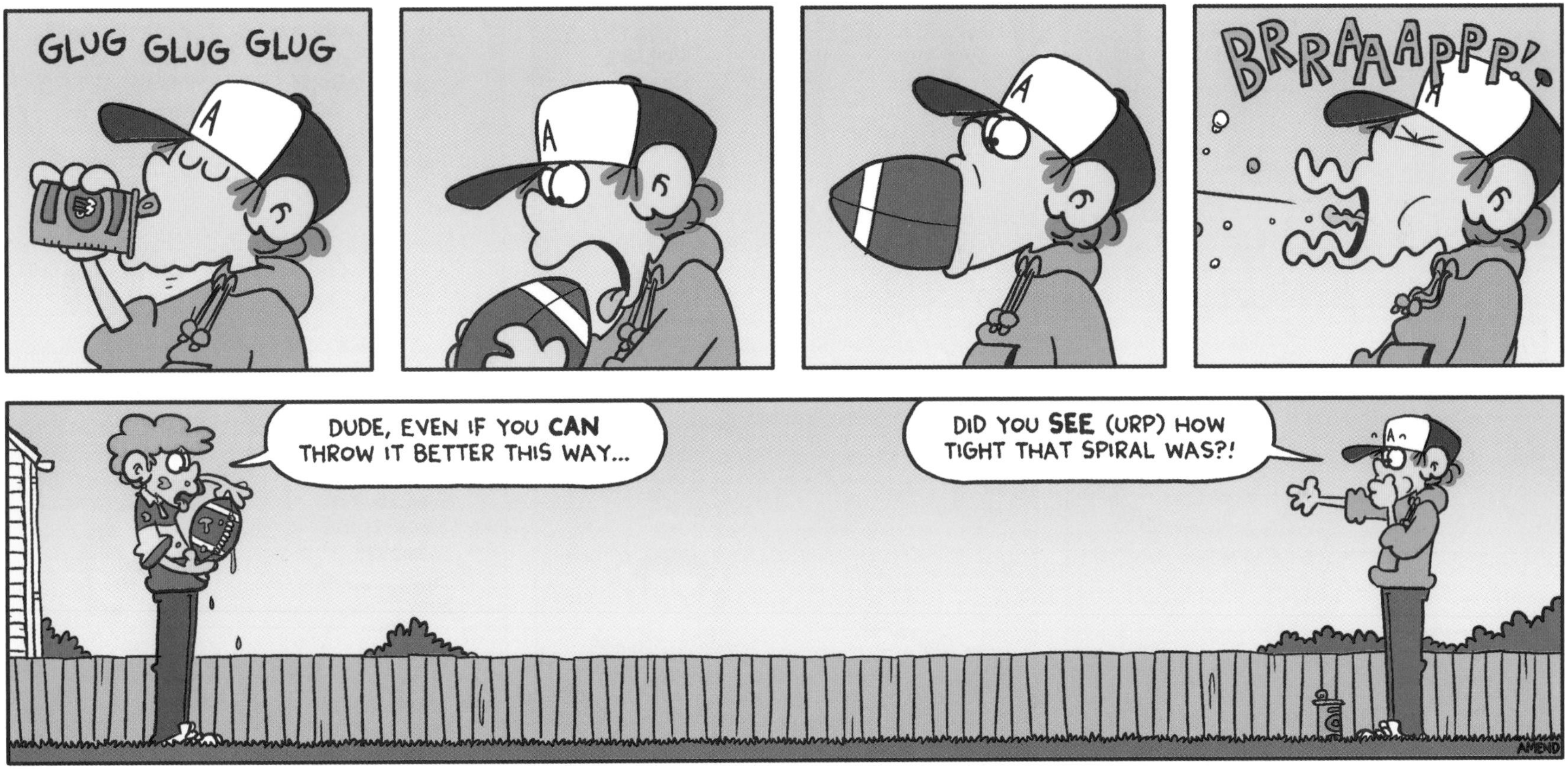
GLUG GLUG GLUG
BRRAAAPPP!
DUDE, EVEN IF YOU **CAN** THROW IT BETTER THIS WAY...
DID YOU **SEE** (URP) HOW TIGHT THAT SPIRAL WAS?!
AMEND

Rouge One

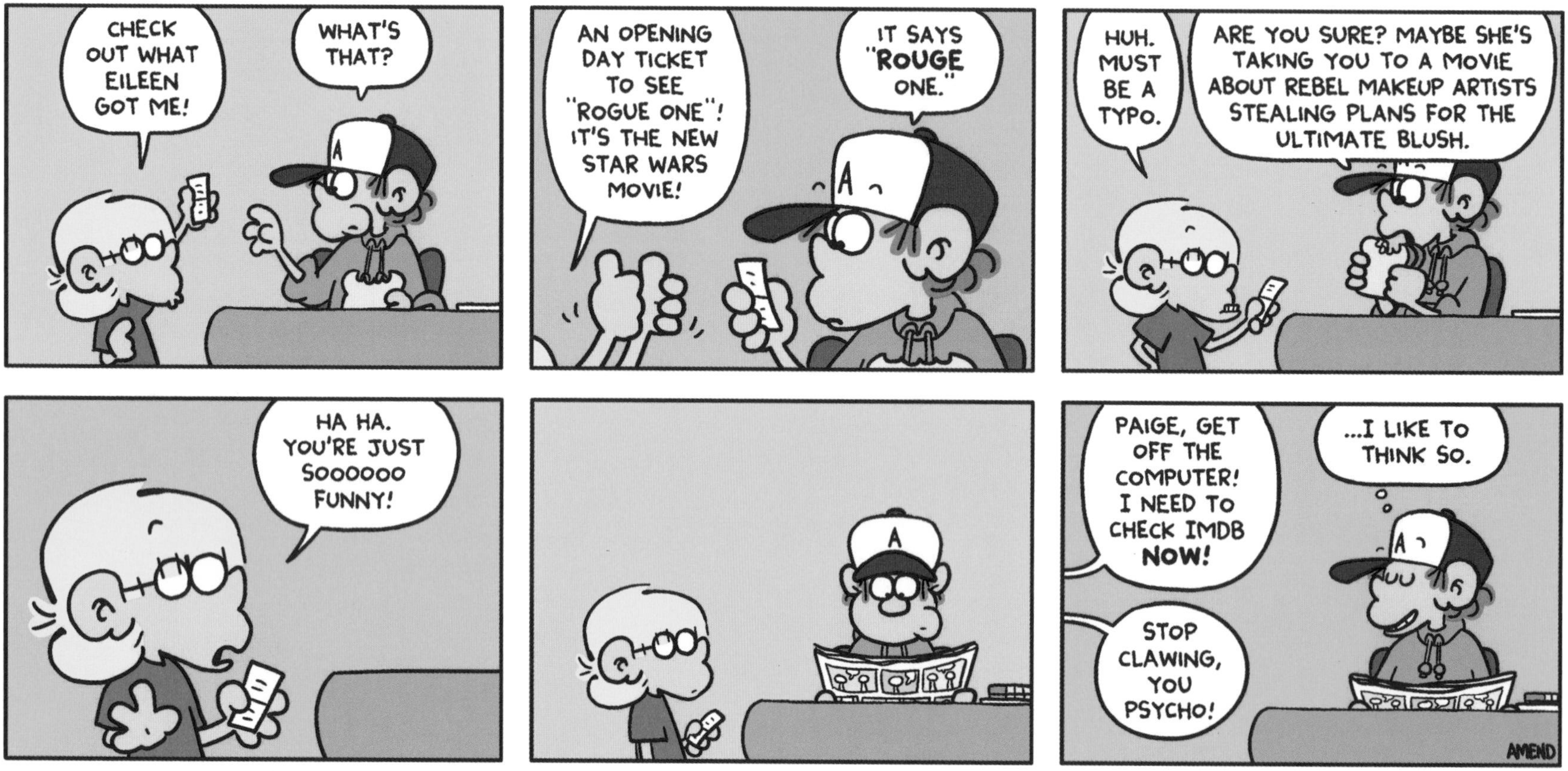
CHECK OUT WHAT EILEEN GOT ME!
WHAT'S THAT?
AN OPENING DAY TICKET TO SEE "ROGUE ONE"! IT'S THE NEW STAR WARS MOVIE!
IT SAYS "**ROUGE** ONE."
HUH. MUST BE A TYPO.
ARE YOU SURE? MAYBE SHE'S TAKING YOU TO A MOVIE ABOUT REBEL MAKEUP ARTISTS STEALING PLANS FOR THE ULTIMATE BLUSH.
HA HA. YOU'RE JUST SOOOOOO FUNNY!
PAIGE, GET OFF THE COMPUTER! I NEED TO CHECK IMDB **NOW!**
STOP CLAWING, YOU PSYCHO!
...I LIKE TO THINK SO.
AMEND

Silent Night's Watch

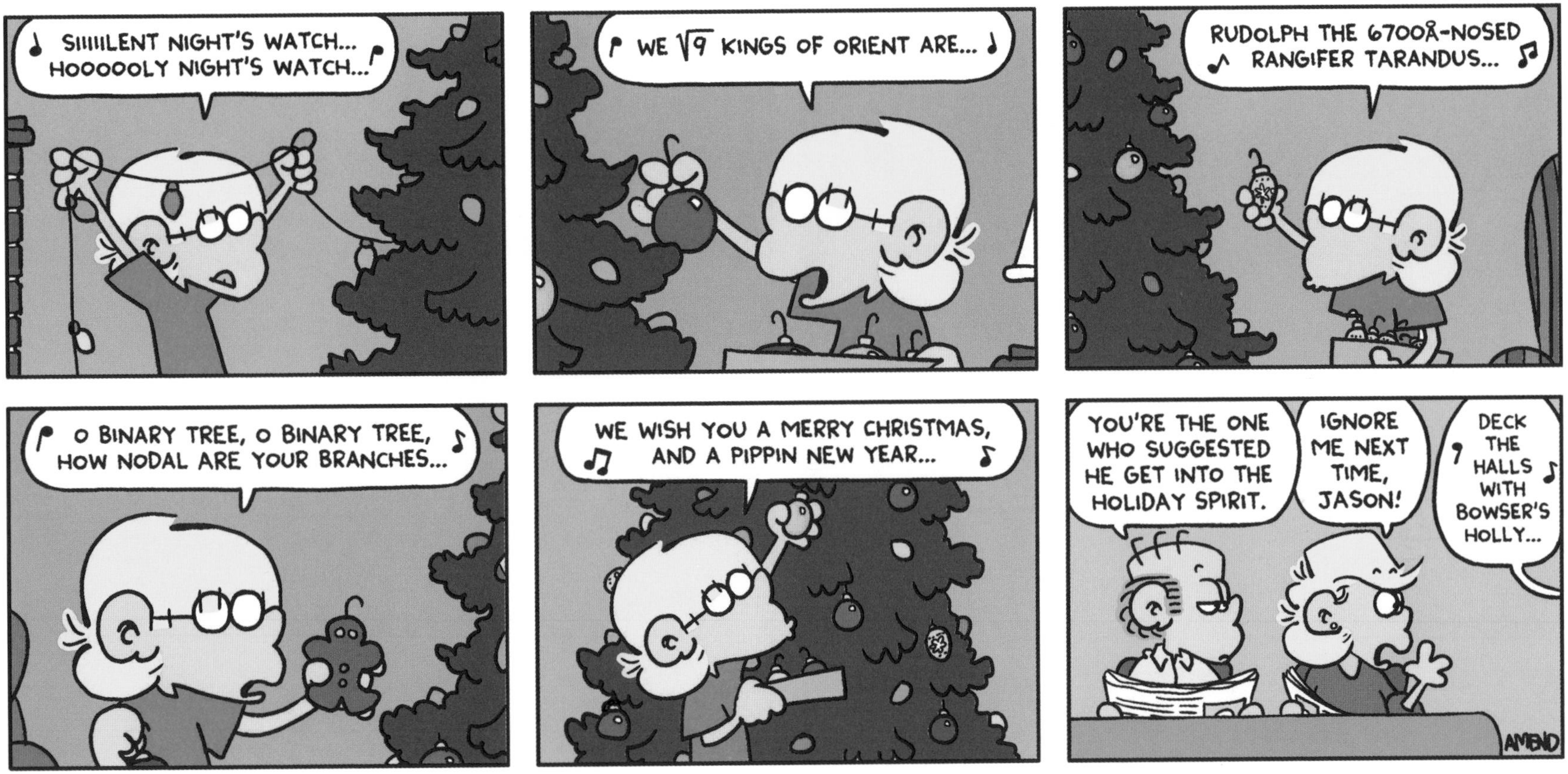
SIIIIILENT NIGHT'S WATCH... HOOOOOLY NIGHT'S WATCH...
WE √9 KINGS OF ORIENT ARE...
RUDOLPH THE 6700Å-NOSED RANGIFER TARANDUS...
O BINARY TREE, O BINARY TREE, HOW NODAL ARE YOUR BRANCHES...
WE WISH YOU A MERRY CHRISTMAS, AND A PIPPIN NEW YEAR...
YOU'RE THE ONE WHO SUGGESTED HE GET INTO THE HOLIDAY SPIRIT.
IGNORE ME NEXT TIME, JASON!
DECK THE HALLS WITH BOWSER'S HOLLY...
AMEND

Stocking Suffer

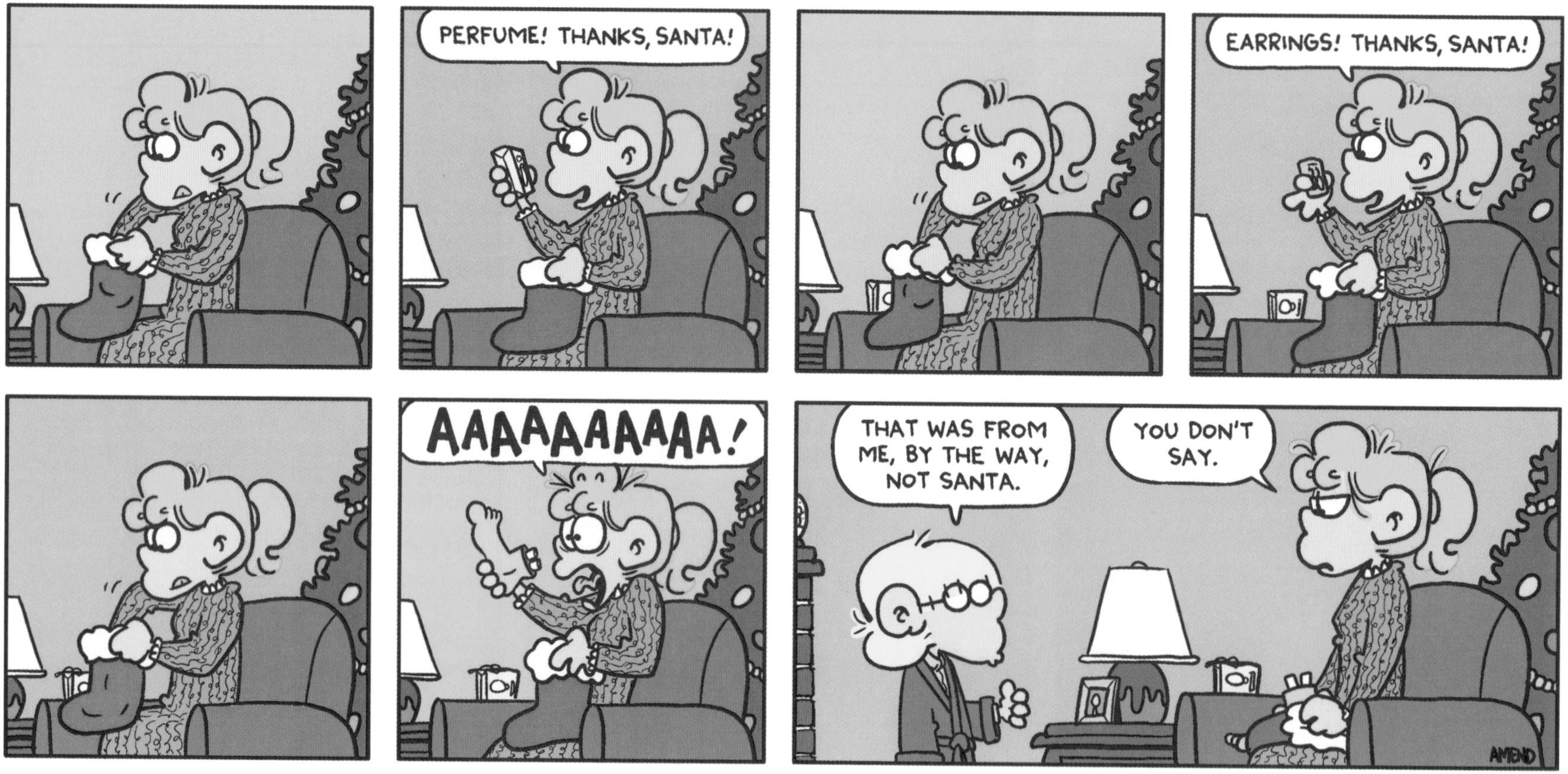
PERFUME! THANKS, SANTA!
EARRINGS! THANKS, SANTA!
AAAAAAAAAA!
THAT WAS FROM ME, BY THE WAY, NOT SANTA.
YOU DON'T SAY.
AMEND

Snowmo

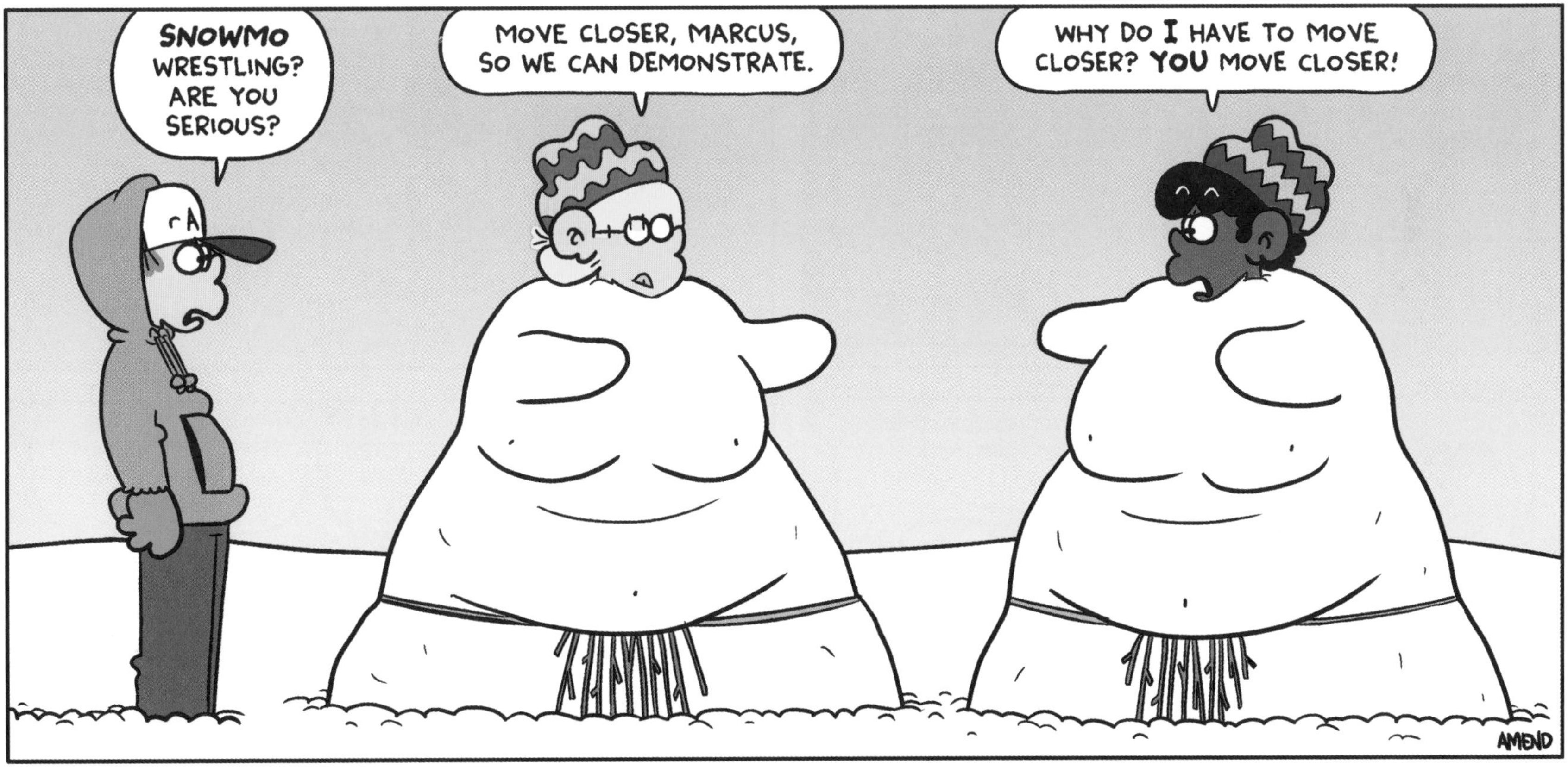
SNOWMO WRESTLING? ARE YOU SERIOUS?
MOVE CLOSER, MARCUS, SO WE CAN DEMONSTRATE.
WHY DO I HAVE TO MOVE CLOSER? YOU MOVE CLOSER!
AMEND

Pink Clothes

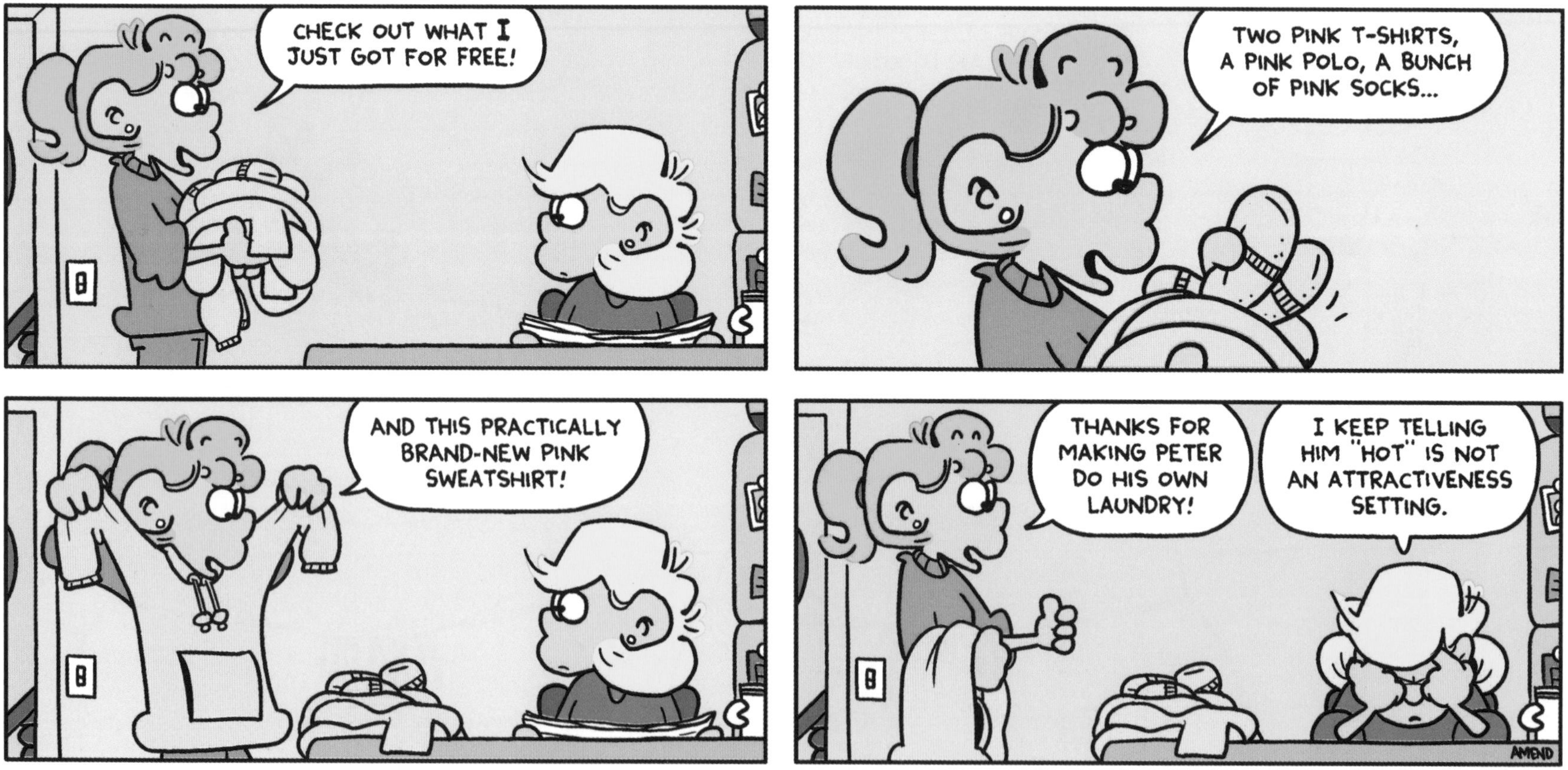

CHECK OUT WHAT I JUST GOT FOR FREE!
TWO PINK T-SHIRTS, A PINK POLO, A BUNCH OF PINK SOCKS...
AND THIS PRACTICALLY BRAND-NEW PINK SWEATSHIRT!
THANKS FOR MAKING PETER DO HIS OWN LAUNDRY!
I KEEP TELLING HIM "HOT" IS NOT AN ATTRACTIVENESS SETTING.
AMEND

Balancing Act

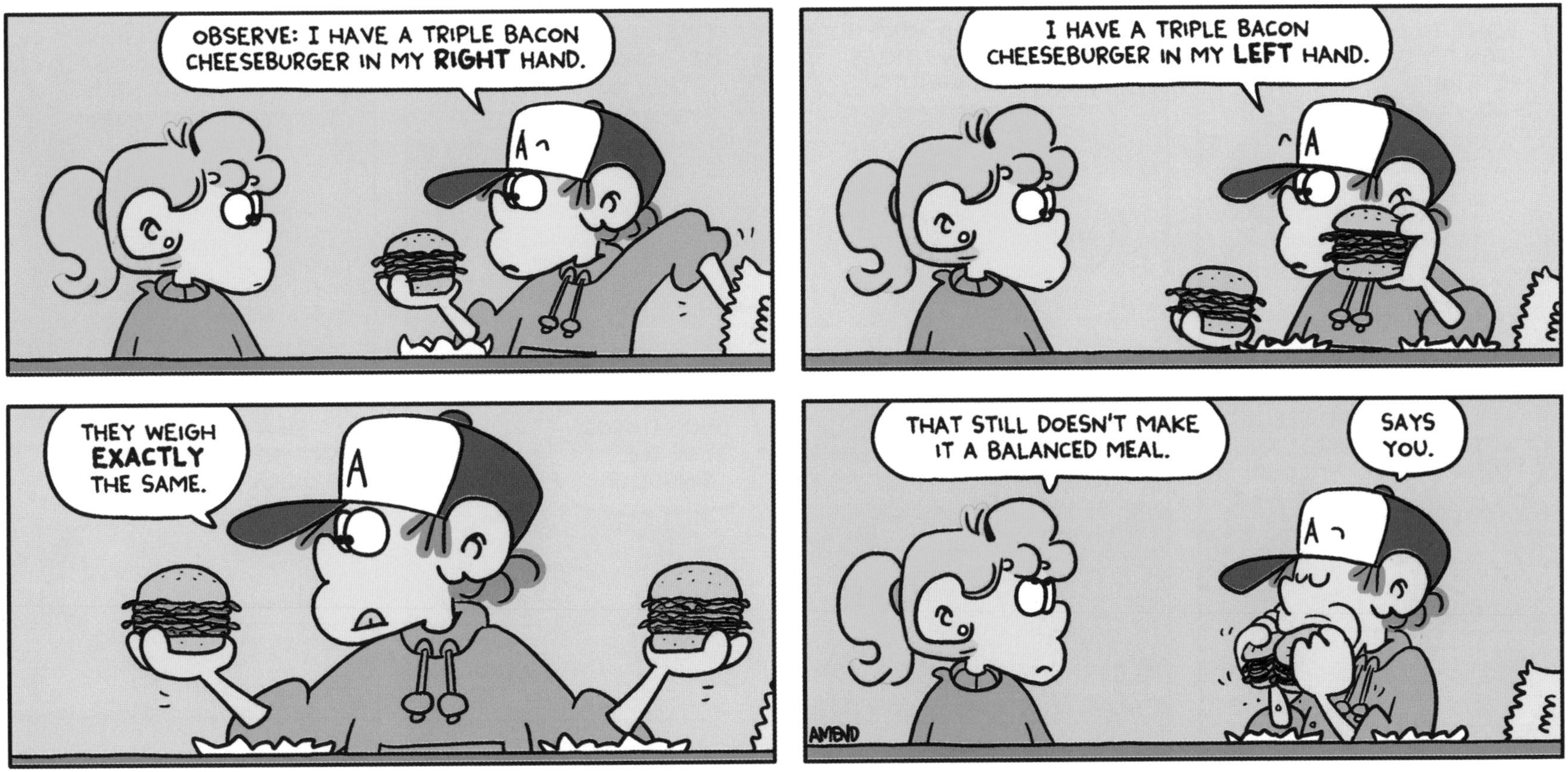
OBSERVE: I HAVE A TRIPLE BACON CHEESEBURGER IN MY **RIGHT** HAND.
I HAVE A TRIPLE BACON CHEESEBURGER IN MY **LEFT** HAND.
THEY WEIGH **EXACTLY** THE SAME.
THAT STILL DOESN'T MAKE IT A BALANCED MEAL.
SAYS YOU.
AMEND

Doughtori

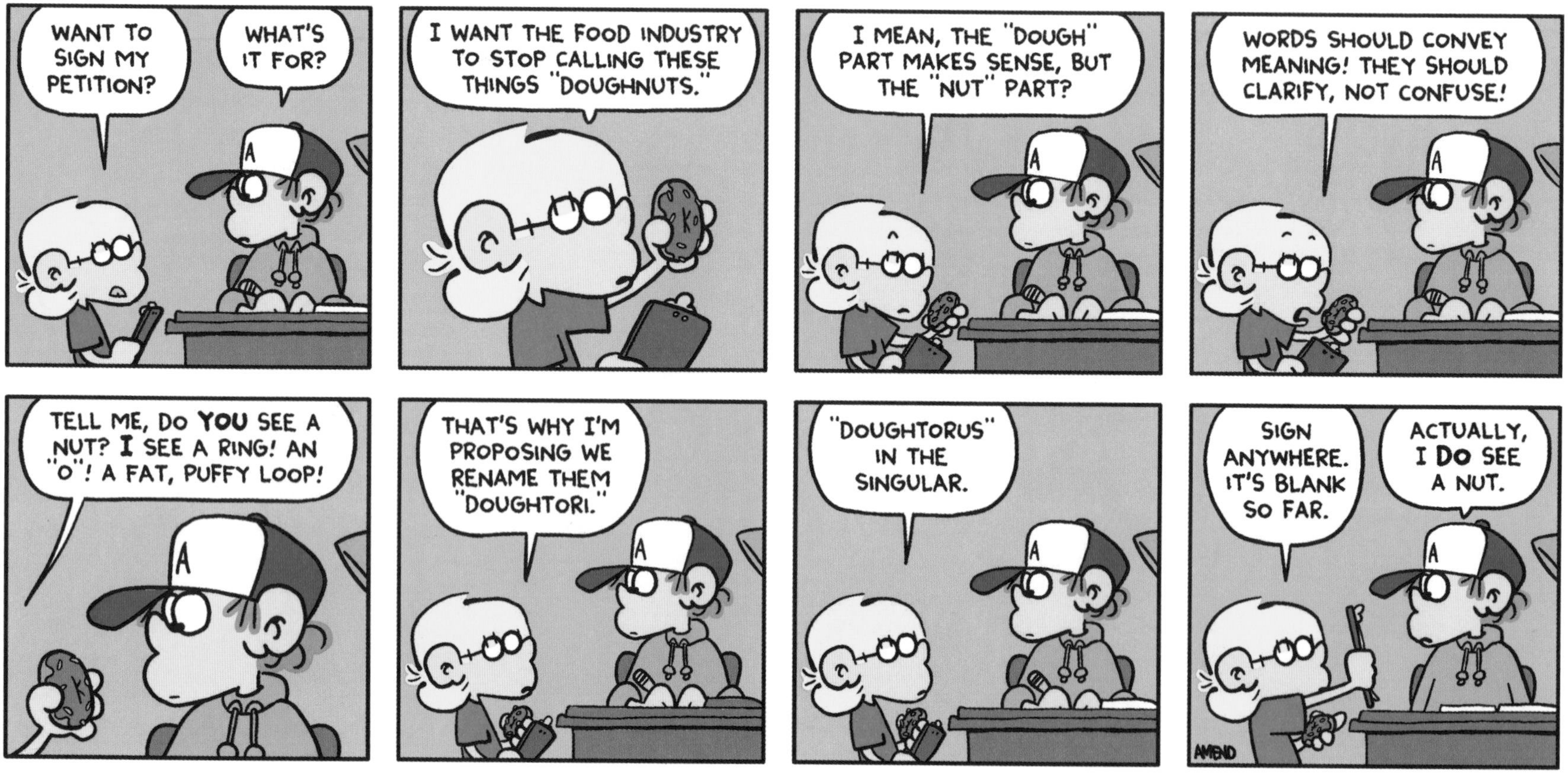
WANT TO SIGN MY PETITION?
WHAT'S IT FOR?
I WANT THE FOOD INDUSTRY TO STOP CALLING THESE THINGS "DOUGHNUTS."
I MEAN, THE "DOUGH" PART MAKES SENSE, BUT THE "NUT" PART?
WORDS SHOULD CONVEY MEANING! THEY SHOULD CLARIFY, NOT CONFUSE!
TELL ME, DO **YOU** SEE A NUT? **I** SEE A RING! AN "O"! A FAT, PUFFY LOOP!
THAT'S WHY I'M PROPOSING WE RENAME THEM "DOUGHTORI."
"DOUGHTORUS" IN THE SINGULAR.
SIGN ANYWHERE. IT'S BLANK SO FAR.
ACTUALLY, I **DO** SEE A NUT.
AMEND

Zero Completions

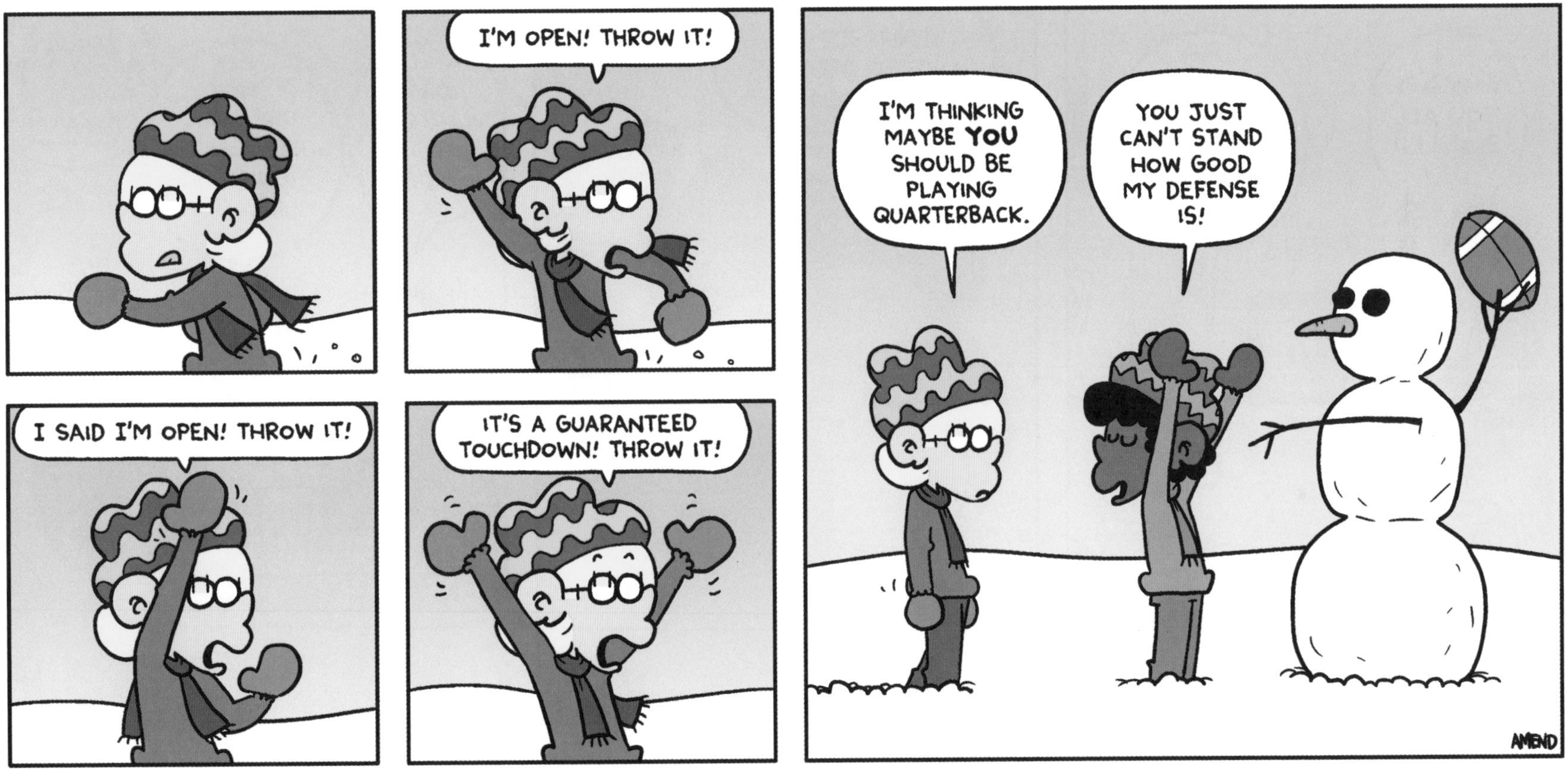

I'M OPEN! THROW IT!
I SAID I'M OPEN! THROW IT!
IT'S A GUARANTEED TOUCHDOWN! THROW IT!
I'M THINKING MAYBE **YOU** SHOULD BE PLAYING QUARTERBACK.
YOU JUST CAN'T STAND HOW GOOD MY DEFENSE IS!
AMEND

Protective Coating

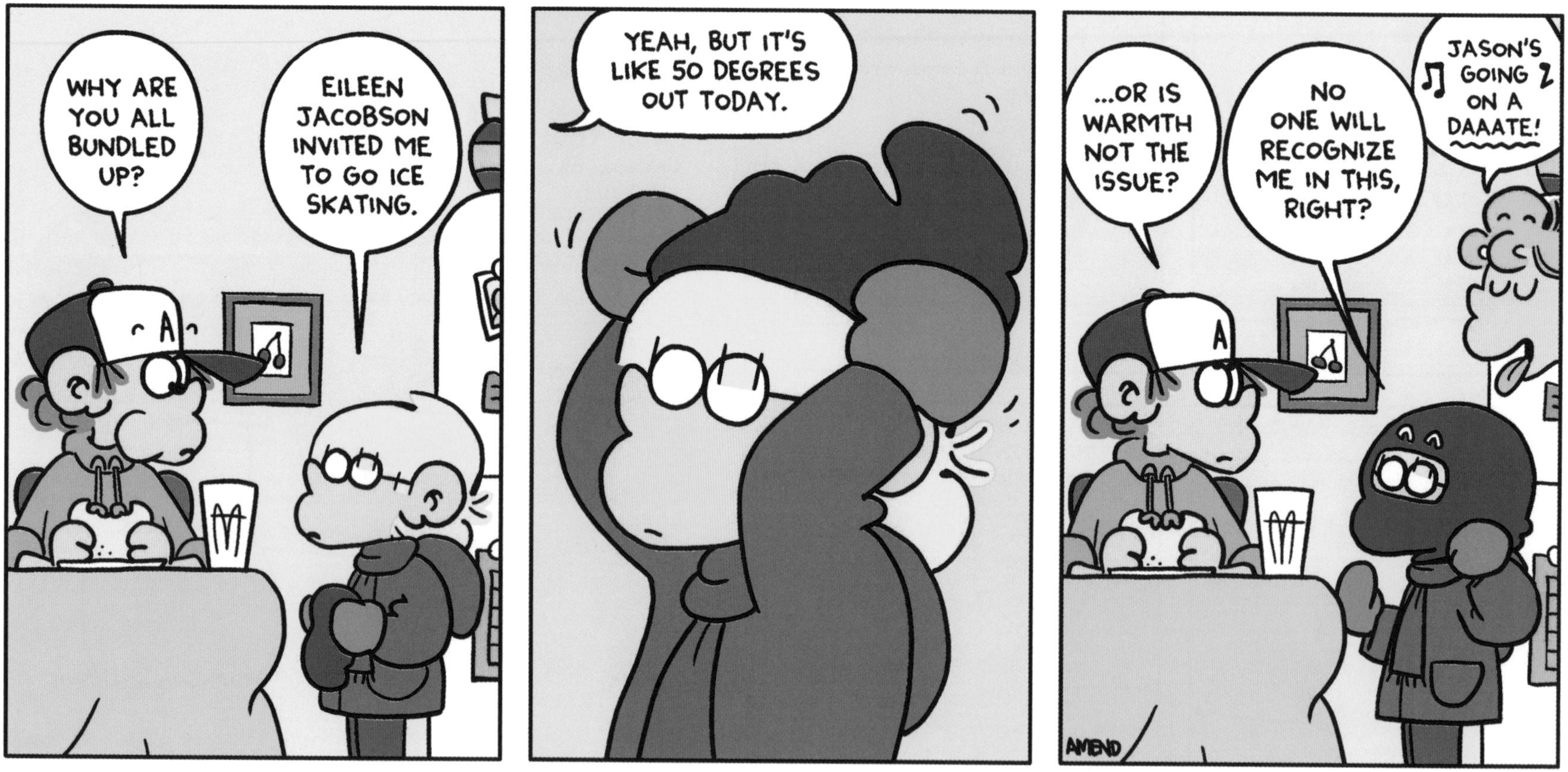
WHY ARE YOU ALL BUNDLED UP?
EILEEN JACOBSON INVITED ME TO GO ICE SKATING.
YEAH, BUT IT'S LIKE 50 DEGREES OUT TODAY.
...OR IS WARMTH NOT THE ISSUE?
NO ONE WILL RECOGNIZE ME IN THIS, RIGHT?
JASON'S GOING ON A DAAATE!
AMEND

Heart Hat

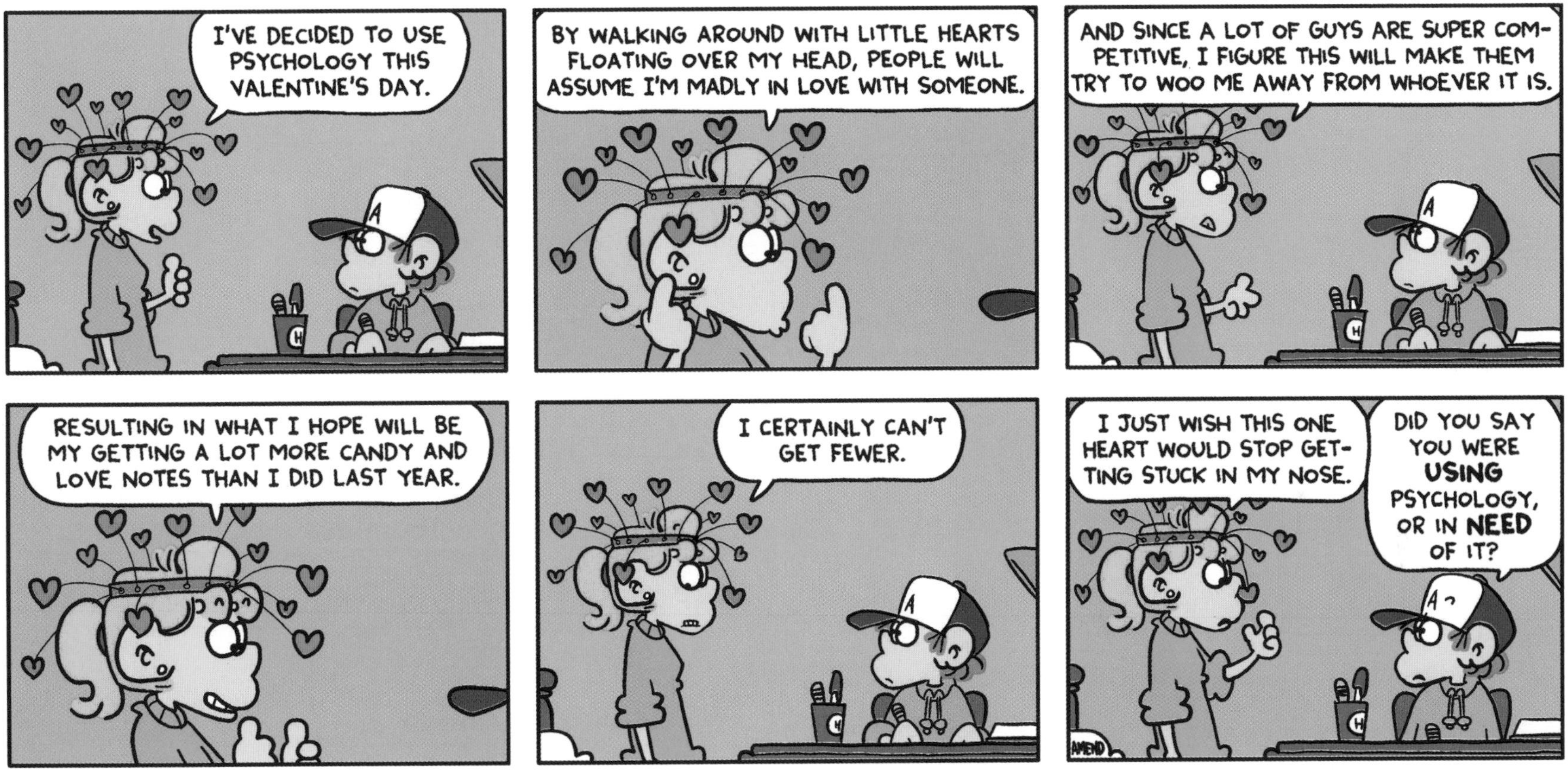
I'VE DECIDED TO USE PSYCHOLOGY THIS VALENTINE'S DAY.
BY WALKING AROUND WITH LITTLE HEARTS FLOATING OVER MY HEAD, PEOPLE WILL ASSUME I'M MADLY IN LOVE WITH SOMEONE.
AND SINCE A LOT OF GUYS ARE SUPER COM-PETITIVE, I FIGURE THIS WILL MAKE THEM TRY TO WOO ME AWAY FROM WHOEVER IT IS.
RESULTING IN WHAT I HOPE WILL BE MY GETTING A LOT MORE CANDY AND LOVE NOTES THAN I DID LAST YEAR.
I CERTAINLY CAN'T GET FEWER.
I JUST WISH THIS ONE HEART WOULD STOP GET-TING STUCK IN MY NOSE.
DID YOU SAY YOU WERE **USING** PSYCHOLOGY, OR IN **NEED** OF IT?
AMEND

Details, Details

AS YOU ENTER THE DUNGEON, YOU SEE AN ORC CENTURIAN, NAPPING AT HIS POST.

MY DWARF WARRIOR ATTACKS!

BUT NOT BEFORE THE BALROG HIDING BEHIND THE DOOR ATTACKS **YOU**! BWAHAHA!

HE SLASHES YOUR DWARF WITH HIS SWORD, CAUSING (ROLL ROLL) FIVE POINTS OF DAMAGE!

WHERE DOES HE SLASH HIM? ON HIS BACK?

PROBABLY.

HOW DEEP IS THE CUT? WOULD YOU SEE BONES?

DID HE HIT AN ARTERY? WOULD BLOOD BE SPRAYING OUT?

DUDE, IT'S ONLY FIVE HIT POINTS.

OK, OK, HOW'S THIS LOOK?

YOU KNOW, THERE'S SUCH A THING AS PUTTING **TOO** MUCH DETAIL INTO YOUR MINIATURES.

IS IT MY DWARF'S TURN TO ATTACK? LET ME GIVE HIM SCARED-YET-ANGRY EYEBROWS.

Blecchteria

INTERESTING. I'VE NEVER SEEN BACTERIA DO THAT.
SEE?! EVEN **THEY** THINK THIS LAB ASSIGNMENT IS GROSS!
AMEND

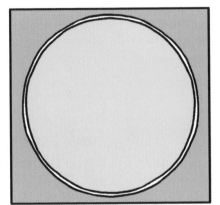

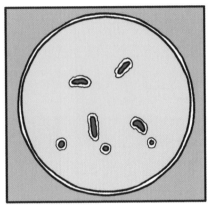

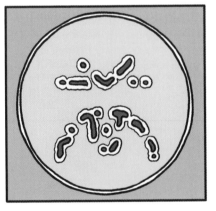

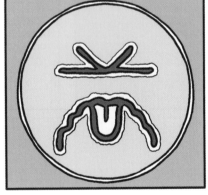

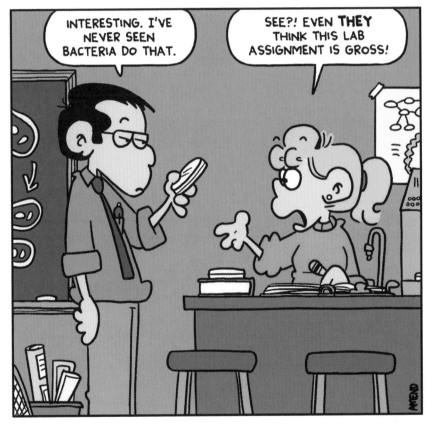

Jason John's

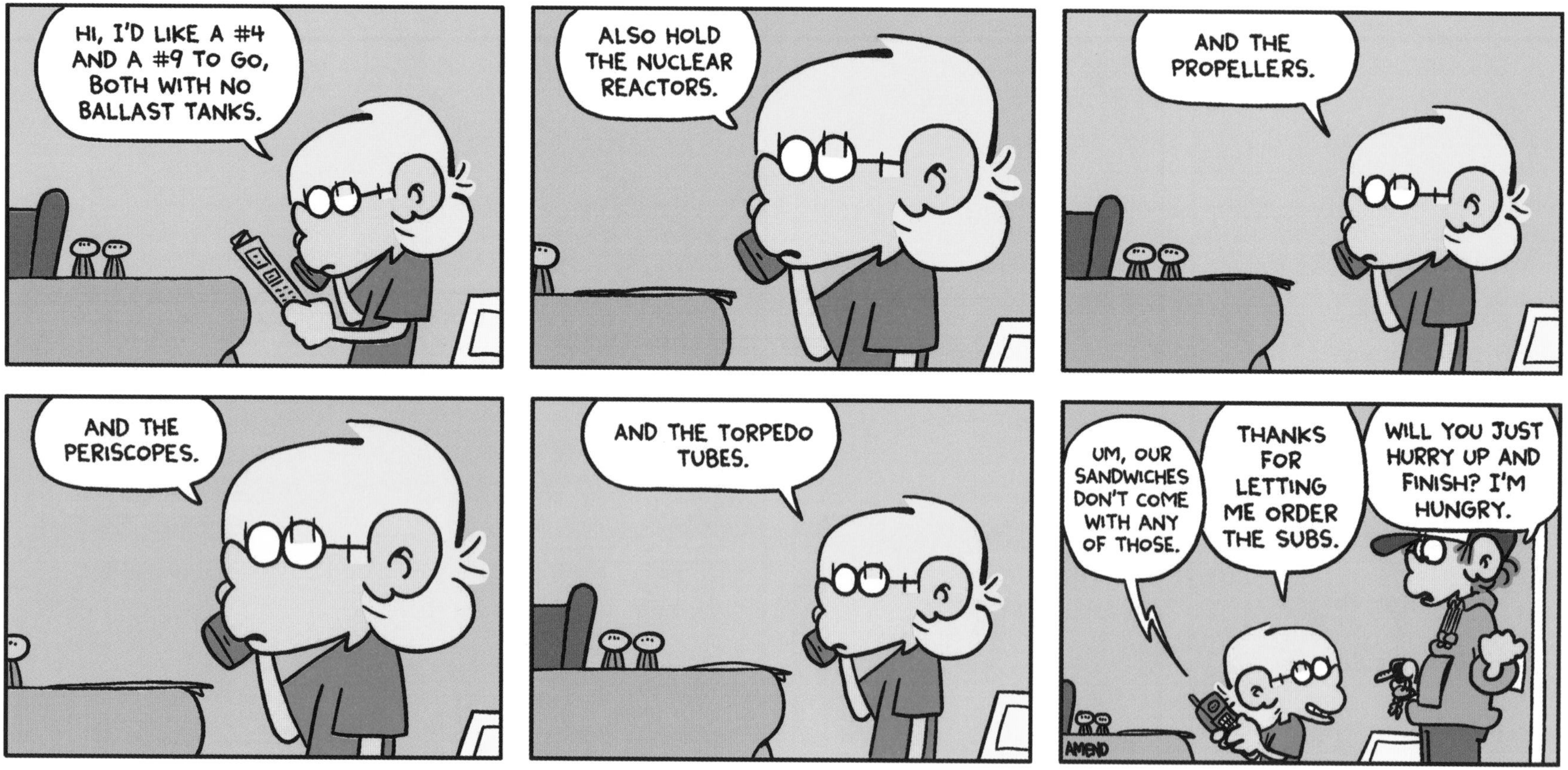
HI, I'D LIKE A #4 AND A #9 TO GO, BOTH WITH NO BALLAST TANKS.
ALSO HOLD THE NUCLEAR REACTORS.
AND THE PROPELLERS.
AND THE PERISCOPES.
AND THE TORPEDO TUBES.
UM, OUR SANDWICHES DON'T COME WITH ANY OF THOSE.
THANKS FOR LETTING ME ORDER THE SUBS.
WILL YOU JUST HURRY UP AND FINISH? I'M HUNGRY.
AMEND

Madness

YOU PICKED FROGS TO BEAT HERONS??
I LIKE FROGS.
YEAH, BUT THEY DON'T HAVE A PRAYER!
WHATEVER. I HAVE THEM LOSING TO WATER SNAKES IN THE NEXT ROUND.
I'M A LITTLE WORRIED ABOUT THE MOSQUITOES VS DRAGONFLIES MATCHUP.
I WENT WITH DRAGONFLIES. I HATE MOSQUITOES.
ME TOO. WHO DO YOU HAVE IN THE FINAL FOUR?
BEAVERS, WATER SNAKES, TURTLES AND ALGAE.
ALGAE?? SERIOUSLY??
I LIKE TO ROOT FOR THE LITTLE GUYS.
HEY, DAD, YOU WANT TO FILL OUT A MARSH MADNESS BRACKET?
YELL LOUDER. HE'S NOT LOOKING.
AMEND

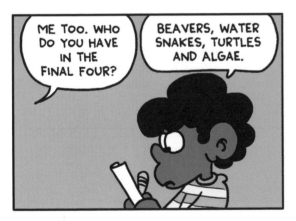

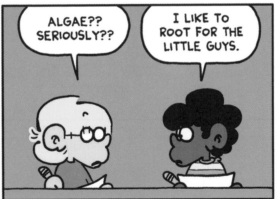

Battle Lines Drawn

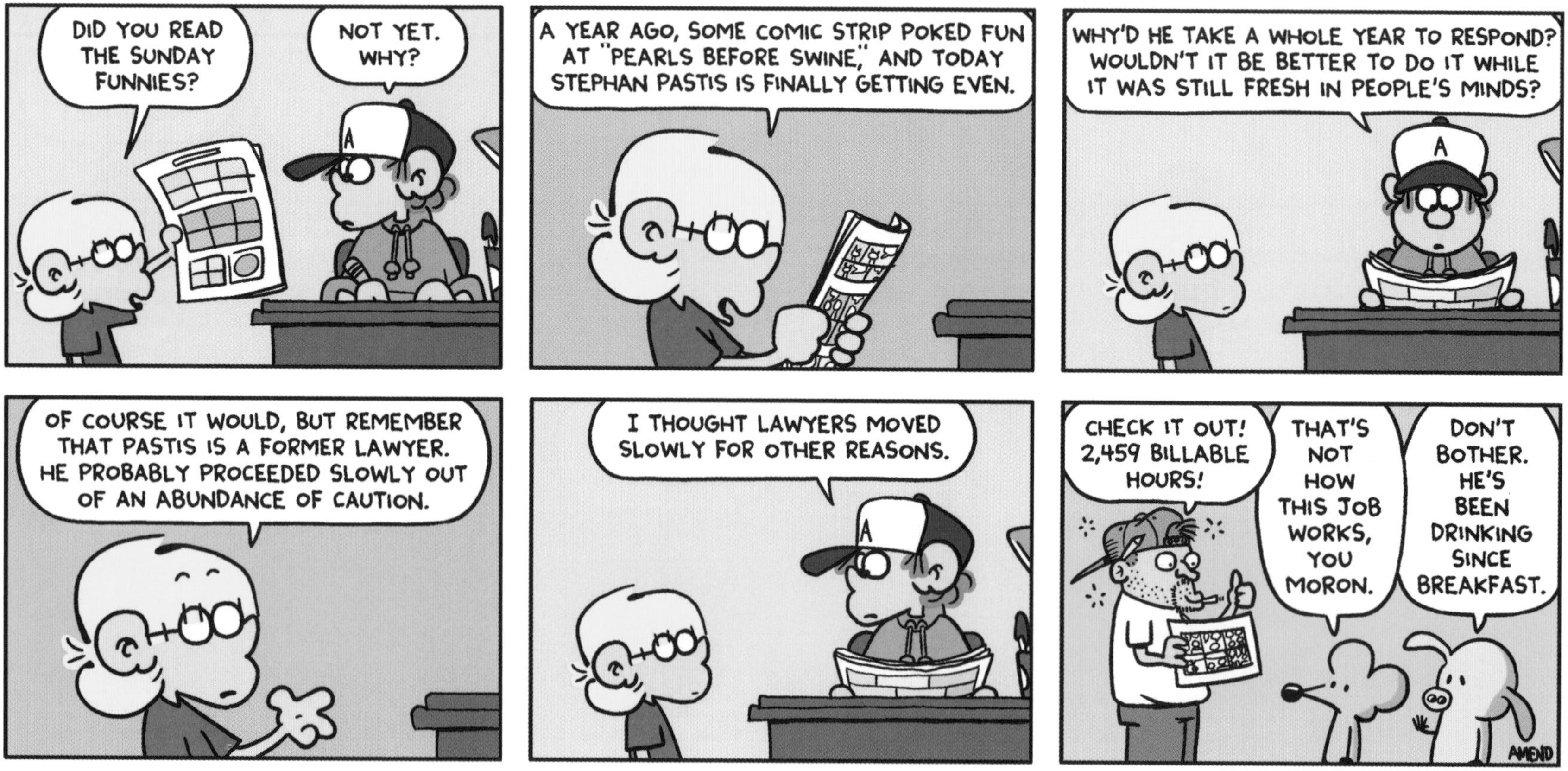
DID YOU READ THE SUNDAY FUNNIES?
NOT YET. WHY?
A YEAR AGO, SOME COMIC STRIP POKED FUN AT "PEARLS BEFORE SWINE," AND TODAY STEPHAN PASTIS IS FINALLY GETTING EVEN.
WHY'D HE TAKE A WHOLE YEAR TO RESPOND? WOULDN'T IT BE BETTER TO DO IT WHILE IT WAS STILL FRESH IN PEOPLE'S MINDS?
OF COURSE IT WOULD, BUT REMEMBER THAT PASTIS IS A FORMER LAWYER. HE PROBABLY PROCEEDED SLOWLY OUT OF AN ABUNDANCE OF CAUTION.
I THOUGHT LAWYERS MOVED SLOWLY FOR OTHER REASONS.
CHECK IT OUT! 2,459 BILLABLE HOURS!
THAT'S NOT HOW THIS JOB WORKS, YOU MORON.
DON'T BOTHER. HE'S BEEN DRINKING SINCE BREAKFAST.
AMEND

Plum Position

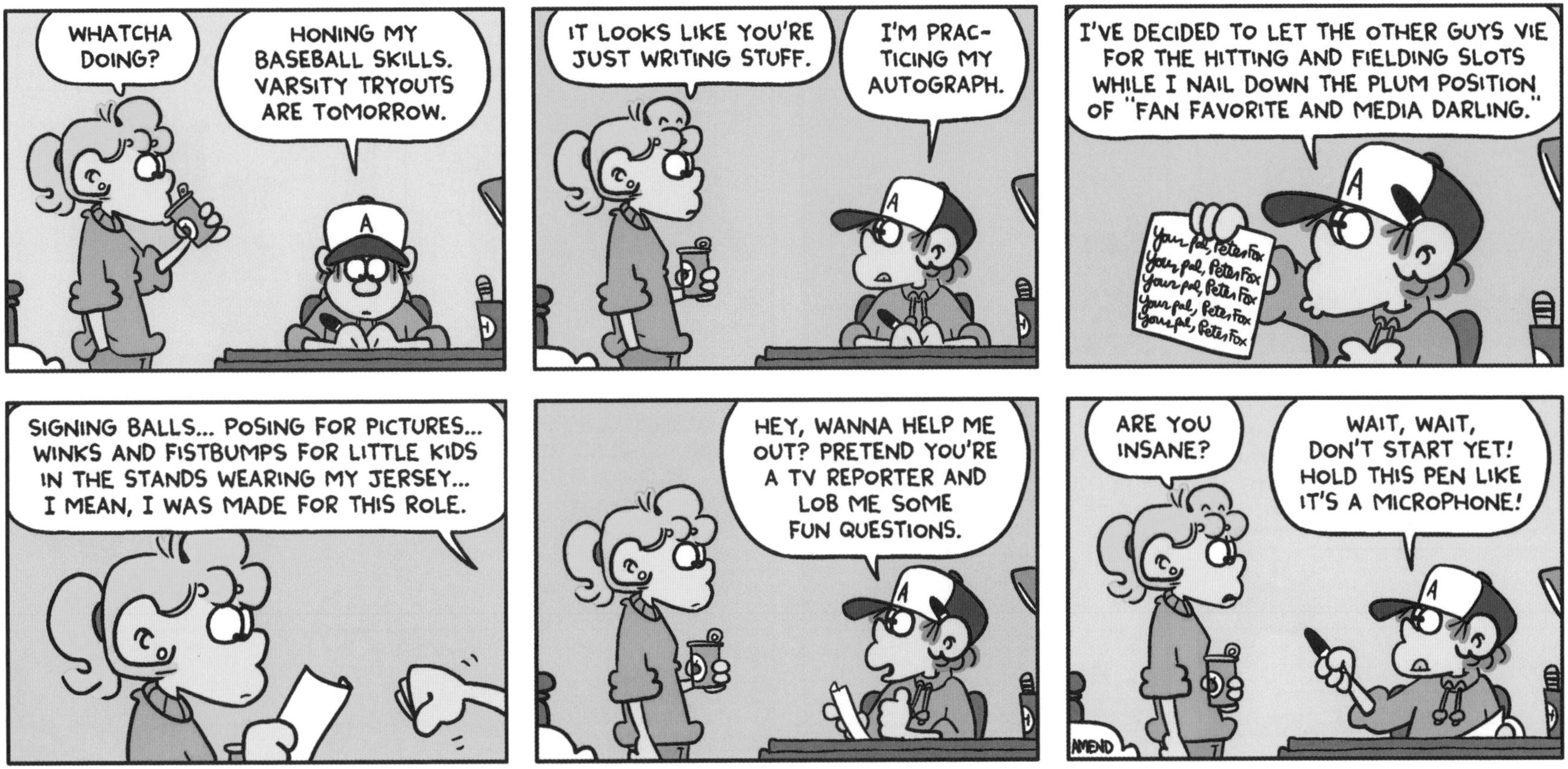
WHATCHA DOING?
HONING MY BASEBALL SKILLS. VARSITY TRYOUTS ARE TOMORROW.
IT LOOKS LIKE YOU'RE JUST WRITING STUFF.
I'M PRAC-TICING MY AUTOGRAPH.
I'VE DECIDED TO LET THE OTHER GUYS VIE FOR THE HITTING AND FIELDING SLOTS WHILE I NAIL DOWN THE PLUM POSITION OF "FAN FAVORITE AND MEDIA DARLING."
Your pal, Peter Fox
Your pal, Peter Fox
Your pal, Peter Fox
Your pal, Peter Fox
Your pal, Peter Fox
SIGNING BALLS... POSING FOR PICTURES... WINKS AND FISTBUMPS FOR LITTLE KIDS IN THE STANDS WEARING MY JERSEY... I MEAN, I WAS MADE FOR THIS ROLE.
HEY, WANNA HELP ME OUT? PRETEND YOU'RE A TV REPORTER AND LOB ME SOME FUN QUESTIONS.
ARE YOU INSANE?
WAIT, WAIT, DON'T START YET! HOLD THIS PEN LIKE IT'S A MICROPHONE!
AMEND

Good Eats

Once upon a time, there was a beautiful princess who lived in a tower guarded by a dragon.

zzzz

One day, a handsome prince came to slay the dragon and rescue the princess.

So the dragon ate him. The princess cried and called the dragon names.

Stupid dragon!

So the dragon ate her, also.

Eventually, word reached her father the king, who ordered his entire army to fight the dragon.

So the dragon ate them, too. The end.

zzzz

QUINCY SLEEPS BETTER WHEN I READ HIM HAPPY BEDTIME STORIES.

YOU ARE SO WEIRD!

AMEND

Pyramidal

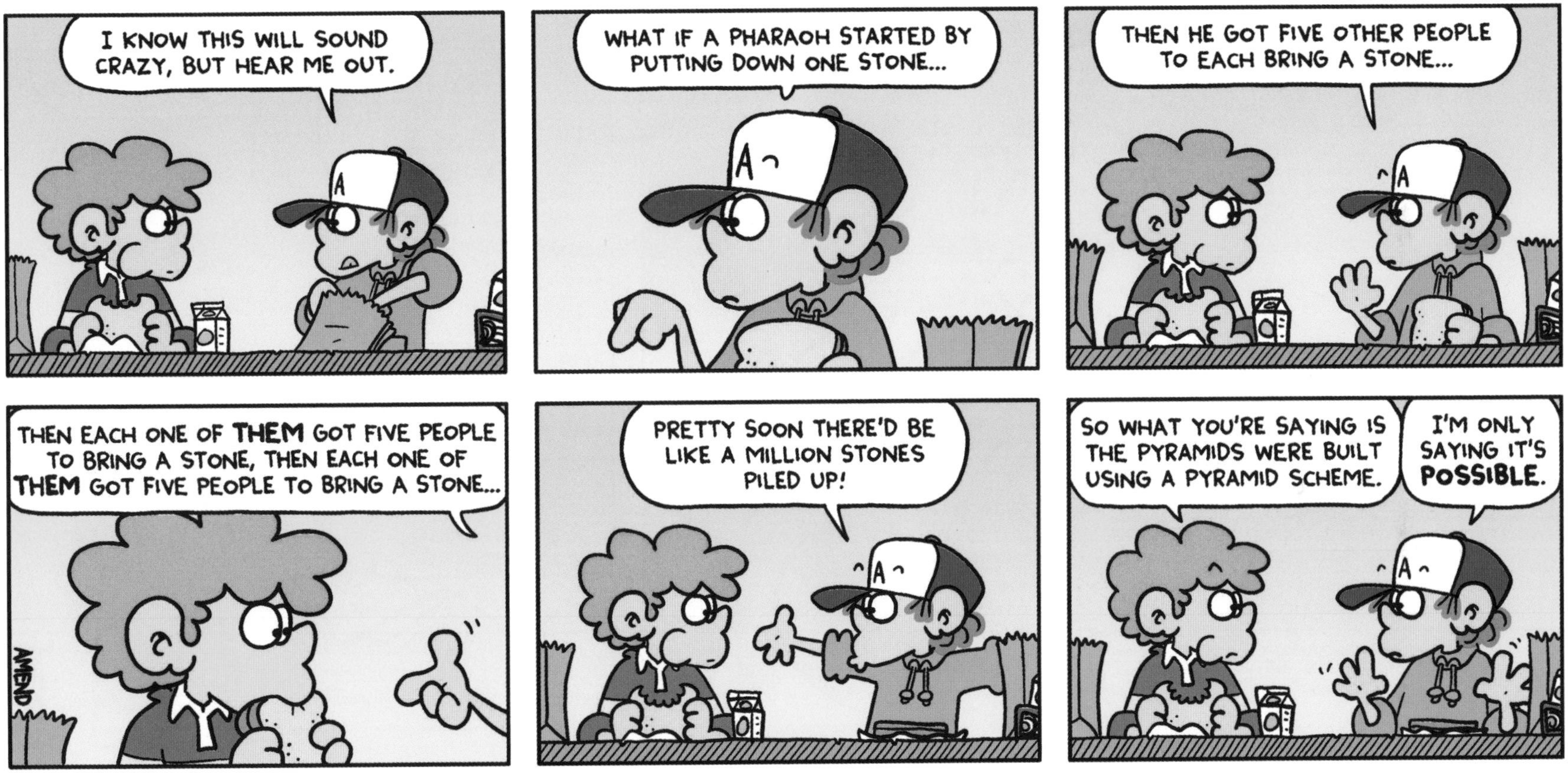

I KNOW THIS WILL SOUND CRAZY, BUT HEAR ME OUT.
WHAT IF A PHARAOH STARTED BY PUTTING DOWN ONE STONE...
THEN HE GOT FIVE OTHER PEOPLE TO EACH BRING A STONE...
THEN EACH ONE OF **THEM** GOT FIVE PEOPLE TO BRING A STONE, THEN EACH ONE OF **THEM** GOT FIVE PEOPLE TO BRING A STONE...
AMEND
PRETTY SOON THERE'D BE LIKE A MILLION STONES PILED UP!
SO WHAT YOU'RE SAYING IS THE PYRAMIDS WERE BUILT USING A PYRAMID SCHEME.
I'M ONLY SAYING IT'S **POSSIBLE**.

Overly Easy

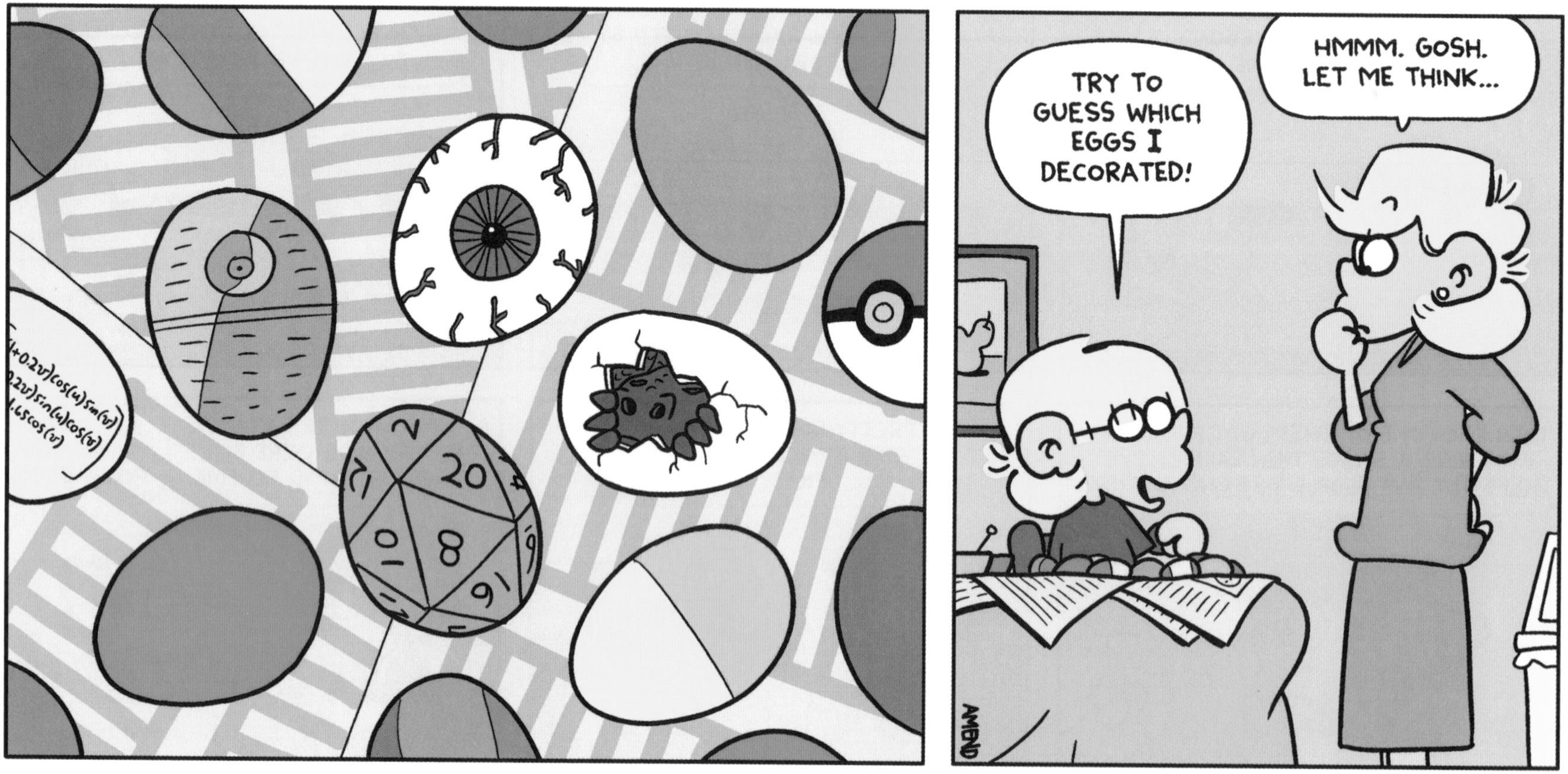
TRY TO GUESS WHICH EGGS I DECORATED!
HMMM. GOSH. LET ME THINK...
AMEND

Problematic

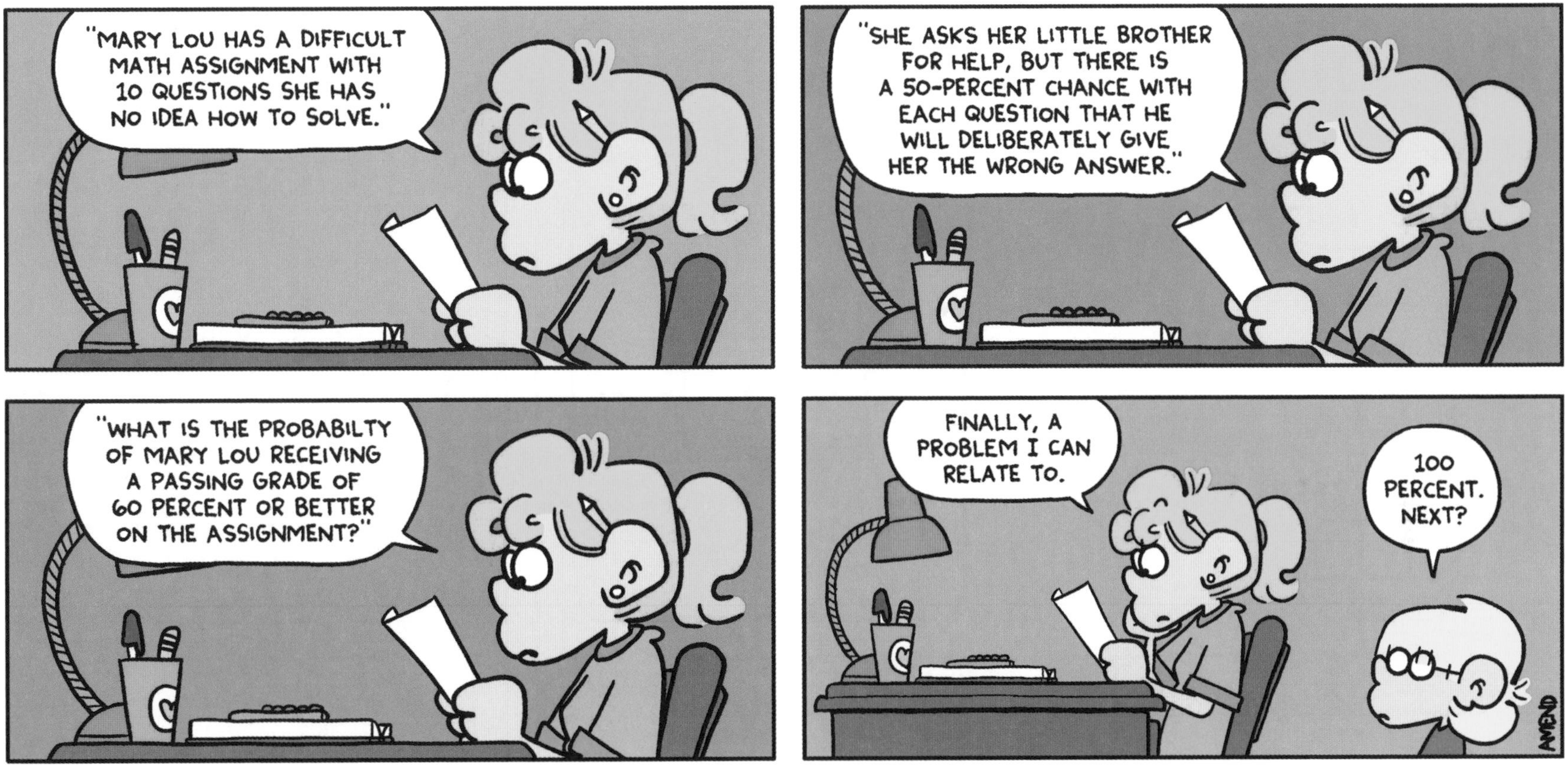
"MARY LOU HAS A DIFFICULT MATH ASSIGNMENT WITH 10 QUESTIONS SHE HAS NO IDEA HOW TO SOLVE."
"SHE ASKS HER LITTLE BROTHER FOR HELP, BUT THERE IS A 50-PERCENT CHANCE WITH EACH QUESTION THAT HE WILL DELIBERATELY GIVE HER THE WRONG ANSWER."
"WHAT IS THE PROBABILTY OF MARY LOU RECEIVING A PASSING GRADE OF 60 PERCENT OR BETTER ON THE ASSIGNMENT?"
FINALLY, A PROBLEM I CAN RELATE TO.
100 PERCENT. NEXT?
AMEND

Numble

JASON'S JUMBLE ®™©®©™
Special Math Edition!!!

Unscramble the numbers to reveal...

A multiple of 117: 0882

□ □ ○ □

A prime number: 134

□ □ ○

An integer cubed: 6409

□ ○ □ □

12 factorial: 601040907

□ □ □ ○ ○ □ □ ○ ○

Woohoo! I'm rich!

How the computer scientist requested his 64-dollar paycheck be written...

○ ○ ○ ○ ○ ○ ○ ○ Dollars

IF THAT'S TOO EASY, I'VE GOT AN ORGANIC CHEMISTRY ONE THAT'S HARDER.

UM, THIS IS FINE.

Oh Gee

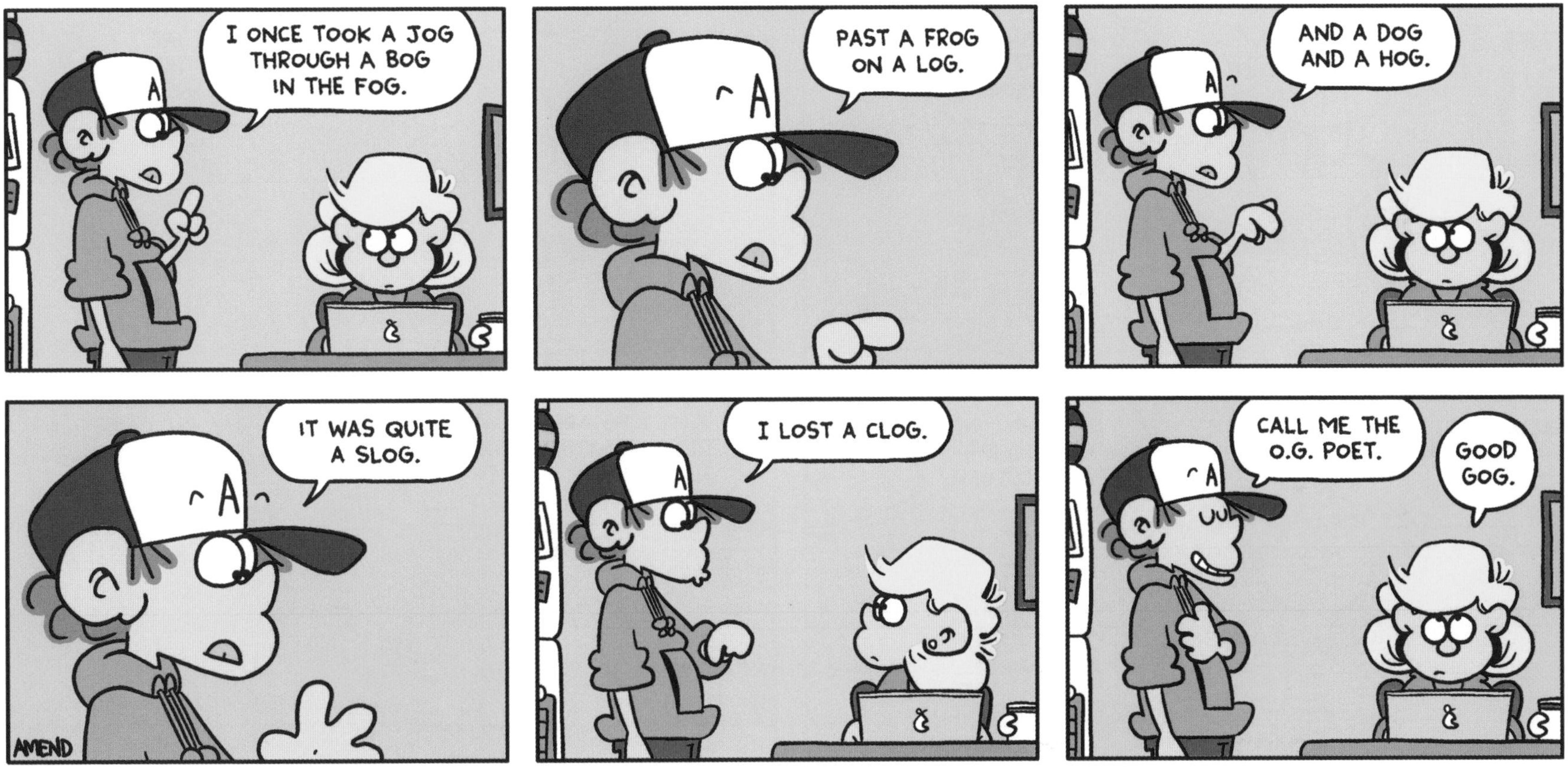
I ONCE TOOK A JOG THROUGH A BOG IN THE FOG.
PAST A FROG ON A LOG.
AND A DOG AND A HOG.
IT WAS QUITE A SLOG.
AMEND
I LOST A CLOG.
CALL ME THE O.G. POET.
GOOD GOG.

Burning Love

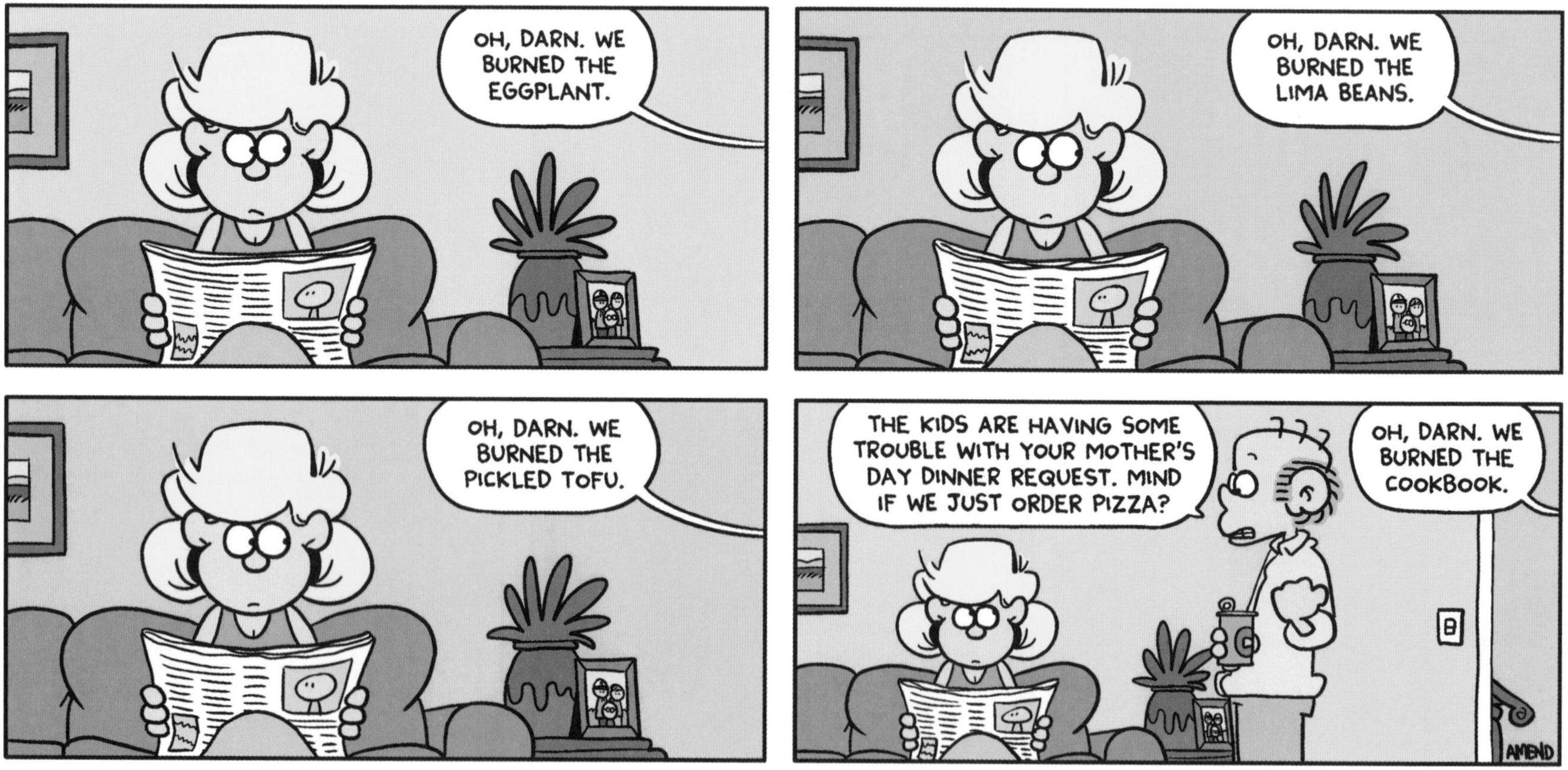
OH, DARN. WE BURNED THE EGGPLANT.
OH, DARN. WE BURNED THE LIMA BEANS.
OH, DARN. WE BURNED THE PICKLED TOFU.
THE KIDS ARE HAVING SOME TROUBLE WITH YOUR MOTHER'S DAY DINNER REQUEST. MIND IF WE JUST ORDER PIZZA?
OH, DARN. WE BURNED THE COOKBOOK.
AMEND

Maximum Something

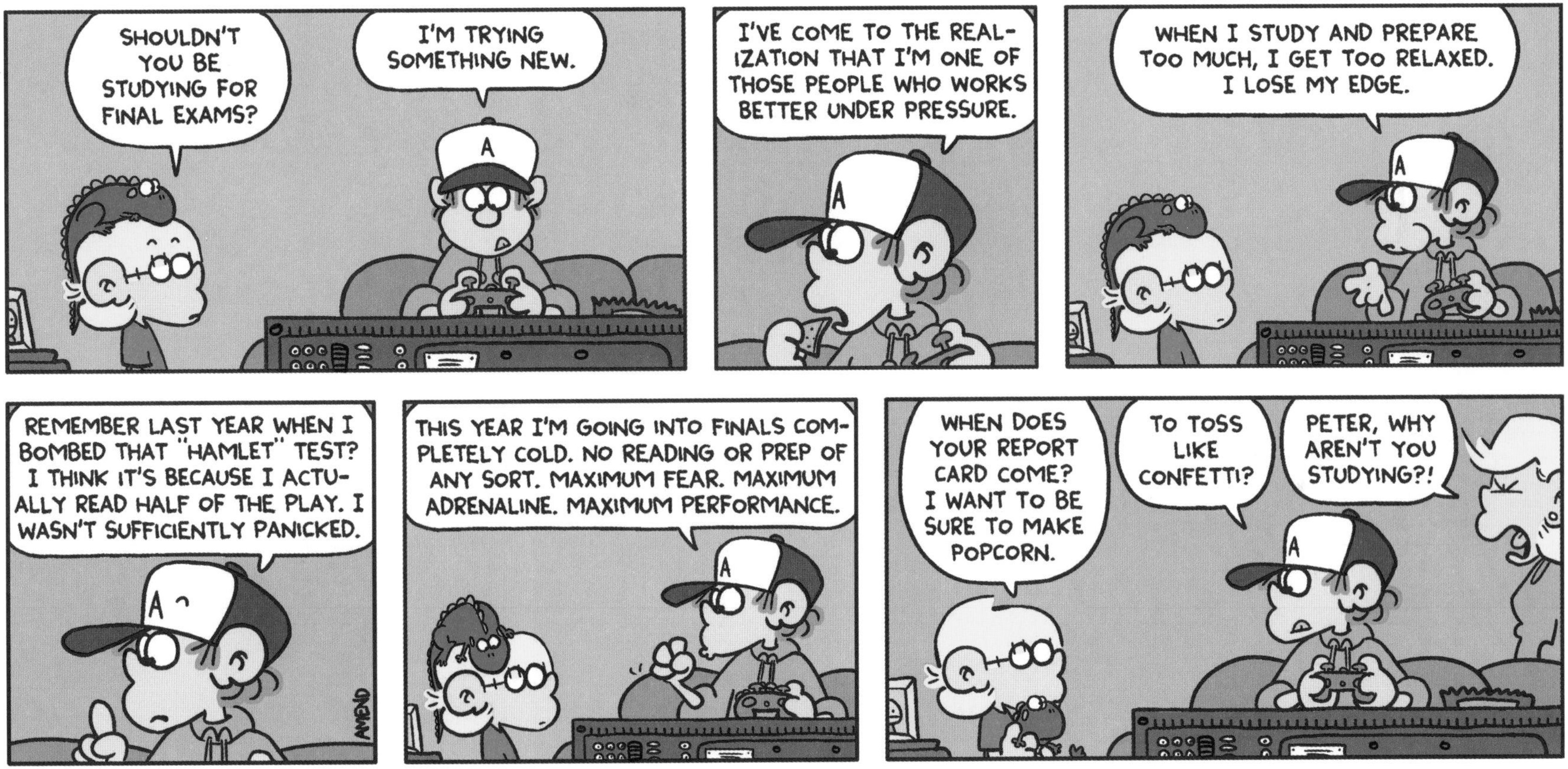
SHOULDN'T YOU BE STUDYING FOR FINAL EXAMS?
I'M TRYING SOMETHING NEW.
I'VE COME TO THE REAL-IZATION THAT I'M ONE OF THOSE PEOPLE WHO WORKS BETTER UNDER PRESSURE.
WHEN I STUDY AND PREPARE TOO MUCH, I GET TOO RELAXED. I LOSE MY EDGE.
REMEMBER LAST YEAR WHEN I BOMBED THAT "HAMLET" TEST? I THINK IT'S BECAUSE I ACTU-ALLY READ HALF OF THE PLAY. I WASN'T SUFFICIENTLY PANICKED.
AMEND
THIS YEAR I'M GOING INTO FINALS COM-PLETELY COLD. NO READING OR PREP OF ANY SORT. MAXIMUM FEAR. MAXIMUM ADRENALINE. MAXIMUM PERFORMANCE.
WHEN DOES YOUR REPORT CARD COME? I WANT TO BE SURE TO MAKE POPCORN.
TO TOSS LIKE CONFETTI?
PETER, WHY AREN'T YOU STUDYING?!

Busted Rhymes

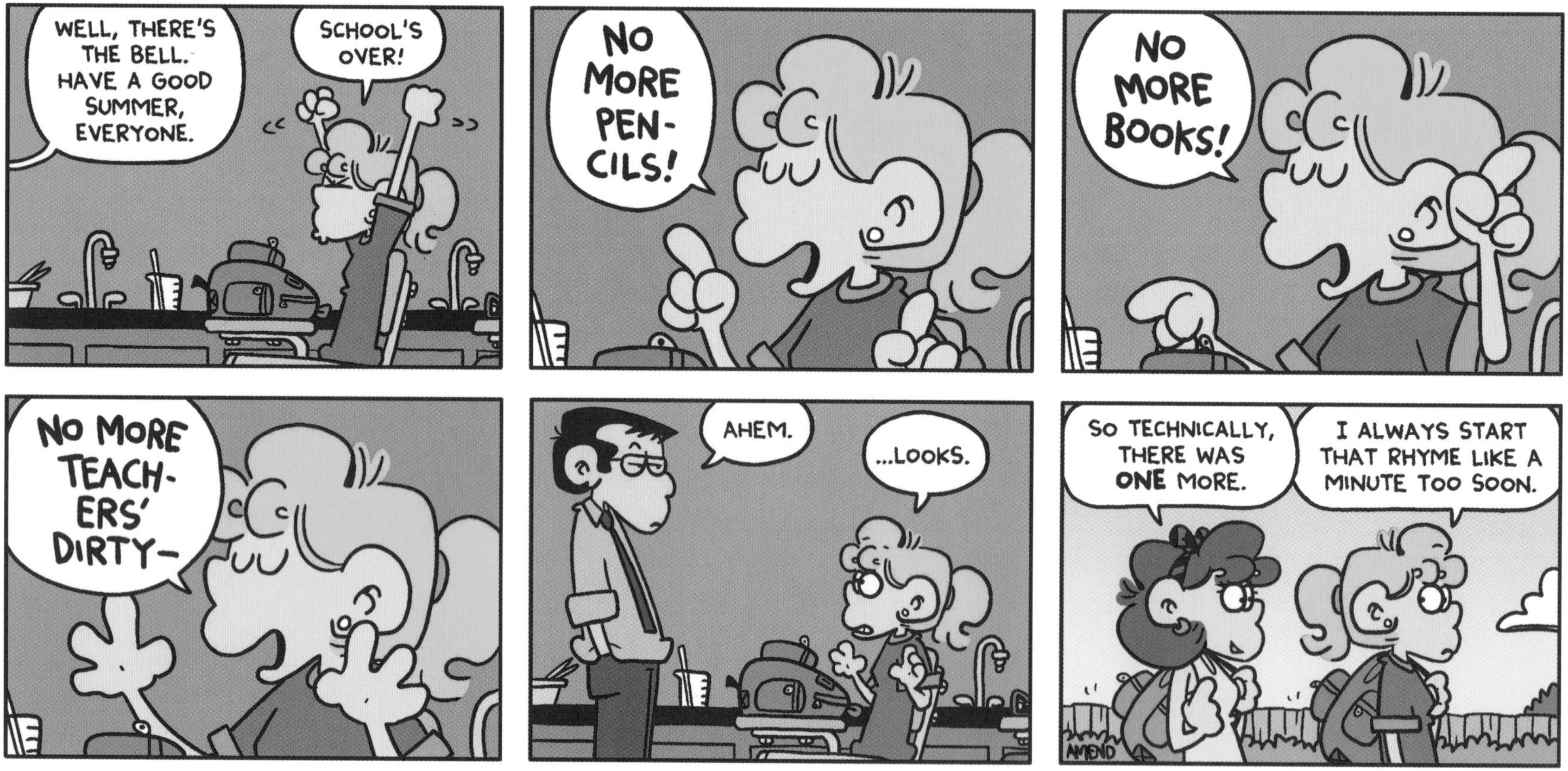
WELL, THERE'S THE BELL. HAVE A GOOD SUMMER, EVERYONE.
SCHOOL'S OVER!
NO MORE PEN-CILS!
NO MORE BOOKS!
NO MORE TEACH-ERS' DIRTY-
AHEM.
...LOOKS.
SO TECHNICALLY, THERE WAS ONE MORE.
I ALWAYS START THAT RHYME LIKE A MINUTE TOO SOON.
AMEND

A What?

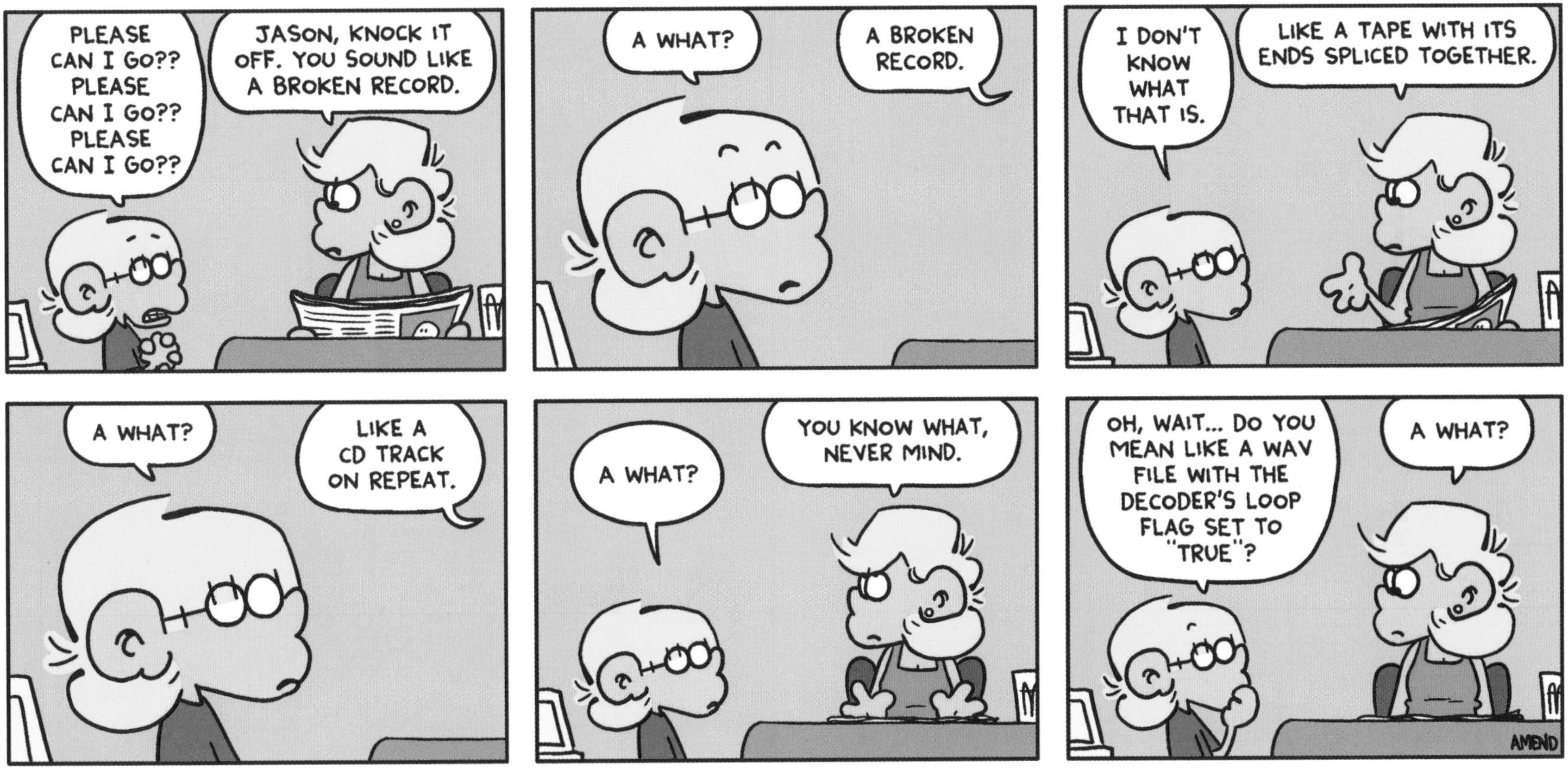

PLEASE CAN I GO?? PLEASE CAN I GO?? PLEASE CAN I GO??
JASON, KNOCK IT OFF. YOU SOUND LIKE A BROKEN RECORD.
A WHAT?
A BROKEN RECORD.
I DON'T KNOW WHAT THAT IS.
LIKE A TAPE WITH ITS ENDS SPLICED TOGETHER.
A WHAT?
LIKE A CD TRACK ON REPEAT.
A WHAT?
YOU KNOW WHAT, NEVER MIND.
OH, WAIT... DO YOU MEAN LIKE A WAV FILE WITH THE DECODER'S LOOP FLAG SET TO "TRUE"?
A WHAT?
AMEND

Cool App

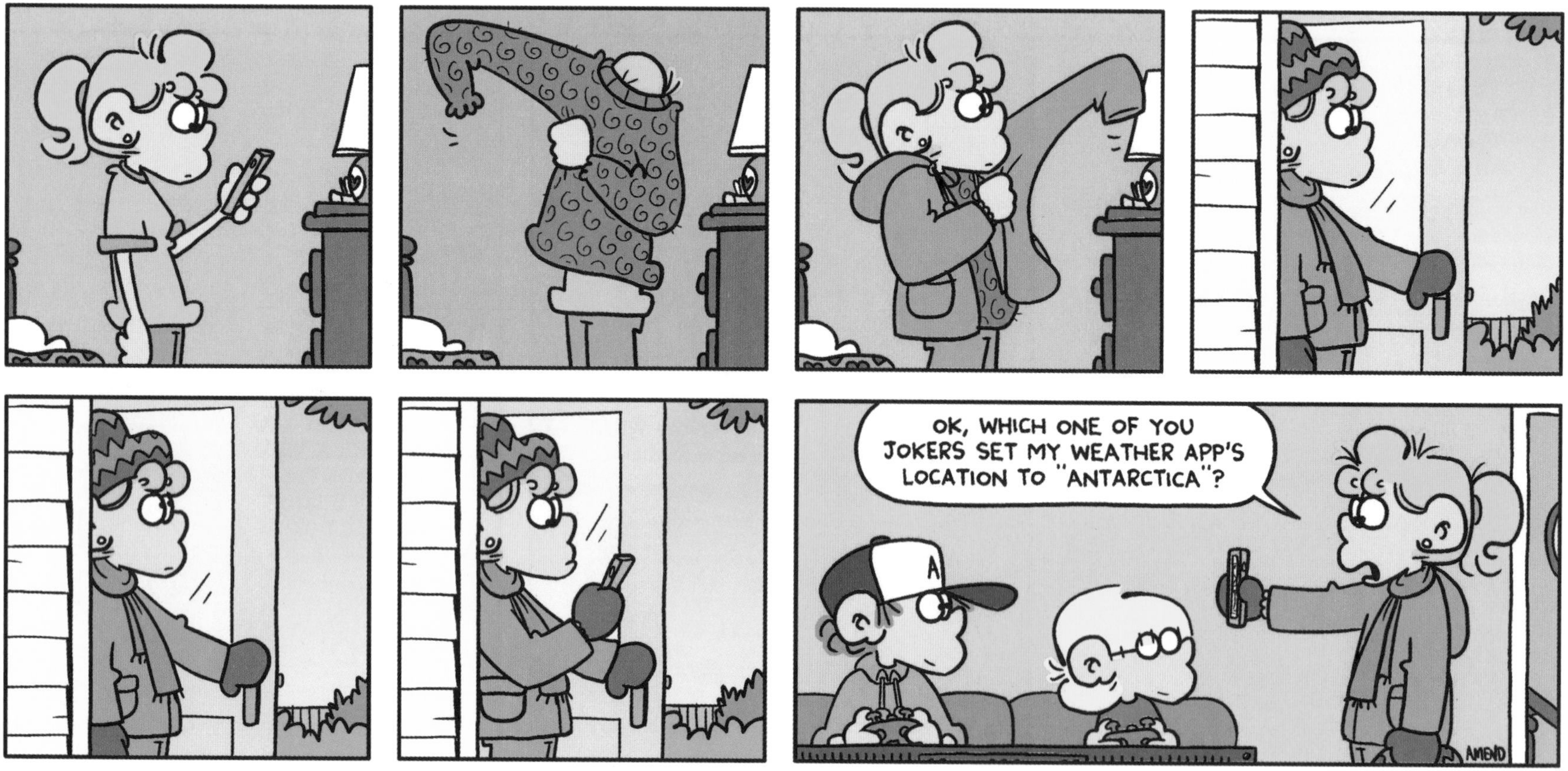
OK, WHICH ONE OF YOU JOKERS SET MY WEATHER APP'S LOCATION TO "ANTARCTICA"?
A
AMEND

Gutsy

WHY DO YOU HAVE A PILLOW UNDER YOUR SHIRT?

IT'S MY FATHER'S DAY GIFT TO YOU!

AS YOU CAN SEE, I NOW HAVE THE BIGGEST BEER BELLY IN THE FAMILY! NOW YOU CAN DRINK BEER AND EAT JUNK FOOD ALL DAY, AND IF MOM ROLLS HER EYES, YOU CAN POINT AT ME AND SAY, "HEY, WORRY ABOUT **HIM**! HIS GUT IS SLIGHTLY BIGGER!"

THANKS, SON. I THINK.

ALSO, IT'S FOUR PILLOWS, NOT ONE.

End Game

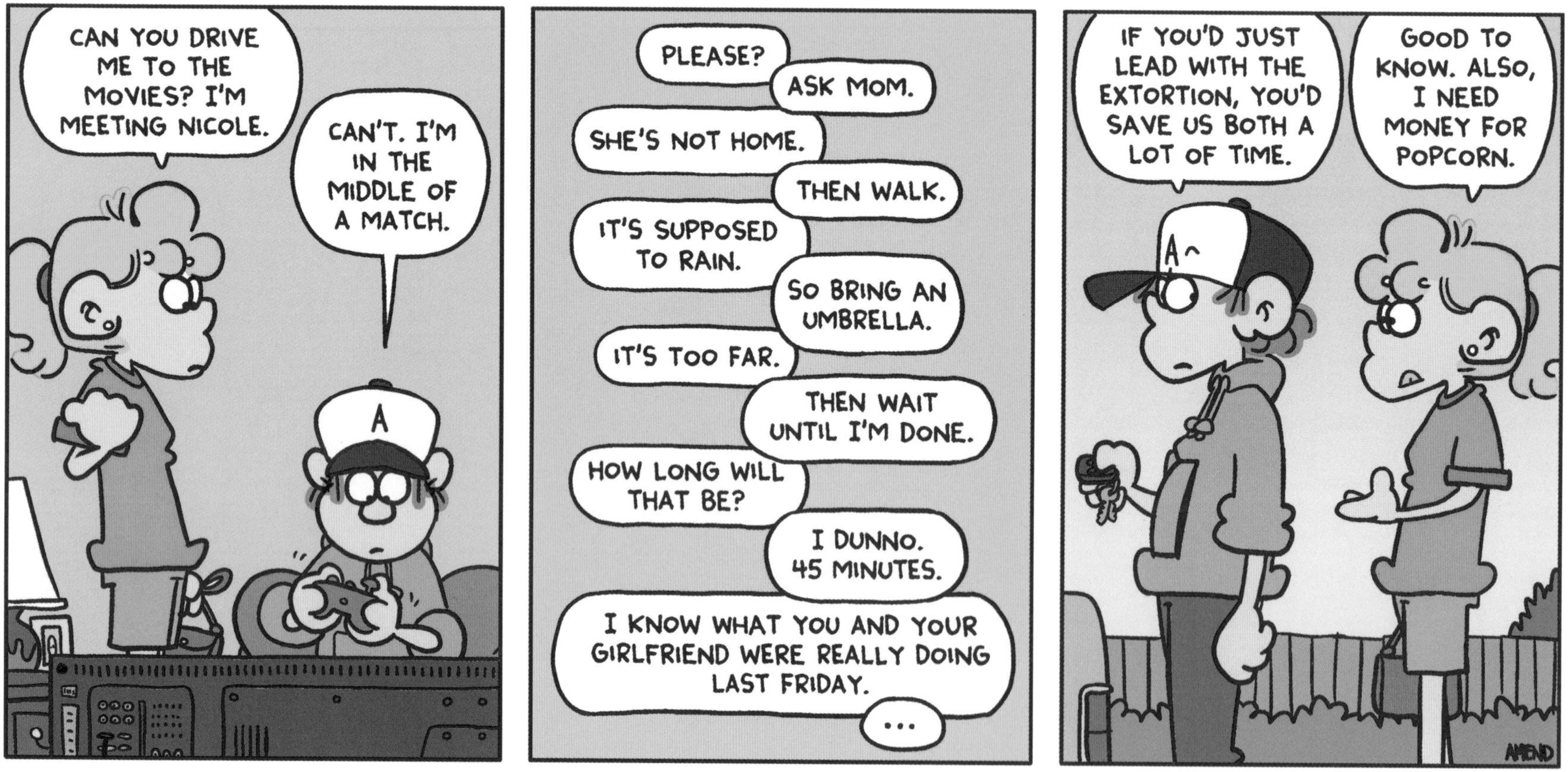
CAN YOU DRIVE ME TO THE MOVIES? I'M MEETING NICOLE.
CAN'T. I'M IN THE MIDDLE OF A MATCH.
PLEASE?
ASK MOM.
SHE'S NOT HOME.
THEN WALK.
IT'S SUPPOSED TO RAIN.
SO BRING AN UMBRELLA.
IT'S TOO FAR.
THEN WAIT UNTIL I'M DONE.
HOW LONG WILL THAT BE?
I DUNNO. 45 MINUTES.
I KNOW WHAT YOU AND YOUR GIRLFRIEND WERE REALLY DOING LAST FRIDAY.
...
IF YOU'D JUST LEAD WITH THE EXTORTION, YOU'D SAVE US BOTH A LOT OF TIME.
GOOD TO KNOW. ALSO, I NEED MONEY FOR POPCORN.
AMEND

Patriotic Appetite

PETER WANTS TO KNOW IF YOU CAN MAKE 1776 BURGERS FOR OUR FOURTH OF JULY COOKOUT.

WHAT'S A 1776 BURGER?

IS IT LIKE SOME MARTHA STEWARTY THING WITH RED, WHITE AND BLUE CONDIMENTS?

OR WITH THE CHEESE CUT INTO THE SHAPE OF A NOTABLE FOUNDING FATHER?

OR WITH JOHN HANCOCK'S SIGNATURE SEARED INTO THE MEAT?

I'M A LITTLE SURPRISED. I WOULDN'T HAVE PEGGED YOUR BROTHER AS A FANCY FOOD SORT OF PERSON.

YOU MISUNDER-STAND. HE WANTS 1776 INDIVIDUAL HAMBURGERS.

AH, OK. THAT'S THE PETER I KNOW.

AMEND

Remote Chance

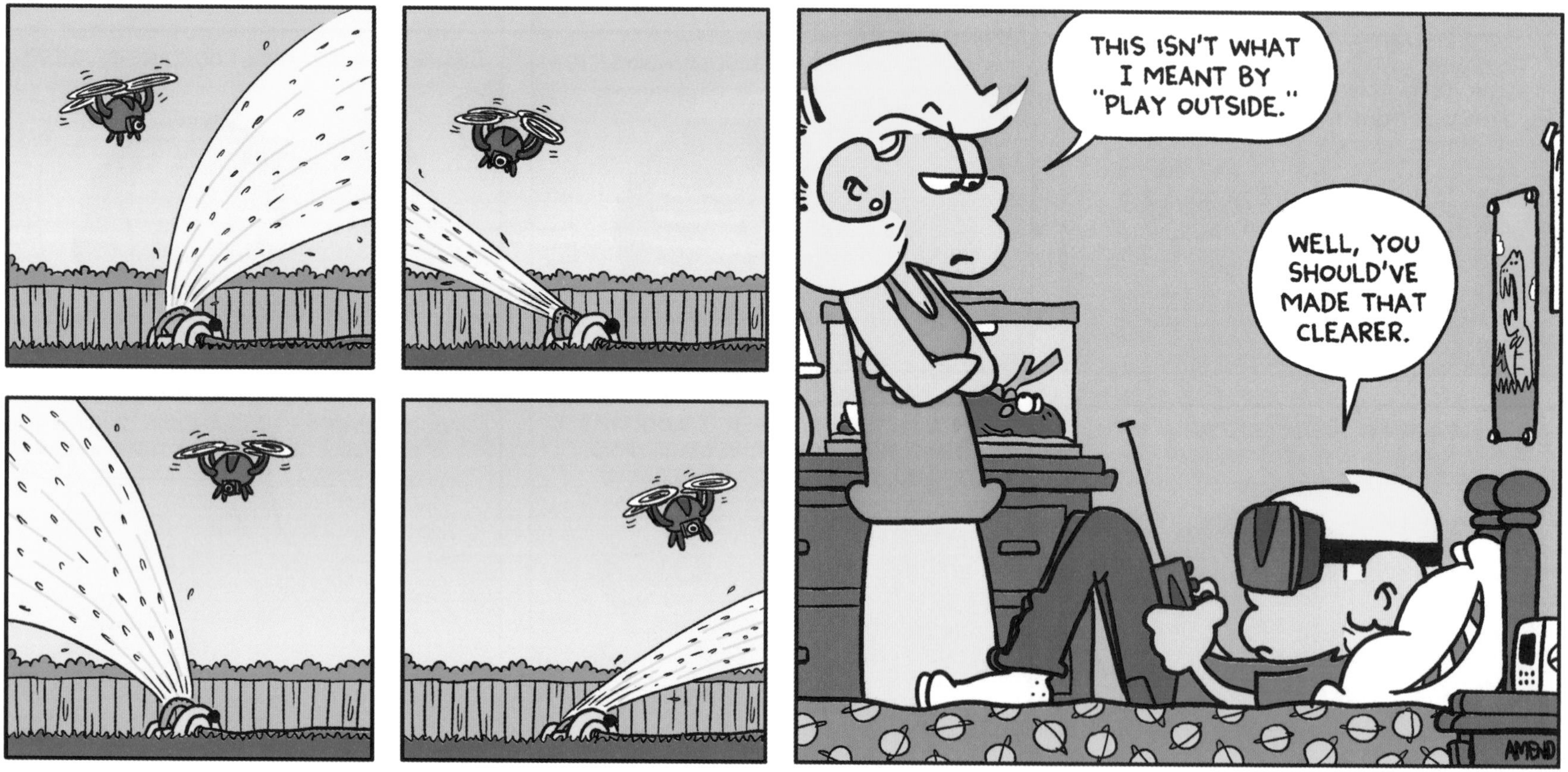
THIS ISN'T WHAT I MEANT BY "PLAY OUTSIDE."
WELL, YOU SHOULD'VE MADE THAT CLEARER.
AMEND

HBO No

IS IT OK IF I WATCH "GAME OF THRONES" TONIGHT?

WE'VE HAD THIS DISCUSSION BEFORE, JASON.

"GAME OF THRONES" IS NOT A SHOW FOR KIDS! IT'S FULL OF GRAPHIC VIOLENCE AND CRUELTY AND ADULT CONTENT THAT YOUR 10-YEAR-OLD EYES SIMPLY AREN'T READY FOR!

MY EYES ARE TOTALLY READY! LET ME TELL YOU SOME OF THE THINGS I'VE SEEN ON THE INTERNET, JUST SINCE BREAKFAST...

I PROBABLY COULD'VE ARGUED THAT BETTER.

YOU CAN HAVE THIS BACK WHEN YOU'RE 50.

AMEND

Coordination

HMM. WHICH ICE CREAM FLAVOR DO I WANT?

STRAWBERRY?

RASPBERRY?

PEPPERMINT?

WOULD IT BE POSSIBLE TO GET SAMPLES OF THOSE?

YEAH, LET'S GO WITH THE STRAWBERRY.

YOU AND YOUR WEIRD NEED FOR COORDINATED COLORS...

I WISH I'D WORN A DIFFERENT SHIRT. I HATE STRAWBERRY.

AMEND

Pool Chemistry

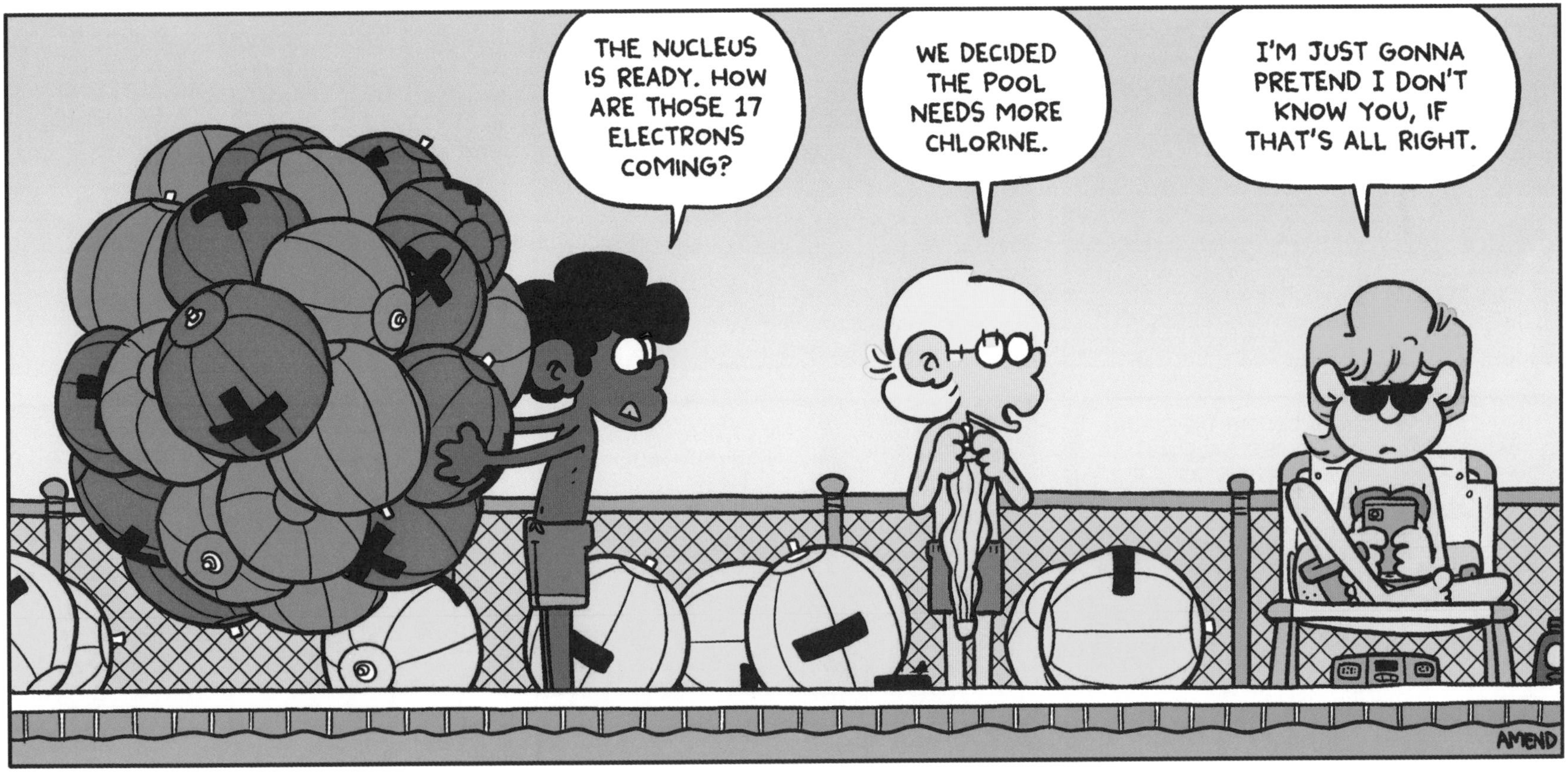
THE NUCLEUS IS READY. HOW ARE THOSE 17 ELECTRONS COMING?
WE DECIDED THE POOL NEEDS MORE CHLORINE.
I'M JUST GONNA PRETEND I DON'T KNOW YOU, IF THAT'S ALL RIGHT.
AMEND

Star or Planet?

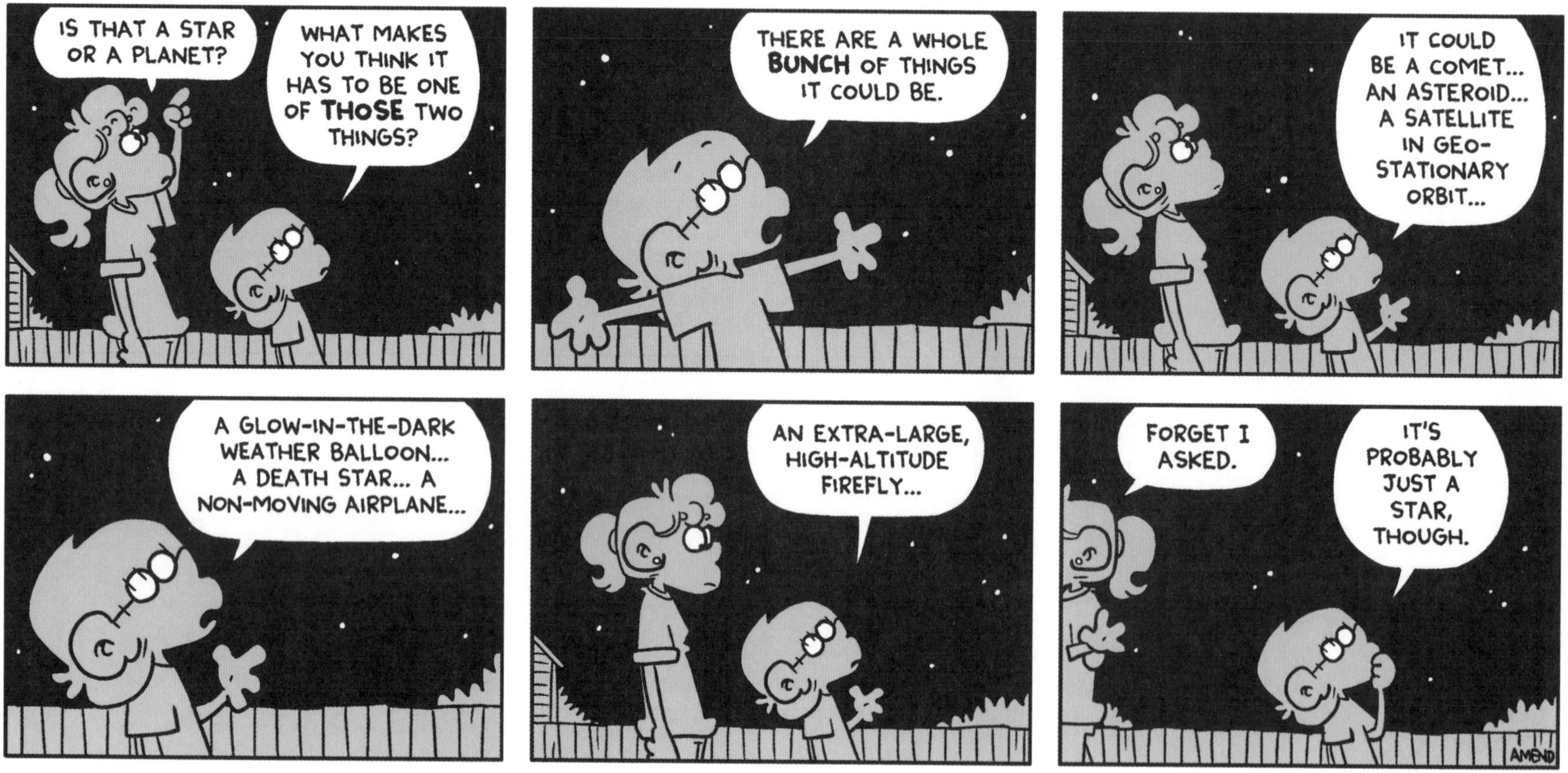
IS THAT A STAR OR A PLANET?
WHAT MAKES YOU THINK IT HAS TO BE ONE OF THOSE TWO THINGS?
THERE ARE A WHOLE BUNCH OF THINGS IT COULD BE.
IT COULD BE A COMET... AN ASTEROID... A SATELLITE IN GEO-STATIONARY ORBIT...
A GLOW-IN-THE-DARK WEATHER BALLOON... A DEATH STAR... A NON-MOVING AIRPLANE...
AN EXTRA-LARGE, HIGH-ALTITUDE FIREFLY...
FORGET I ASKED.
IT'S PROBABLY JUST A STAR, THOUGH.
AMEND

Go! Go! Go!

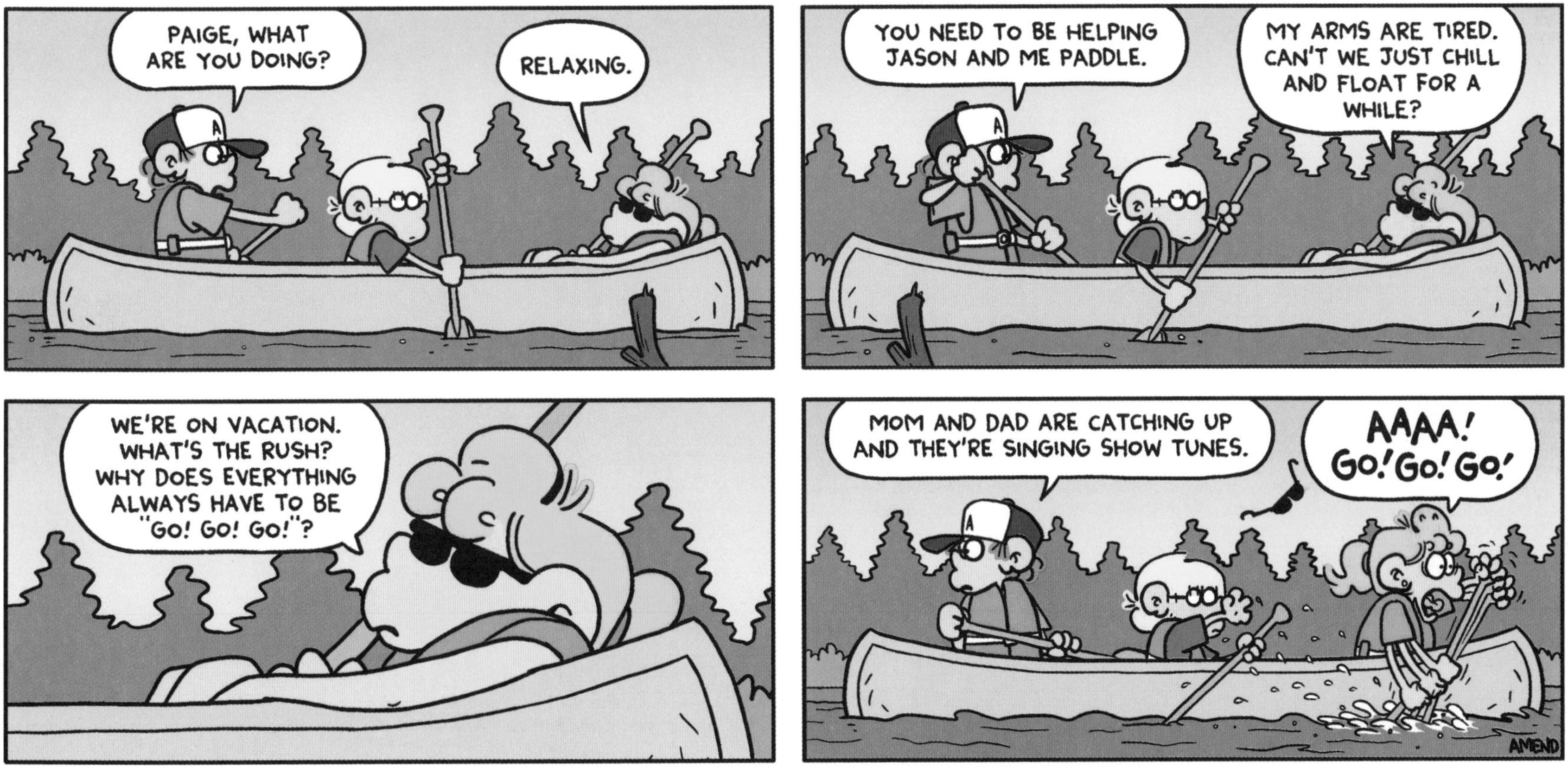
PAIGE, WHAT ARE YOU DOING?
RELAXING.
YOU NEED TO BE HELPING JASON AND ME PADDLE.
MY ARMS ARE TIRED. CAN'T WE JUST CHILL AND FLOAT FOR A WHILE?
WE'RE ON VACATION. WHAT'S THE RUSH? WHY DOES EVERYTHING ALWAYS HAVE TO BE "GO! GO! GO!"?
MOM AND DAD ARE CATCHING UP AND THEY'RE SINGING SHOW TUNES.
AAAA! GO! GO! GO!
AMEND

FoxTrot is distributed internationally by Andrews McMeel Syndication.

Mother Is Coming © 2018 by Bill Amend. All rights reserved. Printed in China. No part of this book may be used or reproduced in any manner whatsoever without written permission except in the case of reprints in the context of reviews.

Andrews McMeel Publishing
a division of Andrews McMeel Universal
1130 Walnut Street, Kansas City, Missouri 64106

18 19 20 21 22 SDB 10 9 8 7 6 5 4 3 2 1

ISBN: 978-1-4494-9646-3

Library of Congress Control Number: 2018941435

www.andrewsmcmeel.com

www.foxtrot.com

ATTENTION: SCHOOLS AND BUSINESSES

Andrews McMeel books are available at quantity discounts with bulk purchase for educational, business, or sales promotional use. For information, please e-mail the Andrews McMeel Publishing Special Sales Department: specialsales@amuniversal.com.